Catholic Schools
Hope in Uncertain Times

Edited by
Anne Benjamin
and Dan Riley

Published in Australia by
John Garratt Publishing
32 Glenvale Crescent
Mulgrave Vic 3170

www.johngarratt.com.au

Copyright of each essay resides with each author. This compilation is copyright © 2008 Anne Benjamin and Dan Riley.

Edited by Cathy Oliver
Designed and typeset by Lynne Muir
Cover photograph by Peter Casamento

All rights reserved. Except as provided by Australian copyright law, no part of this book may be reproduced without permission in writing from the publisher.

First published 2008

The National Library of Australia Cataloguing-in-Publication data:

> Catholic schools: hope in uncertain times / editor Anne Benjamin, Dan Riley.
>
> ISBN: 9781920721800 (pbk.)
>
> Bibliography.
>
> Catholic Church—Education. Catholic schools. Christian education. School management and organization.
>
> 371.0712

Contents

Foreword   5

Introduction   7

PART ONE
FOUNDATIONS OF CATHOLIC SCHOOLS   15

1. A New Ecclesial Context for Catholic Schools
   Michael Putney   17

2. Mission and Catholic Schools:
   Grounding hope in uncertain times
   Therese & Jim D'Orsa   32

3. Stewardship and God's Creation:
   A theological reflection
   Chris Toohey   45

4. Educating Children to Wonder, Wisdom and Stewardship:
   A conversation with Chris Toohey   57

5. Non-Catholics and Catholics in Catholic Schools
   in Australia
   Brian Croke   67

6. The Development of Catholic School Systems
   Kelvin Canavan, fms   82

PART TWO
LEARNING FROM BROADER PERSPECTIVES   97

7. Responding to Leadership Challenges in
   American Catholic Schools
   Timothy Cook   99

8. Challenges to Faith Schools in the United Kingdom
   Oona Stannard   113

9	Fostering a *Globo Sapiens* Attitude amongst Students as the World Becomes More Interdependent Patrick Lynch	127
10	A Shared Hope in Catholic Schools of the South Pacific Kalo Sikimeti	139
11	Islamic Schools : Another faith perspective Silma Ihram	149
12	A School Generation Facing the World's End-Time Hedley Beare	162

PART THREE
LEADING CATHOLIC SCHOOLS INTO THE FUTURE 177

13	Restoring Venice: A call to New Evangelisation Dan White	179
14	Taking the Next Step: Catholic schools and the cry of the poor Anne Benjamin	192
15	A Journey of Healing: One in spirit embracing difference Joan Hendriks	207
16	Both 'Catholic' and 'School': Leading learning with moral purpose Michael Bezzina	220
17	Building Leadership Capacity in Catholic School Communities: Is 'distributed leadership' really the answer? Patrick Duignan	234
18	A Story of Hope: Holy Family Primary School Brenda Kennedy and Patricia Carr	248
	Biographical notes	260

FOREWORD

Since Vatican Council II, several scholarly books and pastoral/theological documents have attempted to capture the essential character and dynamism of a 'Catholic school'. While each carried slightly different emphasis, this body of work constitutes an impressive and consistent effort to provide Catholic schools that serve an international community of 50 million students with a collective sense of their mission and their character. Nevertheless, that body of literature does not tell the whole story. That is also told by the graduates of those schools and by those who teach and have taught in those schools.

Also, unfortunately most of the parents of children in Catholic schools, and most of the teachers in Catholic schools, whether religious or lay, did not read the scholarly documents, or, if they did, found the technical theological vocabulary and the scriptural references of these treatises lacking in any practical application to their lives. By and large, these documents and books, however profound their reformulations of the Catholic identity of Catholic schools, did not reach the minds and hearts of 'ordinary' Catholic adults. At the parish level, for the most part, there had never been a system of adult formation in their Catholic faith which would have provided a tradition of adults who were expected to re-appropriate their faith and their spirituality at a mature level, and thereby integrate that mature faith and spirituality into the practical living out of their everyday lives, and that included raising and educating their children as Catholics.

The issue of the Catholic identity of the school has to be tied to a notion of a flourishing Catholic parish life in which young people can experience the pedagogy of multiple adult examples of Catholic 'practice'. Lacking that experience, the impact of the Catholic school, however orthodox its teaching, will diminish over time.

This book presents a series of essays that brings the reader up to date, so to speak, with some of the best thinking about an integral Catholic education. The foundational essays are very well grounded in Catholic theology and scripture, as well as grounded in the realities and challenges facing the schools and the school's dialogue with the world outside the school grounds.

I continue to be genuinely impressed by educators in the Catholic schools of Australia, as well as by the scholarship emerging from the faculty of Australian Catholic University, and from diocesan Catholic school staff. Because Australian Catholic schools, unlike Catholic schools in the United States, enjoy state financial support as well as widespread public legitimacy, they have the resources to provide for leadership support in the staffs of Diocesan Catholic Education Offices, as well as for teacher salaries comparable to salaries in state schools. Because of this state support as well as strong diocesan commitments to quality education, with the considerable value-added dimension of the religious atmosphere and community service orientation, Australian Catholic schools represent, in my opinion, the most outstanding system of Catholic education in the world.

This book reveals, however, little self-complacency. Rather it is outward and forward looking, pointing to the as yet unmet challenges facing Catholic schools. In this effort it has invited dialogue with Catholic educators outside Australia and outside the Catholic system itself. The book serves as a shining light for Catholic educators everywhere to take a fresh look at themselves.

Robert J Starratt
Boston College

INTRODUCTION

We live in a time of immense possibility. It is also a time of change and uncertainty. In such times, hope is a precious gift which provides the mortar in a sound dwelling. Hope is nurtured in many ways. The contributors to this volume argue that all education exercises a critical role in shaping future society which is strong in hope. In particular, Catholic schools have a unique gift to offer through their identification with a specific culture and values.

This book does not seek to deny the complexity or ambiguity, or challenges which confront, or will confront, young people in our societies. It does not try to re-create solutions from a nostalgically-remembered past, for the past carries its own complexities. Rather, this book is premised on the conviction that hope flourishes only when it is grounded in reality. All the writers in this volume are passionate and emboldened by the possibilities offered through good schooling and recognise the role that quality religious schooling can make to society. They are people who in practice and reflection have tried faithfully to honour their vision.

The structure of the book reflects this premise:
- Part One: Foundations of Catholic Schools
- Part Two: Learning from Broader Perspectives
- Part Three: Leading Catholic Schools into the Future.

The authors bring experience and insights from Catholic schools in Australia, New Zealand, the Pacific, United States and the United Kingdom. They also bring different faith perspectives.

Part One: Foundations of Catholic Schools

The foundation of Catholic schools is their Catholic faith. Bishop Michael Putney argues that if Catholic schools are to maintain their 'Catholic' distinctiveness it is essential they take seriously their ecclesial identity and role within the Church's mission. For Bishop Putney, to try to maintain or enhance the 'Catholic' identity of our schools without dealing with their 'ecclesial' identity and mission will see them doomed to failure. It is therefore imperative for leaders in Catholic schools to have knowledge acquired from serious study and provide witness via practice of their faith.

In contemporary times it is impossible to retreat to the security of a traditional community and concurrently engage people with the message of Jesus 'to the ends of the earth'. No Catholic school whether located in a metropolitan, urban, rural or remote region is isolated from the realities daily reported by the mass media. The Catholic identity is in a process of redefinition generated by global changes. The theme of Therese D'Orsa and Jim D'Orsa is the grounding of hope in these uncertain times. They propose that if the challenges of the Church's mission are grasped, the result will be a richer rather than a diminished understanding of what it means to be Catholic and a member of the Church.

The chapter by Bishop Chris Toohey is a theological reflection on how to responsibly handle our stewardship of God's creation. He advocates that a Catholic faith perspective should be the inspiration and motivation for the way we make use of the goods of the Earth. He acknowledges the tension between exploitation of the Earth and our need to live on it. However, the Earth is a finite resource and the only planet on which we can live. Bishop Toohey wants the response of Catholic schools to have a firm spiritual and theological foundation while listening carefully to the very best science has to offer. In a subsequent interview with Anne Benjamin, Bishop Toohey reflects on the implications for Catholic educators of the current ecological crisis. He considers what climate change means to Catholic educators, the need for a faith perspective as our foundational orientation to the natural world, the challenge of living with uncertainty in uncertain times and ways Catholic schools may provide leadership in such times.

To accept the Church's mission requires an appreciation of the contemporary history of Catholic schools. Brian Croke explains the radical changes in the Australian Catholic school over the past 30 years and explores some of the implications for the coming generation of Catholic schools. It is well documented that a significant proportion of non-Catholic students is a natural and integral element of the modern Australian Catholic school. Today, greater attention is paid to the faith experience of those enrolled in Catholic schools and the implications for individual schools. At the same time the proportion of non-Catholic teachers has also begun to rise although much more slowly. These realities have immediate and long-term implications especially in the context of the issues developed by Bishop Putney and the D'Orsas. However, Croke views these realities as new and hopeful opportunities for Catholic schools.

Perhaps the major development in the coordination of Catholic schools in the last 40 years has been the establishment of Catholic Education Offices throughout Australia. Kelvin Canavan reviews the factors contributing to the development of the Catholic Education Office (CEO) of the Archdiocese of Sydney and provides an overview of its contribution to the educational mission of the Church. The growth of large and influential CEOs has had a significant impact on almost every aspect of Catholic education in Australia. Br Canavan identifies the years ahead for CEOs as a time of new challenges as schools respond to a weakening of the Catholic culture and religious practices symptomatic of a more secular society.

Part Two: Learning from Broader Perspectives

As Catholic schools in Australia address contemporary challenges and prepare for the future, the experiences and insights of others provide an opportunity for critical reflection upon current practices. Timothy Cook provides a glimpse at the reality of being a Catholic educational leader in the United States context. He considers the top three challenges facing these leaders and how such leaders have responded to these challenges to date. The challenges relate to funding, Catholic identity, and leadership. Finally, he provides comments about the way ahead for Catholic schools.

Oona Stannard's informative overview of the challenges before Catholic schools in England and Wales reveals Catholic schools as a vital part of the dual school system but one that is presently being subjected to spurious remarks and attacks. At the heart of the public challenge are firstly the issue of admissions and who has access to education in a Catholic school, and secondly the promotion of community cohesion. Oona argues the attacks are due to a lack of understanding about community cohesion and the role Catholic schools play in helping to build community cohesion. To the argument that faith-based schools are divisive, discriminatory and unnecessary, Oona puts a strong and comprehensive argument that Catholic schools are not ghettos but places that work in partnership with many others, both within and beyond the Catholic sector.

Patrick Lynch continues these themes by detailing the challenges and opportunities experienced by Catholic schools in New Zealand. Although New Zealand Catholic schools enrol about 9% of the total number of school students of New Zealand they, like Australian Catholic schools, are part of a strong international network of 50 million students. For Lynch, Catholic schools will constantly need to transform themselves so they became fundamentally global in their outlook, accepting that their students are international citizens with responsibilities to their fellow global citizens, wherever they happen to be living on the planet.

This theme of global responsibility is evident at the regional level in the chapter by Kalo Sikimeti. It provides critical insights into the realities confronting Catholic schools in the South Pacific during one of its bloodiest periods in its history. This chapter proposes that Catholic schools can work successfully to involve every person in their school communities and the whole society. The purpose is to give a sense of connectedness, a feeling of commitment and purpose to one another and to the children. Prayer is very powerful and Kalo Sikimeti sees it as a pillar of hope for the young children.

In an effort to prepare leaders of Catholic schools for the future it is important to consider leadership through the eyes of those of other faith-based schools. Silma Ihram's chapter provides insights into the realities of providing Muslim schools in Australia. Muslim schools are one of the newest additions to the independent school sector in Australia. The insights discussed in this chapter are salutary for leaders in all religious schools. Silma demonstrates how Muslim schools face similar problems as Catholic schools in a secular, modern and liberal society, but also face greater accountability, difficulty in obtaining approval through local Councils, and a range of student-related identity and faith-related problems. Administrators of Muslim schools continue to struggle with how to assist their students to resolve their identity issues, instil faith in a spiritual, non-politicised religion while preparing them for life in a liberal, even permissive, post-school environment.

As Catholic schools endeavour to contribute to the Church's mission and Australian society they are confronted by global questions regardless of where they are located. Echoing elements of the themes raised by both Bishop Toohey and Lynch, Hedley Beare, an internationally recognised Australian educational leader answers two pivotal questions. How many people can the planet support? And what happens when the earth's resources actually run out? His discussion of these confronting questions is important to the generation of students now in school whose daily lives throughout the 21st Century will be affected by climate. The chapter provides a macro perspective on the realities within which we live and contrasting a perspective to the theological perspective of Bishop Toohey. The chapter offers questions that need to be answered by those in Catholic schools.

Part Three: Leading Catholic Schools into the Future

In an effort to move from the diverse experience of others and macro perspectives of global challenges to the realities of daily leadership in Australian Catholic schools the following chapters provide an increasingly Australian perspective. In 2006 the Archdiocese of Hobart initiated an ongoing process of dialogue and critical reflection surrounding the evangelising mission of Catholic Schools in Tasmania. A Day of Discernment was conducted involving pastors, principals, representative of various governing bodies and senior personnel from the Catholic Education Office. Dan White articulates a range of challenges identified by the Day of Discernment associated with the evangelising mission of the Church within the Archdiocese of Hobart. The chapter explores, in a practical manner, the emerging policy initiatives and strategies being formulated in response to the challenges associated with the identity and mission of Catholic schools raised in Part 1.

Within the foundations established in Part 1, Anne Benjamin focuses on the Church's mission of Catholic schools to serve those who are neediest. For the marginalised of any society to experience the love of God demands a deliberate stance of hospitality and welcome to be evident in Catholic schools. This continuing concern offers an ideal opportunity for school leaders to revisit the issues of access and take Catholic schools into a new chapter of their history. Anne advocates that in the future Catholic schools will need to serve a more comprehensive cohort of children, especially those who are poor and disadvantaged, if they are to give witness to their 'ecclesial' identity.

Aboriginal people are widely recognised as the neediest group in Australian society. Joan Hendriks addresses the pathways to reconciliation against a backdrop that what has happened in the past cannot be mended overnight and requires justice when dealing with one another. Joan acknowledges more Australians are seeking involvement in the unfinished business of reconciliation through processes that promote dignity and respect of all. Her insights and reflections better inform members of Catholic schools of their role within the Spirit of Reconciliation.

Michael Bezzina also accepts the challenge to identify what makes Australian Catholic education explicitly Catholic, doing so through the lens of learning. The chapter provides an overview of an emerging framework for understanding the privileged work of leading learning in Catholic schools. The *Leaders Transforming Learning and Learners (LTLL)* pilot project revealed an enthusiasm among participants for working closely with the fundamental concerns of Catholic education in a way that is holistic, well-founded in the research and reflects accurately their unique values stance. This is a chapter for aspiring leaders in Catholic schools because it recognises current practice and points the way to the future.

Patrick Duignan also argues the idea of a collective responsibility for leadership in Catholic schools is desirable and attainable. The concept of distributed leadership, which is widely promoted as the preferred model for sharing leadership in schools and school communities, needs to be critiqued and challenged as it may well involve conflicting assumptions and/or a clash of paradigms. He believes a number of *Catholic imperatives* suggest an alternative paradigm that provides a framework for growing and nurturing the breadth and depth of leadership in Catholic schools. And the concept of love-inspired leadership overcomes many of the shortcomings of distributed leadership and incorporates the essence of these Catholic imperatives. The chapter by Bezzina and that by Duignan provide a conceptual framework for future research into what makes Australian Catholic schools distinctive in approach and their contribution to the Church's mission.

How do Catholic schools reflect commitment to the Church's mission and provide witness to their 'ecclesial' identity? In telling the story of one school, it is possible to understand Catholic schools a little better. Brenda Kennedy and Tricia Carr bring this anthology to conclusion appropriately with the gritty realities of how one school set out on its journey of hope for a group of children and families in Western Sydney. This story carries echoes of so many other Catholic schools throughout Australia, each endeavouring in its own way to honour its mission to children and to the Church.

We trust readers will recognise our efforts to deliberately integrate a diversity of perspectives as to how to meet the opportunities of these uncertain times.

Anne Benjamin and Dan Riley

PART ONE
Foundations of Catholic Schools

1
A New Ecclesial Context for Catholic Schools

Michael Putney

Catholic schools are an integral part of the Church's mission and their participation in the life of the Church is crucial to their identity. For Catholic schools to continue to be Catholic, it is essential for them to take seriously their ecclesial identity and their role in the Church's mission. To try to maintain or enhance the 'Catholic' identity of schools without dealing with their 'ecclesial' identity and mission would be doomed to failure (cf.Putney, 2005).

For example, we will adequately introduce students to the truths of the faith, and where possible to the One in whom we believe, only if they discover that our faith is *ecclesial*. It is ecclesial because it has come from Jesus himself through the proclamation of the apostles which has been transmitted through written record and the great living Tradition of the Church. Through the centuries, Tradition has faithfully reinterpreted and reappropriated the original experience of Christ which gave birth to the first proclamation. It is also ecclesial because it is shared with Catholic communities of faith around the world, is shaped by shared creedal formulations and recognises an authoritative teaching authority which interprets it.

Identity is shaped not only by one's own tradition but also by engagement with 'the other' which in this case is a multi-faceted other, including other Christians, other believers and above all the secular postmodern culture of Australia today. So we must focus not only on the schools' ecclesial identity, but also deal with their cultural context – not an easy task given the pervasive nature of our secular culture and those aspects of it which are antithetical to the Christian tradition (Putney, 2008).

Catholic schools also work within a Church still assimilating the teaching of Vatican Council II and the influence of Pope John Paul II while simultaneously responding to a vast array of new challenges from within and without. Features of the contemporary ecclesial context include: the centrality of an ecclesiology of communion, the Church's missionary calling, the Church's ecumenical and inter-religious commitments, its commitment to justice, its role as bearer of the Tradition, its contemplative character, and the universality of vocations within it. It is important to analyse this new ecclesial context and to explore its implications for Catholic education.

The Church is a communion

In contemporary theology the Church is most fundamentally understood as a *communion* – a biblical and patristic understanding embraced by Vatican Council II and by contemporary ecumenical dialogue.

To describe the Church as a communion is to say something much more than that the Church is a community: we are referring to the deeper foundation for what may be called community. The relationship between Christians is based upon their shared relationship with Jesus Christ through the Holy Spirit. Because each Christian is in Christ, each Christian thereby becomes a member of the Body of Christ and is intimately related to all other Christians. As a communion, the Church is intensely interpersonal, because it is based upon personal relationships with Jesus Christ through the Holy Spirit, drawing each Christian into the very inner life of the Triune God. We belong to each other because we belong to Christ. Therefore we have a fundamental calling to reach out to each other, to forgive each other, to respond to each other, no matter how difficult this may be. Everyone matters. Broken relationships can never simply be accepted.

Pope John Paul II referred to a 'spirituality of communion' at the heart of the Church's life which should be 'the guiding principle of education wherever individuals and Christians are formed' (John Paul II, 2000, p. 58).

This spirituality of communion, he wrote, 'indicates above all the heart's contemplation of the mystery of the Trinity dwelling in us, and whose light we must also be able to see shining on the face of the brothers and sisters around us'. It also means:

- An ability to think of our brothers and sisters in faith within the profound unity of the Mystical Body, as 'those who are a part of me'. This makes us able to share their joys and sufferings, to sense their desires and attend to their needs, to offer them deep and genuine friendship

- The ability to see what is positive in others, to welcome it and prize it as a gift of God: not only as a 'gift for me', and
- To know how to 'make room' for our brothers and sisters, bearing 'each other's burdens' (Gal 6:2) and resisting the selfish temptations which constantly beset us and provoke competition, careerism, distrust and jealousy (n43, pp.59-60).

Many in our secular culture, especially young people, have a desire for community or for belonging. What the Church offers is not community but *communion*, occurring at the deepest possible level with other human beings and with the whole of creation. This is a communion established by the Holy Spirit in Christ, and with God. In other words, the Church offers something more.

The implications for Catholic education are obvious. All the structures, processes and educational methodologies of our schools and offices are subject to a larger criterion against which they must always be judged. Does what we do/plan enhance or inhibit students, staff and families' experience of communion – remembering that this has a more profound significance than simply 'community'?

The Church is missionary

The Church continues the mission of Christ by the power of the Holy Spirit given at Pentecost. This mission flows from the mission of the Holy Trinity revealed in the sending of the Son and the Holy Spirit. Once the Church is understood as a communion, then the mission of the Church can be understood as flowing from, and leading to, communion. Consequently, one's definition of mission or evangelisation can rightly include many elements of the Church's work, such as work for justice and peace along with the explicit proclamation of the Gospel of Jesus Christ. The Church's mission can be described as working for the establishment of communion between God and humanity, and between human beings among themselves, and with the whole cosmos — a communion to be fully realised only at Christ's second coming.

Explicit proclamation of the Gospel of Jesus Christ draws people to communion with God and to the deeper communion with others that flows from a shared relationship with Christ. Working for justice, peace and reconciliation among people furthers communion because it breaks down the sinful barriers keeping people apart. The different elements of the Church's mission are never sufficient in themselves. Work for justice can easily become secularised without the eucharist or prayer. Eucharist and prayer without work for justice can easily become self-indulgent.

The implication of this for Catholic schools is that everyone involved in Catholic schools is a missionary. Each plays their part in a divine mission begun by the sending of the Son and the Holy Spirit and carried forward by the Church. No one is baptised only for their own sake but for the sake of the world which depends upon them to serve the cause of God's reign in everything they do. This is certainly true of the service our schools offer to the poor, to those who do not know Christ or believe in God, to those who hunger for authentic communion, to all who can be encouraged and formed to become missionaries in turn.

A New Evangelisation

In *Ecclesia in Oceania*, Pope John Paul II wrote that 'school staff who truly live their faith will be agents of a new evangelisation in creating a positive climate for the Christian faith to grow, and in spiritually nourishing the students entrusted to their care' (John Paul II, 2001, n33, p.78).

He continually called this responsibility for evangelisation in a country like our own a *New Evangelisation* because of the new situation in which we find ourselves at the end of the modern era. For such an evangelisation to be effective Catholic teachers will need the skills 'to give an account of the hope that is within us' (I Peter 3:15). They will need to discover the cause of their own hope anew through a particular kind of spiritual or faith formation and education.

A key element in this missionary task is leading students immersed in a post-modern culture to faith in God who has been revealed to them in Jesus Christ. This is no easy task today. David Tacey writes of Australians today:

> We are quite content to be unconsciously possessed by religious expectations and transcendental desires, but, perversely, we will not allow these expectations and desires a religious outlet or goal, but must always direct these desires towards the human and material level. And so we seek all manner of vulgar substitutes for spiritual satisfaction (Tacey, 1995, p.114).

The entry point for the Christian gospel to find its home in the culture of Australian young people in a way that is truly contemporary and yet authentically the gospel as it has been transmitted to us is not easily discernable. The Church needs to find doorways through which contemporary Australians can enter.

Some doorways may be found in their quest for community, the hunger for spirituality and the increasing sense of connectedness with the created order. If the gospel proclaimed by the Church helps people to more deeply belong to each other, to the larger created order and to God, then it may enable them to discover again the real identity of the Church which as a divinely established communion is the focus of such belonging.

When so defined, this task has implications for religious education and the total project of Catholic formation in our schools. These are being increasingly acknowledged and addressed but the task of effective evangelisation still lies ahead of us.

The Church is ecumenical

Pope John Paul II said 'the way of ecumenism' was 'the way of the Church' (John Paul II, 1995), evocatively describing the centrality of ecumenism in the life and mission of the Catholic Church. Previously, in June 1985, he spoke to the Roman Curia about ecumenism as 'a necessary dimension of the whole of the Church's life' to which everything must contribute:

> I have already asked on more than one occasion that the re-establishment of unity among all Christians must be considered a pastoral priority. We are committed together with our brothers and sisters of the other churches and ecclesial communities in the ecumenical movement (Information Service, 1985, p.2).

Each of those words is extremely important. It is 'necessary': it is not optional; it is an imperative arising from the very nature of the Church itself. It demands of us a response. 'It is a dimension of the Church's life,' meaning it is not only a task, or a ministry, or a particular mission; it is interior to the Church itself. The very existence, nature, and life of the Church have an ecumenical dimension.

Moreover, Pope John Paul II said that there is no moment of the Church's existence – no place where it exists, no aspect of its life, its members, its ministries, none of its activities, no decisions it makes, missions it undertakes, policies it formulates, relationships it establishes, tasks it undertakes or goals it seeks – that do not have an ecumenical dimension. Obviously this has very real implications for Catholic education.

Pope Benedict has shown an equal commitment to ecumenism. In his address to the cardinals before his inaugural mass he linked his new ministry as Pope with that of Peter, announcing that:

> his present successor aims, as a primary commitment, to work without sparing energies for the reconstitution of the full and visible unity of all the followers of Christ. This is his ambition, this is his imperative duty. (Benedict XVI, 2005, n724).

A practical articulation of the approach of the Catholic Church to ecumenism is the *Directory for the Application of Principles and Norms on Ecumenism,* published by the Pontifical Council for Promoting Christian Unity in 1993. The *Directory* describes the ecumenical imperative in terms of a theology of communion. This is consistent with all of the Church's ecumenical teaching since Vatican Council II, which sees the divisions between churches in terms of imperfect communion. Such 'imperfect forms of communion' do

> not correspond to the will of Christ, and weaken his Church in the exercise of its mission. The grace of God has impelled members of many Churches and ecclesial Communities, especially in the course of this present century, to strive to overcome the divisions inherited from the past and to build anew a communion of love by prayer, by repentance and by asking pardon of each other for sins of disunity past and present, by meeting in practical forms of cooperation and in theological dialogue. These are the aims and activities of what has come to be called the ecumenical movement (Pontifical Council, 1993, n19, pp.15-16).

Ecumenical activity must not be confused with non-denominational activity. One is not being ecumenical when one avoids dealing with differences between Christians out of a desire to show respect or tolerance or to build friendship. Ecumenical relationships are based upon a real encounter of Christians who bring their respective identities and so their differences into the relationship.

> In Catholic schools and Institutions, the Directory says, every effort should be made to respect the faith and conscience of students or teachers who belong to other Churches or ecclesial Communities. In accordance with their own approved statutes, the authorities of these schools and institutions should take care that clergy of other Communities have every facility for giving spiritual and sacramental ministration to their own faithful who attend such schools or institutions (ibid, p.67).

The phrase 'respecting the faith and conscience of students or teachers' challenges Catholic schools to take seriously the different Christian groupings represented in their student body. Other Christians ought not be treated as if they were Catholics (Putney, 2002).

James J Digiacomo sj writing recently about the goals of Catholic religious education posited that 'for non-Catholic students, the goals are necessarily different'. They include

> that they take seriously the religious dimension of life. The school's religious instruction and activities support and encourage commitment to their own religious tradition. They have an understanding and appreciation of the religious traditions and points of view of the Catholic community. They show signs of growth in moral maturity and practice (2007, p.13).

A goal so consistent with the Directory has very real implications for the preparation of teachers in Catholic schools who are called upon to give such ecumenically sensitive religious formation.

The Church is engaged in inter-religious relations

Catholics now take for granted that the Church is engaged in collaboration and dialogue with other Christian Churches. They have begun to recognise as well its commitment to a very special relationship with the Jewish people, which includes repentance for a history of oppression and persecution climaxing in the horrific events of the Holocaust. They are sometimes less aware of the Church's relationship with representatives of Islam and other world religions.

For example, Pope John Paul II reiterated the Church's commitment to a special relationship with Moslems in one of his General Audiences held in preparation for the Year of Great Jubilee:

> We Christians joyfully recognise the religious values we have in common with Islam. Today I would like to repeat what I said to young Moslems some years ago in Casablanca: 'We believe in the same God, the one God, the living God, the God who created the world and brings his creatures to their perfection (John Paul II, 1999).

He then spoke of the 'significant correspondence' between Christianity and Islam because of this monotheism, while still affirming very clearly our Christian faith in 'the unity of God being expressed in the mystery of three divine Persons' (ibid.).

He continued:

> In today's world where God is tragically forgotten, Christians and Moslems are called in one spirit of love to defend and always promote human dignity, moral values and freedom. The common pilgrimage to eternity must be expressed in prayer, fasting and charity, but also in joint efforts for peace and justice, for human advancement and the protection of the environment. By walking together on the path of reconciliation and renouncing, in humble submission to the divine will, any form of violence as a means of resolving differences, the two religions will be able to offer a sign of hope, radiating in the world the wisdom and mercy of that one God who created and governs the human family (ibid).

Pope John Paul II invited Catholics to collaborate with Moslems because they share with them a religious belief in a secular world. The beautiful image of members of the two religions 'walking together on the path of reconciliation' and thereby offering a sign of hope to the world illustrates just how different his vision was from that of some today who would wish to forge a chasm between the two religions and indeed to see Muslims as antagonists in the contemporary world.

Pope Benedict committed himself to continuing the Church's co-operation with and dialogue with the members of other world religions in his address to the cardinals before his inaugural Mass in Rome when he spoke of his task 'to make the light of Christ shine before the men and women of today, not his own light but that of Christ':

> Conscious of this, I turn to all, also to those who follow other religions or who simply seek an answer to the fundamental questions of life and have not yet found it. I turn to all with simplicity and affection, to

assure them that the Church wishes to continue to engage with them in an open and sincere dialogue, in search of the true good of man and of society (Benedict XVI, 2005, n724).

There are very real implications in this for Catholic education. Unlike ecumenical relations, inter-religious relations are not based on a common faith in Jesus Christ and certainly not on a common baptism. They may not even be based upon a common faith in one God. However, students from other world religions must be respected and they cannot be asked to compromise their own religious beliefs.

At the same time a Catholic school cannot in any way minimise its Catholic identity simply because its student body includes non-Christians. It is too easy to do so out of a false desire to show respect; whereas true respect occurs when a truly Catholic school welcomes non-Christian students in a way which allows each to maintain their own religious integrity.

The Church works for justice

Last century, the Church developed a vast and profound teaching on social justice, unsurpassed anywhere or any time in history, which was reinforced by the Vatican Council II and continued by the post-conciliar papal magisterium. Pope Benedict has made his own contribution in *Deus Caritas Est*. Firstly he situated the ministry of charity at the centre of the church identity as

> expressed in her three-fold responsibility: of proclaiming the word of God (kerygma-martyria), celebrating the sacraments (leitourgia), and exercising the ministry of charity (diakonia). These duties presuppose each other and are inseparable. For the Church, charity is not a kind of welfare activity which could equally well be left to others, but is a part of her nature, an indispensable expression of her very being (Benedict XVI, 2006, n39).

After affirming work for justice as essential to this commitment to charity, he then described the Church's role in achieving justice in a nuanced way within this larger commitment to love.

> The Church cannot and must not take upon herself the political battle to bring about the most just society possible. She cannot and must

not replace the State. Yet at the same time, she cannot and must not remain on the sidelines in the fight for justice. She has to play her part through rational argument and she has to reawaken the spiritual energy without which justice, which always demands sacrifice, cannot prevail and prosper. A just society must be the achievement of politics, not of the Church.

Yet the promotion of justice through efforts to bring about openness of mind and will to the demands of the common good is something which concerns the Church deeply (ibid, n45).

Some of the implications for schools of this commitment to justice have long been recognised. Students ought not only be encouraged to have a commitment to working for justice but also educated about our Catholic social justice tradition and its theological foundations. If graduates of our schools are to play their role in building a just society they need to have at their disposal the rich body of Catholic social justice teaching and at the same time be committed to making their own contribution even at personal cost and despite opposition from others.

The Church is the bearer of the Tradition

An essential responsibility of the Church is to bear anew to each generation the Apostolic Tradition which enables them to make their own the life-giving revelation of God in Jesus Christ. Sometimes people fear we have lost our firm grasp of the Tradition and seek some kind of 'restoration'. This could involve restoring the ecclesiastical culture of a previous generation which would not serve the present one. What is needed is a reclaiming of the wholeness of the Tradition which has come to us from previous generations but in a way which allows it to speak in new ways to this generation.

To reclaim the life-giving truths at the heart of the Catholic Tradition is to rediscover a God who is Trinity. This becomes very challenging in the context of a variety of world religions which are non-Trinitarian, and of a secular society which has left no place for God. The Church also needs to reclaim a truly 'Christian' faith, which is to reaffirm that Jesus Christ is the centre of human existence and human history and that we have been 'saved' by him. This may require a new language in order to become a gospel of liberation for young people. We also need to rediscover the Eucharistic faith which we take for granted and the Marian faith which has yet to find a contemporary expression in the Australian church.

The relationship we enter into with God through Jesus Christ – encountered in the Word and in the Eucharist – introduces us to a whole communion which includes Mary, the saints, and Christians throughout the ages and around the world. This is the fundamental ecclesial experience of Catholic faith.

That Catholics today sometimes have a weaker grasp of their Trinitarian faith is not just a sign of the erosion of our faith tradition, but also of the Church's difficulty in communicating God to the contemporary world. We have to learn again to speak of the Triune God shown to us through Jesus Christ as the most liberating and enlightening of all truths.

Catholics stand for something. They believe in truth about the world, themselves, and God, as they have come to understand it through their religious tradition. In a post-modern world where one becomes very conscious of different perspectives on the truth, there needs to be a certain humility in the way this is proposed, while still believing that truth can be grasped and truth claims can be made about the teachings enshrined in our Tradition. As believers, we offer an interpretation of the whole of reality and not just a part of it, because of our conviction that there is a divine source for all that is and a divine future as well.

This is not simply an intellectual journey of understanding. Rather, it is an encounter with a mystery in which we participate. There can be no separation between faith as an intellectual exercise and faith as a spiritual process. To introduce people to the truths of our faith is to introduce people to the Truth whom we worship and love.

We are not only called to find new ways of saying what we believe. More importantly, we need to find new ways of believing. The former without the latter can appear to be merely new packaging. The latter, though more demanding, is essential.

At the beginning of the third millennium, the Church, above all, will need to be a community which enables peoples to experience a deeply, authentic Christian spirituality. Doctrines alone do not satisfy the hunger in the heart of contemporary Australians though they remain vitally important. Discourse about God is not the only thing people are seeking. Experience of God is also what they are longing for. Clarity about God without the possibility of experiencing a relationship with God will never be enough.

This has real implications for Catholic schools which are privileged locations for introducing young people to the great Tradition. Religious education and catechesis serve this larger goal. Not all will enter into a life-giving relationship with this Tradition but they have the right to be introduced to it in a Catholic school.

The Church is contemplative

One of Pope John Paul II's most important contributions to our reflection on the mission of the Church at the beginning of the new millennium was to emphasise the deepest spiritual dimension of the Tradition of which the Church is the bearer:

> Is it not one of the 'signs of the times' that in today's world, despite widespread secularisation, there is a widespread demand for spirituality, a demand which expresses itself in large part as a renewed need for prayer? Other religions, which are now widely present in ancient Christian lands, offer their own responses to this need, and sometimes they do so in appealing ways. But we who have received the grace of believing in Christ, the revealer of the Father and the Saviour of the world, have a duty to show to what depths the relationship with Christ can lead (John Paul II, 2000, n45-46).

He referred to the great mystical tradition of the Church of both East and West and described prayer 'as a genuine dialogue of love' and as 'a journey totally sustained by grace, which nonetheless demands an intense spiritual commitment'. He then concluded:

> Yes, dear brothers and sisters, our Christian communities must become genuine 'schools' of prayer, where the meeting with Christ is expressed not just in imploring help but also in thanksgiving, praise, adoration, contemplation, listening and ardent devotion, until the heart truly 'falls in love'. Intense prayer, yes, but it does not distract us from our commitment to history: by opening our heart to the love of God it also opens it to the love of our brothers and sisters, and makes us capable of shaping history according to God's plan (ibid. n33).

The implication of this for Catholic schools is that students ought to have the possibility of experiencing a relationship with God, through learning to pray deeply in their hearts and not just to know prayers. The Catholic tradition of prayer is not only liturgical but also contemplative.

Too often Catholics look elsewhere for formation in prayer of the heart, prayer of silence, or contemplation when they deserve to know about it and to know how to pray in this way through their own Catholic religious formation.

In the Church everyone has a vocation

The most important of all vocations in the Catholic tradition is the fundamental vocation to holiness and to participation in the life and mission of the Church, which is common to all through their baptism. Only in this context can we speak of the four states of life or vocations – priesthood, religious life, single life and marriage. But there is a further vocation: the personal vocation unique to each one. It is this which really gives the passion and the motivation whereby Catholics live out their fundamental baptismal vocation. Each person is called to make their own unique contribution to the life and mission of the Church and only the discovery of this personal call is likely to inspire young Australians to commit themselves to the mission of the Church (Grisez and Shaw, 2003, pp.34-35).

In *Ecclesia in Oceania* Pope John Paul II wrote concerning the vocation of teachers in Catholic schools:

> For the lay people involved, teaching is more than a profession: it is a vocation to form students, a widespread and indispensable lay service in the Church (n77. See also Hahenenberg, 2007).

This is the great challenge for Catholic schools – to help teachers discover their personal vocation and to engage in it with passion.

People often speak of the loss of Religious from our Catholic schools and then rightly affirm the continuation of the mission of the schools by lay people. However, unless one recognises that the personal vocation of the Religious was what mattered and not just that they were Religious, one can fail to recognise that it is the personal vocation of lay people in our schools that matters and not just that they are lay Catholics.

One of the crucial implications of this for Catholic schools is that teachers have the support they need to discover their personal vocation.

Conclusion

Catholic schools are continuing a role that has always been part of the

Church's mission. That role is changing because of the changing culture within which they are situated but also because of the changing ecclesial context itself. Catholic schools will flourish if they make the adjustments necessary to deal with these new contexts. They are already trying to do so and as they reflect more upon the task they will, by God's grace, make the responses necessary to meet the challenge.

References

Benedict XVI, (2005) The New Pope's First Speech, *Origins* 34:45, April 28, n724.

Benedict XVI, (2006) *Encyclical Letter Deus Caritas Est of the Supreme Pontiff. Benedict XVI to the Bishops, Priests and Deacons, Men and Women Religious and all the Lay Faithful on Christian Love.* Strathfield: St Paul's.

Digiacomo, James J. (2007) Educating for a Living Faith. *America* 197:6. September 10.

Grisez, Germain and Shaw, Russel. (2003*) Personal Vocation. God Calls Everyone by Name.* Huntington: Our Sunday Visitor.

Hahenenberg, Edward. (2007) The Vocation of Lay Ecclesial Ministry, *Origins* 37:12 August 30.

Information Service, (1985) Twenty-Fifth Anniversary of the Secretariat for Promoting Christian Unity, *Information Service* 59.

John Paul II, (1995) *Encyclical Letter Ut Unum Sint of the Holy Father John Paul II on Commitment to Ecumenism.* Vatican City: Libreria Editrice Vaticana.

John Paul II, (2000) *Apostolic Letter Novo Millenio Ineunte of His Holiness Pope John Paul II to the Bishops, Clergy and Lay Faithful at the Close of the Great Jubilee of the Year 2000,*Vatican City: Libreria Editrice Vaticana.

John Paul II, (2001) *Post Synodal Apostolic Exhortation Ecclesia in Oceania of His Holiness Pope John Paul II to the Bishops, Priests and Deacons, Men and Women in the Consecrated Life and all the Lay Faithful on Jesus Christ and the Peoples of Oceania: Walking His Way, Telling His Truth, Living His Life.* Vatican City: Libreria Editrice Vaticana.

John Paul II. (1999) General Audience Wednesday 5 May. *http://www.vatican.va/holy_father/john_paul_ii/audiences/1999/documents/hf_jp-ii_aud_05051999_en.html* [accessed 9 October 2007].

Pontifical Council, Pontificium Consilium ad Christianorum Unitatem Fovendam (1993) *Directory for the Application of Principles and Norms on Ecumenism.* London: CTS.

Putney, M. (2002) Catholic Schools and Ecumenism. *Catholic School Studies* 75:11 May.

Putney, M. (2005) The Catholic School of the Future. *Australian Catholic Record* 82:4, pp.387-398.

Putney, M. (2008) 'Catholic Identity and Mission' in Neil Ormerod (ed) *Identity and Mission in Catholic Agencies*, Strathfield, St Paul's Publications, pp. 15-37.

Tacey, D. (1995) *Edge of the Sacred. Transformation in Australia.* Blackburn: Harper Collins.

2
Mission and Catholic Schools: Grounding hope in uncertain times

THERESE D'ORSA AND JIM D'ORSA

Always be ready to make your defence to anyone who demands from you an accounting for the hope that is in you… (1 Peter 3:15)

Catholics share faith in a Trinitarian God, a God understood as a community of persons. Catholics also believe human beings are made in the image of God, created to be persons-in-community. To be a person-in-community is, however, to be a person-in-culture, since all human communities exist in cultures. It is also to participate in the dialogues which create and sustain cultures.

Created in the image and likeness of God, ideally Catholics seek to be committed to God's mission in the manner taught and witnessed within human history by Jesus. The dynamic of mission is the creation of communities-for-mission, communities which are, at the same time, embedded in culture and maintained through dialogue.

The Catholic Church world-wide is a communion of these communities-in-mission. The emerging vision of what these communities, both individually and linked together can be, in the service of the Kingdom of God, provides a basis for profound hope.

Mission community and culture

A time of disconnection and uncertainty

Today's young people are, indisputably, growing into adulthood in uncertain times. If the times are uncertain for young people, they are scarcely less so for those responsible for their education. In the religious domain, for example, the extraordinary advances in biblical scholarship whilst potentially very enriching for teachers of the faith and their students, also bring with them the added requirement that teachers access appropriate and ongoing study and formation in order to carry out their ministry of teaching. There may also be the necessity of a sometimes painful 'letting go' of what has been one's previous grasp of the scriptural foundations of faith.

Advances in biblical scholarship have occurred at the very time when the salience of the Christian story continues to diminish for many people. There is much work to be done, with the help of these advances, in rebuilding Christianity as a contemporary metanarrative so that our young people may not only be proud of it as a principal source and shaper of their own personal worldview, but may contribute to its ongoing enrichment.

God's mission in a Church 'becoming'

Beyond the revolution in biblical scholarship, it is also important to note other ecclesial factors. In terms of historical experience, students attending Catholic schools today do so in a unique ecclesial environment. They are one of the first generations to grow up in a Church which is becoming truly global, no longer a European Church with branch offices in other cultural regions of the world as had been the case for many centuries. The potential of these communities networked across the globe to welcome and help form today's young people as global citizens and as Chrisians is enormous.

A feature of this new ecclesial environment is the emergence at the most official level, of a dramatic change in the understanding of the Church's mission. As an outcome of the work of Vatican Council II (1962-65), God's mission is being re-situated at the centre of ecclesial understanding of mission. The key insight on mission adopted by the Council is expressed in *Ad Gentes* 2 – 'The Church on earth is by its very nature missionary since, according to the plan of the Father, it has its origin in the mission of the Son and the Holy Spirit'.

Instead of focusing on the various goals of missionary engagement as was expected, the Council switched focus onto the nature of the Church itself, and declared it to be fundamentally missional. Over time the implications of this shift in mission understanding are being worked through.

A cluster of associated insights has accompanied the major shift. If the whole Church is missionary by its very nature, then one of the most important corollaries is that each baptised member is called to embrace God's mission in some way. Jesus identified his mission as making present God's dream for humanity, which he called the Kingdom of

God. Each one of the baptised is, therefore, similarly called to help God's Kingdom break into the milieus that form the matrix of human life. How can young people and their teachers make sense of this?

With this key insight of Vatican Council II, mission has once again taken on a Trinitarian character, as in the period prior to the first expansion of Europe into the Americas in the 16th century. The God of Jesus Christ is understood as a Trinity of persons whose essence is community. God's life is shared with others through creation which ushered in the beginning of history. Within history God's mission is carried forward in the making whole of all creation (cf Mark 16:15). The pursuit of this mission across time is carried forward in ways known fully only to God.

In the years following Vatican Council II, the word which quickly became synonymous with the Church's mission was 'evangelisation'. It is a broad term covering what the Church does in pursuing its mission. As the Gospels clearly show us, it implies both the speaking of Good News (proclamation) and the living of Good News (witness). In any era the shape of witness to the good news will vary with the circumstances impacting on people's lives. In our times, witness obviously must include work for justice, human liberation and reconciliation, and an imperative to care for God's creation.

Jesus' mission and the Kingdom of God

When, as a metaphor for God's mission, Jesus used the phrase 'the Kingdom of God', he was employing words redolent with meaning for his hearers (Fuellenbach, 1995). Jesus drew on these understandings but also gave them added, and sometimes different significance, particularly in his Kingdom parables.

The community of disciples (the Church) is not only at the service of this Kingdom, but themselves constitute a social space where people can actively experience the Kingdom in the here and now. The invitation to young people to make a positive choice for the Church community must, therefore, be clearly accepted by them as an invitation to join a community whose goal is to create, both within and beyond itself, the Kingdom of God.

Discipleship means accepting the challenge to learn to create and maintain a religious and social space where people actually experience the Kingdom, as well as gain the formation and spiritual strength to increase its scope. This occurs in families, schools, parishes, and the many other communities which are influenced by the movement of the Holy Spirit.

Jesus identified his own life and mission with the covenantal requirement of his own people when he gave his own 'mission statement':

> The Spirit of the Lord is upon me because he has anointed me to bring good news to the poor. He has sent me to proclaim release to the captives and recovery of sight to the blind, and to let the oppressed go free, to proclaim the year of the Lord's favour (Luke 4:18-19).

Contrast communities

The Hebrew tradition on which our Christian tradition stands, grows out of an experience of being called by God to be of significance in God's pursuit of wholeness for creation. This was expressed in the covenant as an agreement to be a 'contrast society' that is a society in which relationships with, and action on behalf of, the most marginalised were to mark the essential difference between God's people and surrounding peoples (Fuellenbach, 1995, p.30). Through the mediums of narrative, law and liturgy Israel assembled over time an oral and written tradition whose interpretation was central in establishing its identity as a contrast society.

The Christian tradition focuses on a second deliberate intervention by God in regard to the inauguration of a contrast community through the life and ministry of Jesus. The call to discipleship that lies at the heart of God's mission is a call to be co-creators of contrast communities. Contrast communities live within a culture and, in mission, challenge certain expressions of the culture when they do not align with the values of the Kingdom. The Christian conception of contrast community differs from the earlier Jewish conception of Israel's covenantal responsibilities. Whereas the Hebrew conception defines identity as separation from other societies, the Christian community lives within society, not separate from it.

Rebuilding the Catholic sub-culture for mission

Sub-cultures, particularly major ones such as Australian Catholicism, are multi-dimensional constructs. If we are to rebuild our Australian Catholic sub-culture so as to be effectively missional, that is composed of contrast communities, then the work needs to proceed at a number of levels.

Whatever model of culture one works from, it is the ideational area within culture which must be affected if indepth change is to occur (Cote, 1996; Luzbetak, 1988; Tanner, 1997). This area is comprised of the beliefs, values, symbols and ideas which, coupled with the dynamic myths, lie at the heart of a people's culture. Change at this level is difficult to achieve, but once it does occur, it is pervasive in its effects.

Changes in the understanding of mission are undoubtedly among the most significant to occur in the ideational area of Catholicism worldwide in recent centuries. Such changes and their implications lie at the heart of the reconstruction of Australian Catholicism, affecting the way it construes its various ministries, including those to young people in schools.

As with other Catholic Churches world-wide, our re-building takes place not only in our unique context, but also within the global context. The factors that impact on all societies and cultures, viz globalisation and the increased pluralisation in many facets of human life, are also affecting us. Western societies such as our own are also experiencing advanced secularisation (Rolheiser, 2006).

In dealing with the extreme pluralism within society (Congregation for Catholic Education (1997)), the challenge is to put in place processes of dialogue so that the many understandings and expressions of truth, beauty and goodness held among humans may be appropriately evaluated and shared, with the resulting insights brought to bear constructively on human living.

Communities sustaining persons for mission

Insight into God as a community of persons with a mission or purpose in regard to the whole of creation is implicit in the Christian scriptures. Coupled with this is the understanding, common to both Hebrew and Christian scriptures, of the human person as made in the image and likeness of God. The human person, then, is created as a person-in-community with a mission to make whole all of creation.

Since all communities exist within a broader culture, to be a person-in-community is to be a person in a culture. Christian communities carry a responsibility to be aware of the extent to which the seeds of the gospel are present in their local culture and where the culture constrains the freedom to love. As contrast communities their members are also concerned with how the public culture impacts on the lives of other groups besides themselves. Contrast communities need to look outwards as well as inwards when it comes to building God's Kingdom. Their mission is to address local realities in terms that make sense within the parameters of the local culture.

Renewing the sense of mission

A renewed sense of mission is more likely to take life in our Catholic sub-culture if the community is involved in dialogical processes which engage the community's members. This dialogue needs to be carried on at three levels and involves asking very fundamental questions:

At the level of mission
- Is our school community life an end in itself, or does it exist for a purpose beyond itself. If so, what?

At the level of culture
- In what ways does our Australian culture both liberate and constrain our freedom in understanding and pursuing the mission of our school community?

At the level of community life
- To what extent does our school community proclaim and witness to Jesus and his mission, in our particular context?

Because not everyone views community life and mission from the same perspective, dialogue is absolutely essential, even among those ostensibly committed to participation in mission. Dialogue is carried on not only in words, or formal processes, but also in the acts of living, acting, and reflecting. It is a dialogue embedded in the praxis of the community. Christian identity emerges from the sense of belonging which results from active engagement in this praxis.

Orientations within a living Tradition

A biblical model for dialogue

Walter Brueggemann (1982), a highly respected biblical scholar and commentator particularly on the Hebrew Bible, explores the orientations which the Old Testament faith communities brought to bear on their religious experience, and which took shape in the canon of their scriptures. His classic work has exceptional relevance for contemporary educators.

Brueggemann's thesis is that the process of differentiation within the canon of the Hebrew Bible into Torah, Prophets and Writings is not a matter of chance but presents us with a model of dialogue which is fundamental to Israel's identity and to its living out that identity as a contrast society.

In the Hebrew Bible, the Torah combines both the central narrative of Israel and the Law which gives the community life and direction. It is the most sacred and fundamental part of the Jewish tradition, but not the final word on the whole of the tradition.

Within Israel's social structure, the Torah orientation characterised the leadership, whose responsibility it was to ensure that God's covenant with the people was honoured. It was a responsibility shared between the priests and the king. As history attests, the kings found it difficult to lead Israel as a 'contrast society', not surprisingly since there were few models to follow. The tendency was always to move towards cultural accommodation with surrounding peoples, with the result that the Torah orientation was often co-opted to serve the king's ends.

Moving the analysis onto a biblical canvas encompassing both Hebrew and Christian scriptures, people within the faith community with a Torah orientation are those who see it as their essential responsibility to preserve the essence of God's disclosure to God's people. This is because such disclosure is fundamental to the faith of the community. It provides the ethos which underpins both identity and mission.

All faith communities, irrespective of the cultures in which they exist, need members who have a Torah orientation, a sense of what is fundamental and non-negotiable in defining the identity and mission of the group. Obviously, difficulties arise when such people impose their own views of what is fundamental and non-negotiable in place of what God has disclosed, thus introducing distortion with consequent division, and the pursuit of self-interest.

In the life of Israel, the corrective to this form of distortion was the prophets. As Brueggemann expresses it, the perspective of the prophet was shaped by the gap identified between what God had promised and what the religious leaders and the king were delivering.

The ministry of the prophets proceeded on the twin bases of love of the Tradition and critique of current practice. They spoke strongly against lack of justice for and exploitation of the most vulnerable members, incompetence and poor judgement of rulers, lack of vision including incapacity to frame an alternative vision to present practice, and liturgy which in consequence was problematic and dishonoured God. Prophets also denounced cultural accommodations that undermined Israel's covenantal relationship and subverted it as a contrast society.

The prophets recognised the power of symbolic action in communicating their message, and were adept at marshalling the symbols of their culture to enhance the impact of their message. Such action often generated a dialogue which shaped Israel's identity. Despite this, their role was not always appreciated. In addition, leaders sometimes recruited false prophets to justify courses of action, or to provide religious legitimation to various forms of cultural accommodation which were inconsistent with God's covenant and with Israel's commitment to be a contrast society.

Whilst the dialogue, which resulted from prophecy, helped establish Israel's identity and mission, another 'voice' also participated in the shaping of this identity and mission, viz 'the Writings'. This sector of the Old Testament is comprised of the Psalms and the Wisdom literature. It continued to shape Israel's narrative into the Hellenistic period.

By comparison with the two previous authoritative forms of knowing and their allied orientations held within the faith community, the Writings represent a more muted voice in the dialogue of identity. Within the Psalms and the Wisdom literature, the concern is not what God has done for Israel in the past, nor how secular and religious leaders are delivering God's promise, but rather how God's presence is discovered and celebrated in ordinary human experience. How is God's presence experienced in the prayer life of our community? How does the wisdom of Israel compare with that of other communities? What has been learned about living as a contrast society? How do these understandings bear on day to day decisions? The concern in the Writings is less with God's disclosure in regard to mission and identity (Torah), or with critique (Prophets), than with what needs to be done in the here and now to keep community life purposeful and on an even keel. The Wisdom orientation is pragmatic, focused on what works for the community within its cultural context.

Pluralism as a strength in community life

Brueggemann's contention is that a healthy religious community recognises and encourages the development of all three 'voices' among its members. The Torah voice focuses on what is central and always essential. The Prophetic voice challenges in terms of the vision and performance, that is, it identifies the gap between the promise which follows God's disclosure and the experience of people in the here and now. The Wisdom voice is concerned with making sense of things in the here and now and effectively using the resources of culture to their full potential, including in worship. All three voices share a common love of the tradition and narrative of the community, albeit appreciated from different perspectives (See also Malcolm, 2002, pp.24-30).

In working to create genuine hope for young people, it is essential that the education offered is not indulging a particular, perhaps unwitting, preference for one orientation to the neglect of the others. Not only do young people have the right to a thorough grounding in the whole Tradition, but it is essential that they see and experience the interconnectedness between the three orientations. They need to learn that dialogue-in-community is a consequence of being a person-in-community, a person made in the image of God. As in Israel, none of us has the right to author the Tradition in the sense of providing a less-than-holistic or distorted introduction to the whole. The substance of our religious task lies in the whole. How competent are our teachers to deliver in this regard? Do such considerations feature in discussing the mission of the school?

Grounding hope – educational challenges

It is not difficult to transfer consideration from Brueggemann's canvas, the Hebrew scriptures, to include the Christian scriptures and the experience of the past two thousand years in which communities have attempted to engage in faithful living. Nor is it surprising that, independently of Brueggemann's work, Gonzales (1999), Bevans and Shroeder (2004) have found quite similar orientations in Christian theology, as they have worked on issues of mission and identity. These scholars argue for the recognition and value of the pluralism inherent in our tradition. They also argue the need for dialogue within Christian communities as a way forward in re-configuring Catholic culture, and developing a new sense of belonging consistent with this reconfiguration. This is important in any work of evangelisation.

There are many implications for school leaders which emanate from the above discussion. The following represent some obvious examples.

Educating in the entire Tradition
Teachers and leaders have a grave obligation to educate in the tradition in its entirety. In uncertain times, when we have to work particularly diligently at recognising the points of continuity and discontinuity in the way we relate to the heart of our faith tradition, the tendency to be selective must be avoided. The surest foundation of the hope which

will sustain young people and teachers alike is genuine and imaginative leadership in accessing God's disclosure to us as given in the canon of scripture and offered within a community-in-mission.

Students grow up in a particular youth sub-culture (Crawford & Rossiter, 2006). It is important to understand and have some empathy with its aspirations while being able to recognise its limitations and potential as a vehicle to advance God's Kingdom. There is much that is intuitively prophetic in youth culture.

Communities that are not strongly and clearly mission-oriented are likely to be problematic in our post-modern context, and will struggle with the issue of identity. This is obvious in the case of school practices. Strategic planning, for example, even though rightly attractive to the Wisdom orientation within our tradition, does not in itself demonstrate that a school is mission-oriented, even if it gives lip service to what is fundamental in terms of a Torah orientation. Only if strategic planning is used as a servant of the whole Tradition, and is embedded in the Tradition as the foundation and model of the educational process, can the extent of the present attention and level of resourcing being given to it within Catholic Education be justified.

To encourage young people along the path of prophetic engagement is a core part of the educational enterprise, and one particularly suited to the sensibilities and generosity of the young. However, without capacity to discern the dysfunctionalities in our society so as to provide for human betterment, even the best efforts of generous people can be quickly dissipated. Similarly, without a firm adherence to the core of God's disclosure as given in Christ and lived in community, the prophetic voice tends to grow shrill or off-key, and finally muted.

Living the Tradition

In Brueggemann's analysis the educational challenge is the same as that inherent in the living of the Tradition. It is a challenge to see and live the connectedness of the elements. We see the importance of this only too readily when we recognise that our sacramental life seems to bear little connection with our struggle for justice, or our acceptance of the Holy Spirit seems not to seriously guide the sense we must make of living in a very complex and seriously fragmented world.

Prayer and the willingness to pray are essential ingredients in all three orientations. There is thus no single orientation to prayer either for individuals or for the school community which alone does justice to our Tradition. People will come to value prayer through the experiences of all three orientations. It is important to keep this in mind in preparing liturgies.

Fundamental to all three orientations within one Tradition, and to the sustaining of hope, is life in community. This is a great strength of most Catholic schools and provides a very sound basis on which to build in securing identity and mission.

God's mission in schools

God's mission exists beyond the scope of the Church's mission. Jesus' teaching on the Kingdom of God is a crucial element in taking forward God's mission in our work. Over many years we have had cause to be seriously concerned at the lack of even a basic grasp of Jesus' teaching on the Kingdom amongst Catholic school personnel with whom we have been involved in study programs. Given that such understanding is fundamental to grasping both Jesus' mission and that of his Church, this constitutes a substantial challenge.

Building the culture of the school on the basis that the dignity of each individual lies in being a person-in-community has serious implications for school practices. These implications pertain to what the school promotes, what it asks of its teachers, and how it relates to the local Catholic communities such as family, parish and diocese. They bear directly on the hope students have of a better world and their place in it.

Since community cannot be separated from the culture in which it exists amongst teachers and leaders, more serious attention needs to be given as to what is empowering and disempowering for people who live in Christian communities in Australia. Where is the culture inimical to the Gospel and where does it carry the seeds of the Gospel? What are the implications of the answer to this question for the entire curriculum? A contrast community needs to know what it aligns with, and what it stands in contrast to, if it is to be an effective witness to the Gospel.

Conclusion

The theme of this chapter has been the grounding of hope in uncertain times. We live in a post-modern era, a time of becoming, when it is difficult to discern what the shape of societal and cultural change will be, even in the immediate term. This has forced some fundamental re-evaluation of what it means to be Church and in consequence, what it means to be Catholic. The dynamics at work are complex. It seems impossible to retreat to the security of a traditional community and at the same time engage people with the message of Jesus 'to the ends of the earth'.

The dynamics of change point to the importance of ongoing discernment of God's mission and the responsibility of discipleship carried out by persons-in-community. There are a number of ways of framing responses that will be reached through dialogue, each with its own legitimacy. Mission therefore needs to be formulated in a way that respects the 'dignity of difference' (Sacks, 2002) found in all authentic Catholic communities now and across time. Such an approach provides a basis for hope and unity within diversity.

A time of 'becoming' is also a time for choosing. This chapter has endeavoured to explore some of the parameters of choice opened up by the developing theology of mission which has emerged as a result of Vatican Council II. Catholic identity is in the process of being redefined under pressure of changes occurring globally. If the mission challenges are grasped, the result will be a richer rather than a diminished understanding of what it means to be Catholic and a member of the Church. The outcome rests not only with Catholic leaders but with God's Spirit. In this context wise leaders recognise that young people deserve to be grounded in their tradition in all its richness. They also recognise that young people have their own role in the enrichment of that Tradition, as shapers and not merely inheritors.

References

Bevans, S. and Shroeder, R. (2004) *Constants in Context*. Maryknoll N.Y.:Orbis.
Brueggemann, W. (1982) *The Creative Word*, Philadelphia: Fortress Press.
Congregation for Catholic Education (1997) *The Catholic School on the Threshold of the Third Millennium*. Strathfield: St Paul's Publications, n1.
Cote, R. (1996) *Revisioning Mission: The Catholic Church and Culture in Post-Modern America,* New York: Paulist Press, chs 7 & 8.
Crawford, M. and Graham Rossiter, G. (2006) *Reasons for Living* Camberwell: ACER Press.
Flannery, A. ed. (1975) *Vatican Council II The Conciliar and Post Conciliar Documents*. New York: Costello.
Fuellenbach, J. (1995) *The Kingdom of God*, Maryknoll N.Y.: Orbis, Part 1.
Gonzales, J. (1999) *Christian Thought Revisited*, Maryknoll N.Y.: Orbis.

Lakeland, P. (1997) *Postmodernity*, Minneapolis: Fortress Press.
Luzbetak, L. SVD (1988) *The Church and Cultures: New Perspectives in Missiological, Anthropology,* Maryknoll N.Y.: Orbis.
Malcolm, L (2002) 'An Interview with David Tracey' in *The Christian Century*, February 13-20, pp.24-30.
Moltmann, J. The Church in the Power of the Spirit, quoted in Stephen Bevans and Roger Shroeder (2004) *Constants in Context: A Theology of Mission for Today,* Maryknoll N.Y.: Orbis, pp.298-299.
Pope John Paul II (2001) *Ecclesia in Oceania*, Strathfield: St Pauls Publications, n6.
Rolheiser, R. (2006) *Secularity and the Gospel*. New York: The Crossroad Publishing Company.
Sacks, J. (2002) *The Dignity of Difference*, London: Continuum.
Schreiter, R. (1997) *The New Catholicity*. Maryknoll N.Y.:Orbis ch 1.
Tanner, K. (1997) *Theories of Culture*, Minneapolis: Fortress Press.

3
Stewardship and God's Creation: A theological reflection[1]

Chris Toohey

'In the beginning...' These words open both the Book of Genesis and the Gospel according to John. This wonderfully evocative phrase recalls that creation had a beginning, when time and space began. Before the beginning nothing other than God existed. There was no matter, no space, no time. There was only God – the eternal God who always was.

It is difficult, if not impossible, for us who are bound by space and time in a three dimensional world, to imagine a being who never had a beginning. Little children often ask me, 'Who made God?' When I tell them that no one made God their faces display a mixture of wonder and perplexity.

Faith takes us beyond mere imagination to believe in and relate to the personal presence of the God who has chosen to reveal himself to us. He has let us know who he is, our place in the universe, how we are meant to live and what our final destiny is. God revealed himself to the People of Israel as the one and only true God: there is no other. The living experience of the presence of God in history was the foundation of the faith of Israel.

Creation

The magnificent account of the creation of the universe by God, as told in the Book of Genesis, is an expression of that faith. Genesis reveals a God who is sovereign and free, who decides to create from no necessity. No reason is given. Yet it was no mere impulse: God knew what he was

---

[1] This chapter is an amended version of the *Rerum Novarum* Lecture given by Bishop Toohey in Melbourne on 12 October 2006 and is used here with permission.

doing. The universe was created and unfolds according to the divine plan.

Consider the utterly tremendous power of God who was able to create something as vast as the universe from nothing. When I consider the universe I am staggered not only by it immensity, but that it is so very old (at least by human reckoning). When astronomers look through their telescopes they refer to objects as 'far away and long ago'. Although light travels at 300 000 km per second, it is still relatively slow given the size of the universe and the distances it must travel so that by its radiation we can see. If we were to make a scale model of the universe where the sun was shown as the size of your thumbnail, then the nearest star would be about 250 km away. On that scale light would take just over four years to get there!

We perceive the universe in a certain way because of our place in it. We are small; it is large. An astronomer once asked me, 'Do you think God made all this just to blow our minds?' The question gave me pause to think, but the answer may well be, Yes!

Whichever way you look at it God's creation is amazing. It is evidence of the awesome power, great beauty, intelligence and love of the Person who made it. Today we think there are as many stars in the universe as grains of sand on all the world's beaches, plus the deserts, multiplied by ten. Our sun, itself a star, fuses millions of tons of hydrogen molecules every second. The energy emitted by its nuclear furnace radiates out into space in every direction. A small amount reaches our planet to give us enough light and heat to drive the earth's weather patterns and to enable life to exist on this tiny, fragile, but extraordinarily beautiful planet.

Once upon a time human beings thought that the earth was literally the centre of the universe. Everything rotated around this planet as if it were the hub of a giant wheel. But now we know that the earth orbits the sun in a family of planets, four of which are very much larger than the earth. In fact all the planets of the solar system would fit into Jupiter with room to spare. To our mind the solar system is a big place but it exists in a galaxy known as the Milky Way which has over 250 billion stars. These islands of stars, as the galaxies are sometimes described, are scattered throughout the universe in their billions. In the scheme of things the earth would appear to be of little consequence, as would the creatures that inhabit it.

Yet we know it as our home. It is a beautiful benign planet despite its raging storms and awesome geological activity. It may also be quite unique in the universe because the factors, which must converge to allow the earth to exist in the form it does, are such that they are not likely to be repeated.

Our belief is that none of this happened by mere chance or accident. It was by God's will that the earth came to be. Faith, informed by divine revelation, gives us the stance and attitude we should have towards the earth in particular and the universe in general. All of it is the work of God's creative action. We live in the space and time of this world by God's choice and gift. It is given to us on trust to enjoy, to use and to manage responsibly.

Called to stewardship

We also know that God saw all that he had made and found it very good (Gen 1:4). God placed human beings in a privileged position at the summit of creation. Our privileged position with regard to God's Creation is tempered by the knowledge that God is God and we are not. We know that we are not the explanation for our own existence nor can any of us secure our eternal existence. And with privilege comes responsibility: to be accountable for our actions and to respect the wishes of the donor for what has been given on trust.

Our relationship with the world in conformity with God's plan makes up part of our human identity. That relationship is in turn the result of another still deeper relationship between God and ourselves. We are God's partners by his choice and plan. God has chosen to reveal himself to us and seeks always to remain in dialogue with us whom he loves beyond our comprehension. In the context of this never-ending conversation with the Creator, we find truth and inspiration, and the understanding we need to make sound moral judgments concerning the present use of the world's goods and the future of the world.

This partnership involves God as Creator and human beings as stewards of what God has made. Our vocation to be stewards of creation is no mere added-extra consideration of our place in the scheme of things. It stems, rather, from the reality of God and the truth about us with whom the Creator is in constant dialogue.

We know this earth as the garden which we have been given to look after so that it can produce its fruits. We know this as a privilege and a duty. For the People of God, the creation was an object of praise.

O Lord how great are your works! In wisdom you have made them all. (Psalm 104) When I see the heavens the work of your hands, the moon and the stars which you have made, what is man that you care for him? Mortal man that you keep him in mind? (Psalm 8:3-4).

God walked among us

As if all of this were not wonderful enough, consider the truth proclaimed in the Gospel: The author of the universe came and dwelt among us. As the prologue of St John's Gospel expresses it,

> In the beginning was the Word and the Word was with God and the Word was God. Everything that exists had its existence through him and for him. And nothing exists except through him...And the Word became flesh and lived amongst us (John 1:1).

The sheer scope of this message means that only faith can embrace its mystery. Only through faith can we know the person responsible for the Universe who is now as human as you or I (though he is without sin).

Vatican II's document on divine revelation says it beautifully and simply. 'God chose to walk among us as a friend' (*Dei Verbum*, #2). The image reminds me of the garden in which God placed Adam and Eve. God came looking for them in the cool of the evening but they were in hiding because of their shame. And now God has come looking for us in the most definitive way possible. He has come to this garden planet to seek us out, to enter into a profound dialogue with us, to show us the way, to teach us the truth and to secure a life for us that will never end.

Are we hiding from him still, refusing to admit the truth? Have we really accepted him? Do we really want to do things his way?

God has chosen to offer salvation to the human race not from a distance, but by dwelling in the world as a true human, with a human body and a human soul, without ever ceasing to be God. He has made all things new. Jesus has inaugurated a new world in which everything is subjected to him (1 Cor 15).

What sin has broken down he will build up into a new harmony. St Paul writes,

> Therefore, if anyone is in Christ, he is a new creation: the old has passed away, behold, the new has come (2 Cor 5:17). Nature, which

was created in the Word is, by the same Word made flesh, reconciled to God and given new peace (cf Col 1:15-20).

The letter to the Romans describes the whole of creation as being in one great act of giving birth as it awaits full liberation.

Human interaction with the natural world

This faith perspective should be the inspiration and motivation for the way the Christian makes use of the goods of the earth. It also sheds light on how best to use technology. *Gaudium et Spes* affirms that we 'judge rightly by an intellect that surpasses the material universe, for we share in the light of the divine mind' (GS, #15). *Gaudium et Spes* continues to state that human beings,

> created in God's image, received a mandate to subject to themselves the earth and all that it contains, and to govern the world with justice and holiness, a mandate to relate themselves and the totality of things to him who was to be acknowledged as the Lord and Creator of all. Thus, by the subjection of all things to the human race, the name of God would be wonderful in all the earth (GS, #34).

Human beings have always laboured to harvest, mine and manufacture that which comes from the earth. The fruit of the earth combined with the work of human hands has produced the basics for sustaining our life. Our God-given appreciation for beauty and form has been expressed through the hands of skilled artisans in every culture on earth as they worked with raw materials from the earth.

With the dawn of science and the scientific method 400 years ago, we found ways to develop technologies to give us more power to use the earth's fruits for our benefit. Human reason is also a gift from God, as are all our talents. They do not exist in opposition to God's power. Rather, they point to the greatness of God and his mysterious plan for the human race. But as our powers increase through scientific and technological advances, our responsibility for the use of those powers in ways that conform with the divine purpose increases proportionally. As good stewards we must use our powers wisely.

As Pope John Paull II stated,

> the Church has repeatedly emphasised that the Catholic Church is in no way opposed to progress, rather she considers 'science and

technology are a wonderful product of a God-given human creativity, since they have provided us with wonderful possibilities, and we all gratefully benefit from them' (25 February, 1981).

Technology is a tool — a way to solve and meet challenges which confront us on a global scale. Hunger and diseases, which can be alleviated with new medicines and strains of plants and crops pose a challenge and an opportunity to make the world a better place.

However, technology is a means to an end which must always be seen as the *good* of humanity. Technology and its use are not neutral. Technology can be used for good or ill; progress or degradation (cf John Paul II meeting with scientists and representatives of the United Nations University, Hiroshima).

The exercise of *prudence* is of critical importance. It is irresponsible to proceed to use technology simply because it is available and without thorough consideration of its effects on the common good, and the health of the earth and biosphere. Such action does not come from a proper use of human reason, nor does it fulfil our vocation of stewardship. The Church teaches as follows:

> A central point of reference for every scientific and technological application is respect for men and women, which must also be accompanied by a necessary attitude of respect for other living creatures (Pontifical Council for Justice & Peace, 2005, #459).

Included in this attitude of respect is the thoughtful appreciation of the nature of each species (human, animal and plant) and the mutual connection and interdependence of each in an ordered system of life.

Indiscriminate use of biotechnology to genetically manipulate human, plant and animal life results in harm being done to the integrity of the human race and to the earth's ecosystems. Pressures that arise from a profit-driven agenda must not blind us to the consequences of our use of technology, nor force us to act without taking the time for prudent consideration. Everything we do must be as good and trustworthy stewards with a deep appreciation for what the Creator has given us on trust.

The earth: a finite resource, given in trust

We must be very careful not to set ourselves up as God's opponents. In that case we would also oppose the very creation which is ordered for our good. In so doing we 'end up provoking a rebellion on the part of nature' (John Paul II, 1991, n37).

Instead, God wants our co-operation to enter into a joint venture with the God who loves us and all that he has made. This honour and invitation is extended only to human beings. All other forms of life are in a way, at our mercy. Yet we abuse that life at our peril.

'The tendency towards an 'ill-considered exploitation of the resources of creation,' states one Church document, 'is the result of a long historical and cultural process' (Pontifical Council, 2005, #461). We live on the most benign planet in the solar system and possibly in the entire universe. Earth is a teeming garden of life. It offers hospitality to all living creatures. Its environment and ecosystems are home to the jewel of God's creation: the human race created in the image and likeness of God.

None of us would use our family home in a way that would threaten its ability to provide us with comfort, protection and shelter. Similarly, to use the earth only as a 'resource' risks threatening its viability as our 'home' (cf. Pontifical Council, 2005, #461). So a tension exists between exploitation of the earth and our need to live on it. The earth is a finite resource and the only planet on which we can live. Outside our thin layer of atmosphere is a hostile environment. Considered in this way the earth is like a space vehicle speeding through the vacuum of space with everything on board needed to sustain life.

This view of the earth was given to us by the astronauts of the Apollo programme, who had the joy and privilege of seeing the Earth as it rose above the mountains of the moon. As they stood in the stark loneliness of the lunar surface, they looked back at the Earth in wonder at its sheer beauty and delicate fragility. That little blue-green ball was held in the utter blackness of space and was home to five billion people. On that planet was everyone and all that they knew and loved. Seeing the earth from that vantage point changed them irrevocably.

I will never forget Christmas Eve 1968 when the three astronauts of Apollo 8 read the whole of the seven day creation account from the book of Genesis. All through that wonderful reading the grainy picture from their television camera was of the earth, photographed live in black and white from the window of the command module of their space vehicle. When the reading was over they wished 'everyone on the good Earth a happy Christmas from the crew of Apollo 8'. To hear the astronauts proclaim the word of God from 200 000 miles away in space, 'God saw all that he had made and found it very good,' captured my imagination, appealed to my faith and will remain with me always.

From then on I could never see this lovely planet as merely something to be consumed. This place is where life is sustained; it cannot be reduced to a resource available for mere exploitation.

The unique privilege of being human

The human being has a transcendent dimension. Our openness to God's self revelation in Jesus, our appreciation of the good, the true and the beautiful, set us apart and mark us out as unique in all the creation. Progress in scientific knowledge in itself does not cause human beings to ignore the reality of transcendence. Indeed science could well serve to heighten our awareness of the beauty, intelligence and power of God. But the replacement of God with science and technology in 'scientism and technocratic ideologies' (cf Pontifical Council, 2005, #462) leads to a reduced and narrowed view of things where we do what we want because we can. As stewards we are called to do much better than that.

On the other hand we must be careful not to absolutise nature and the environment. The world of nature is not above the dignity of the human person. There are some who, in the name of ecology, promote a worldview that is contrary to divine revelation tending to 'divinise' or personalise the earth in some way.

Others promote the idea that there is no real difference between human beings and other living creatures, since the biosphere as one entity of 'undifferentiated value'. While it is true that all life on earth is interdependent and that we cannot harm one species without in some way doing damage to all species including our own, it is also true that we have a superior responsibility of stewardship given by God to care for the earth. We share life with all living things, but they do not share our dignity, privilege, responsibility or vocation.

We can only begin to grasp the nature of our responsibility for the environment within the context of relationship with God who made all things.

> This is why Christian culture has always recognised the creatures that surround us as also gifts of God to be nurtured and safeguarded with a sense of gratitude to the Creator (Pontifical Council, 2005, #464).

One of the great contributions of the late John Paul II was his emphasis on the intimate connection between environmental ecology and human ecology. In calling for ecological conversion John Paul wanted to reinvigorate our sense of oneness with God our creator and oneness with all his creatures. He wanted us to be converted to a view that sought to care for the earth with a motivation that sprang from our loving relationship with God, and of God with us, his co-workers and friends.

From assumptions to uncertainty

Across the world today there is a general acceptance that we face an ecological crisis of global proportions. A global crisis can only be met by a global effort. Our interdependence demands such action. We are indebted to the scientists, rural people, foresters, fisher people, writers, artists, photographers, educators, business people, government officials, and all who have helped humanity become aware that the earth is in trouble.

The earth's system is complex and science even now is only beginning to unlock its intricate detail. The land, oceans, atmosphere, lithosphere and living organisms exchange energy, water and chemicals in biochemical cycles. These cycles are our planetary life support systems and earth's climate is the result of their complex interactions. Research has concluded that since the beginning of the industrial revolution, carbon dioxide in the atmosphere has risen by nearly 30%, methane more than doubled, and nitrous oxide has risen by about 15%. The use of fossil fuels accounts for about 80% of human-caused carbon emissions.

Carbon cycles naturally move between the atmosphere, vegetation, the oceans and the lithosphere. The amount of greenhouse gases humans are releasing into the atmosphere exceeds the absorption capacity of the oceans and vegetation on land. Deforestation has further reduced the absorption of carbon dioxide. We are facing consequences that will influence the way we human beings will live on this planet in the future. Carbon stores energy. With a more energetic atmosphere we face severe droughts and floods and more intense storms and cyclones. Poorer countries will suffer disproportionately. Geographic and seasonal patterns of rainfall will alter.

Of overarching importance is the fact that contemporary society has developed on the assumption that the global climate is constant. Science has demonstrated this assumption is false, even in the absence of human-forced climate change. Much of our infrastructure is therefore locked into current patterns of rainfall and temperature and presuppose a stable climate regime. The human and economic costs of climate change will be immense.

Responses to climate change

A critical part of any response lies in the continuing development of alternative sources of energy that can substitute for greenhouse-gas emitting fossil fuels. While 'technological fixes' may be grasped by some as an escape from the reality of global climate change, there is a real need for scientific research into technologies which reduce carbon emissions.

At the international, national and local levels of government there is a developing commitment to secure a safe and healthy natural environment through new legislation. This effort has been stimulated by public opinion which looks to the common good and asks that those who pollute be punished in some way. Laws in themselves are not sufficient. They must be accompanied by attitudinal change, and a lifestyle that seeks to protect the natural environment. From our Catholic point of view our response should have a firm spiritual and theological foundation. It should also involve our careful listening to the very best science has to offer.

At times the available scientific data are contradictory. The research is still a work in progress and of necessity there are uncertainties. Scientists themselves do not always agree and while some devote their energies to defend a particular theory, others will try to disprove it. The general population can and does become confused at times. In these circumstances it seems proper to invoke the 'precautionary principle' which aims at managing a situation of uncertainty. We make decisions conscious of the possibility of modification if and when new data come to hand and admit that science cannot always provide ready assurances about the absence of risk. In other words,

> Prudent policies, based on the precautionary principle require that decisions be based on a comparison of the risks and benefits foreseen for the various possible alternatives, including the decision not to intervene (Pontifical Council, 2005, #469).

In this context, economic decisions regarding the use of natural resources must pay heed to the uncertainties surrounding our present circumstances and the serious responsibility to safeguard the integrity of nature. Safeguarding the environment comes at an economic cost. However, economic development must be in harmony with protection of the natural environment.

> An economy respectful of the environment will not have the maximisation of profits as its only objective, because environmental protection cannot be assured solely on the basis of financial calculations of costs and benefits. The environment is one of those goods that cannot be adequately safeguarded and promoted by market forces (Pontifical Council, 2005, #470).

Ecological conversion

In the end, the issues surrounding the health of the natural environment are not just scientific, technological, political and economic; at their foundation is the very nature of the person and our relationship with our Creator. Economic degradation points to a spiritual imperative to view the earth as sheer gift, given to us by God on trust and our vocation is to be stewards of creation.

Christians believe that the incarnation of the Son of God has given the earth a status above anything else in the universe. At a moment in time, the author of the universe took flesh, had a human body and a human soul, and walked on this extra-ordinary planet. For Christians, believing that the person through whom and for whom the whole of creation exists, actually lived, died, and rose to life again *here* must change the way we view this, our home. This is no ordinary planet and human beings are no ordinary creatures. St. Athanasius said, 'God became human so that humans could become gods'. Through our incorporation as members of Christ's body we are conformed to God in the most profound way. We should see and love the creation as God sees and loves it.

To change our ways to protect the natural environment will require a religious conversion to the will of God so that we will have the courage and motivation under God's grace to do what we need to safeguard this garden planet. John Paul II called this the 'ecological conversion'. A new mentality will lead to new life styles 'in which the quest for truth, beauty, goodness and communion with others for the sake of the common good are the factors that determine consumer choices, saving and investments' (John Paul II, 1991, #36).

This is not a utopian view of the future. Rather, in a hopeful spirit, we must aim at a way of life on earth that conforms to the intentions of the person who gave me life, who knows me by my name, who made the universe and chose me to live as part of it. By 'conversion', I mean a grateful heart which knows that God has saved us from hopelessness and selfishness. Because of this, all our effort on behalf of God's creation is worthwhile.

After all, I know him personally, and he knows me and all my brothers and sisters, he who made and found to be very good everything that exists.

References

Catholic Earthcare Australia, http://catholicearthcareoz.net/
John Paul II, (1991) *Centisimus Annus,* On the Hundreth Anniversary of *Rerum Novarum*, Homebush, St Paul Publications.
Paul VI, (1965) *Dogmatic Constitution on Divine Revelation, (Verbum Dei),* November.
Paul VI, (1965) *Pastoral Constitution on Church in the Modern World, (Gaudium et Spes)*, December.
Pontifical Council for Justice and Peace, (2005) *Compendium of the Social Doctrine of the Church,* London, Burns and Oates.

4
Educating Children to Wonder, Wisdom and Stewardship: The implications of climate change for Catholic educators

A Conversation with Chris Toohey

In 2007 Bishop Toohey visited Britain to deliver a series of lectures on 'The Church and Climate Change'. During this short visit, he addressed many groups of politicians and media. He also visited a number of schools and entered into conversation with students of all ages. He describes his work with young people as the most exciting part of his mission in the search for wisdom in our interaction with nature. The conversation documented in this chapter occurred on the morning he returned to his diocese in Wilcannia-Forbes from Britain.

The conversation explores some of the implications which Bishop Toohey believes are important for Catholic educators in their work with young people.

What does climate change mean for Catholic educators?

One of the responsibilities we have as educators is in some ways to prepare young people for life. The difficulty at the moment with the uncertainty regarding climate change is knowing exactly what it is we are preparing them for.

When Galileo challenged the thinking of his day with the notion that the earth was not the centre of the universe, he was regarded as an eccentric, as dangerous and a heretic. It is hard for us to imagine the impact of the shift in perspective that Galileo brought. Yet the change that we are presently facing is of the same Galileo-like proportion. We have always assumed that the earth is there to give us food, air and water as if what we do does not matter. We are beginning to realise the falsity of the old assumptions. We are beginning to question. We are beginning to ask, 'Can we sustain the way we are living?'

The answer is clear: We cannot! In the first place, 20% of the world's population simply cannot go on consuming 80% of the world's resources. There is injustice in that. Those who are already poor will always feel the impact of climate change more dramatically and they will have far fewer resources to deal with its consequences. Secondly, the developed world cannot expect to maintain its same level of consumption and at the same time bring the developing world to the same level. The earth cannot sustain that. Politicians and scientists agree that our present lifestyle in the developed world is unsustainable and at the same time, we must provide the means for people in developing countries to attain greater levels of prosperity. This is the double bind we are in: our present consumption of natural resources is unsustainable, but it is unjust not to change the poverty in which most of the world lives.

Our lifestyle of addiction to fossil fuels is stressing the earth. A grave crisis exists in the loss of biodiversity. Earth is groaning under this pressure. I cannot think of any other time in history when change has been so urgent and significant. This is a global issue for the whole human family. The last words that Pope John Paul II spoke to me personally were on this issue. On another occasion, in a homily in 2000, Pope John Paul II said: 'Humanity is on the brink of an abyss'. These are strong words and indicate how seriously he viewed the situation.

As educators, where does this leave us? What do we say to young people who are growing up now into this uncertainty?

We need to respond on two dimensions. In the first place, on the socio-political dimension, we have to educate young people that we can and must engage with the *political issues*. We must encourage young people to think creatively about how the issues of injustice and our interaction with nature can be handled politically. I would like to see teachers engage young people in workshops, which simulate the political issues and tensions in this issue. Likewise, the *economic issues* need creative economic thinking. The god of economic growth is closely linked with political strategies and the measures of growth (and political success) are always measured against the previous year's figures. It is a closed loop which fails to take account of other factors. So students need to be educated to be competent and creative in their understanding of economics.

The third set of issues with which to engage and challenge young people are the *technological issues*. We need to educate young people about the urgency of improving solar, wind and water technologies and educate them in the competency to do something about them. By the way, we have uranium to power the whole world for only about 60 years. So nuclear power is a short-term solution and has the problem of long-term waste. Will our students discover other new technologies which we can live with?

The second dimension is the *personal dimension*, and it includes the *spiritual* and the *theological*. We need to educate young people that the present crisis is about more than taking shorter showers, using green bags and watering the garden less. These things are okay as far as they go. As educators, we have to go further and explore with young people about the totality of their – our – whole lifestyle. How sustainable is it? Am I really connected to the natural world? Am I living as the creator God expects? Theology and spirituality run together. In theology, we try to grasp better what we believe; our prayer and spirituality reflect what we believe. Catholic educators have a responsibility to lead young people to see Christ in creation and to respond to him in creation.

Your paper[1] and your conversation keep returning to a faith perspective as the foundational orientation to the natural world and to dealing with the critical situation in which we find ourselves. Yet religious practice itself is just one such an area of uncertainty at the present time.

Faith and doctrine are changeless; they create our Tradition. Yet, that Catholic Tradition is not a 'freeze-frame'. It is more like a movie which develops as the faithful delve into the mysteries of the Gospel within their own context. In many ways, we still haven't caught up with the present time, in our teaching of faith. People will not connect with doctrine if it does not touch them. Religious education curriculum must include doctrine which touches people's lives. If the doctrine we teach is not connected to children (or adults) in their lives it will simply wash over them. It will mean nothing to them. The teachers of divine truth

---

[1] Cf Chapter 3, 'Stewardship and God's Creation: A theological reflection'.

must fulfil their mission within their historic context.

There are universals in the present ecological challenges which apply to everyone as part of their citizenship in the world. Young people grab this idea of spirituality in our interaction with nature 'like bees with nectar', even young children. I did some work in England with Year 6 children from Bristol, and they just loved it. I do not try to 'dumb down' the theology of creation and our responsibility. I think that is a mistake we sometimes make. We would not ever fully understand the mysteries of our faith. I tell teachers that you cannot explain everything, and it does not serve children well in religious education when we do try to explain everything. We run the risk of making mysteries quite bland or even explaining them away.

In Catholic schools, how can teachers create a situation where 'a religious conversion to the will of God' as you describe in your paper is more likely?

I am convinced that we cannot address this challenge without a sense of wonder at creation. I am full of wonder that I am alive to even consider these things. In my paper, I referred to the sense of wonder communicated by the Apollo astronauts as they viewed earth from the moon's surface. In many ways, their sense of wonder has changed my life. Children – all of us – are born with a great sense of wonder. Watch how an infant or a child explores their world: they are alive with wonder. It is a great joy. In the West especially, I think we have lost a sense of wonder of our own existence. Until teachers and children get back a sense of wonder about creation, there will be no change, no matter what curriculum they use. We have really got to address the loss of the sense of wonder.

The things I am talking about, the changes we must make, the attitudes we need to educate our children towards are things like wonder, wisdom, courage, right judgement. We – the human race – will need these qualities, because what we are facing is a profoundly ethical and spiritual challenge. We are talking about a spiritual malaise as much as a physical crisis. And so, teachers need to teach for these things. Wisdom, wonder, courage and right judgement cannot be bottled and bought and sold – as much our generation thinks they can manufacture and buy most things. But we cannot manufacture them. These qualities are gifts of the Spirit and it is the Spirit who will give them.

What is the message you want Catholic educators to hear?

This is an urgent spiritual challenge. Pope Benedict is speaking more and more about the ecological situation we are in. In the past few weeks alone, he has made seven statements about it. Our misuse of the universe, he said recently, is causing it to rise up against us. Or another time, he said very beautifully, that 'the deserts of the world are multiplying because the deserts of our hearts are multiplying'.

However, to address this without hope would be a tragedy especially for young people. In the past, we have sometimes made mistakes in exposing young people to some of the evil in our world, like war and poverty and injustice and nuclear threat, but we have left them powerless and without any sense of hope. That is not helpful. Educators need to be hopeful that we will get the technology right, that we will get the economics right and that we will get the politics right. Teachers need to encourage young people in this hope and engage them in the creativity of getting things right.

I am confident that we will do it. I am amazed and encouraged with what has happened even in the last five years, since the Australian bishops launched 'Earthcare Australia'. Things are starting to happen. We can be very hopeful with our teachers and young people — not in some fairytale way, and not based on faith in ourselves alone, but based in faith in the will of God. God 'who made and found to be very good everything that exists' will not be thwarted as creator. He will continue to create what is very good.

Your paper refers to living with uncertainty and managing uncertainty. What does this mean for young people, their parents and teachers?

People do not like change. Change creates 'dis-ease' in people. We have to think through this situation because people will react in different ways. There are at least four directions people can take when confronted with the monstrous change relating to climate and the environment which is in front of us. The four directions include the following:

- *They deny the crisis.* I call this the 'Parable of the Titanic'. The passengers felt the shudder of the ship as the iceberg struck, but they continued on in the staterooms, eating and drinking. They listened to the music as it played and said, 'This ship cannot sink. It is just a rumour. Take it with a grain of salt. Those people are over-reacting.' This is like the shudder earth felt in the 1980s, but we paid no heed to the message then. At that time, some people warned us to change our way of life, but we shrugged our shoulders and said they were extremists and panicking for nothing. Now another call has come over the ship's speaker systems: 'Come on deck. Board the life rafts.' And still some people again are ignoring the message and calling the messengers alarmists.

- *They panic.* Fear can result in in-action. Panic can cause us to run around in multiple directions, going no-where, achieving nothing.
- *They try to buy a way out of the crisis.* That is, they buy a place in the life boat, so that they can be sure of getting away, regardless of others. This is obscene. It is as if money can save us from the need to engage in the struggle. In some ways, the buying of carbon credits could perhaps fall into this category. They will save themselves, with little regard for those who will be most adversely affected.
- *Finally, they can deal with the change which is demanded:* face the crisis, intelligently and creatively. They inform themselves as best as they can. They explore options and alternatives. They weigh consequences. They work cooperatively with others for the common good. In short, they name the crisis for what it is and develop strategies to deal with it.

I would like to think of this last approach as 'The Parable of Apollo 13'. Apollo 13 was a space mission which blew up 350 000 miles from earth. Against all odds, the team on Apollo 13 arrived back safely home to earth. They survived. How did they do it? The team on Apollo thought creatively. They worked together collaboratively. They got the spaceship to do things that it was not designed to do. They managed the resources that they had left. They stayed calm. They supported each other. They prayed. And amazingly, in the context – the face of likely disaster and death – they looked down on planet earth and marvelled at creation. Even this was not all. The Apollo 13 team returned safely home because they were prepared to trust the people back home, the people who crunched the numbers, relayed messages and gave directions to the astronauts. The astronauts who heeded the directions from their home-team based on earth are an analogy for us to pray for wisdom in seeking from our home-based God's will for us in directing how we live through this crisis.

In working with young people, and in their own reflections as educators on the issues of climate change, teachers might find the 'Parable of Apollo 13' a useful one to use.

In what ways can Catholic schools give leadership in responding wisely to this crisis?

As well as educating students in awareness and understanding across the political, economic, technological, spiritual and theological and social justice dimensions of the human interaction with nature, each school needs to model the best in collaboration, creativity and faith. Students need to be challenged to take responsibility for contributing to managing the future of planet earth.

There are many positive examples and much we can build on. For example, on my recent visit to the United Kingdom, I visited Holyrood School in Edinburgh. The school community has already decided to become 'an eco-oriented school' with a faith dimension. Holyrood is educating children to be advocates for the natural world. To do this, children are being taught how to write to politicians. The Student Representative Council is set up, not to further students' interests, but to promote the interests of the natural world. So that, rather than work for better conditions only for themselves, students advocate on behalf of the environment. This was children learning about mission by being missionary. It was fantastic to see this Catholic school focused outwards with a sense of mission for the world.

On another visit, I was heartened to visit a joint Anglican-Catholic school in an extremely embattled and impoverished area of Liverpool. The formerly cement-grey walls of the school had been painted in bright colours. Each classroom faces onto a glassed atrium, which has been scientifically designed to warm the environment naturally, but which also changed the ambience as well. All children had some garden responsibility. Children monitor power consumption within the school. The school has set aside one classroom as a prayer room with a teacher acting as chaplain. Having once been a so-called 'failing' school, it now has a waiting list. I said to the principal, 'I can see this school is transforming the students.' She replied, 'This school is transforming the neighbourhood.'

I also visited other schools, including secondary schools, whose students come from quite privileged backgrounds. Even though their circumstances were quite privileged compared to others, the students at these schools, just like their peers at Liverpool and Holyrood, were likewise amazing in their willingness to engage with these enormously difficult issues and to respond creatively.

Here in Australia, I recall a small primary school in a rural area in the diocese of Townsville. With a committed focus on the ecological, the school has been transformed. The school has its own eco-systems and nature walks and what happens in the classrooms has been transformed.

These are just some examples which should give us all a lot of hope. In all our schools there are already many good practices we can build on.

What other signs of hope do you see with respect to Catholic schools responding to this crisis?

The leadership in Catholic schools in Australia is absolutely wonderful. There are simply excellent people in the Catholic school system. Schools already work with children on working collaboratively and creatively. But sometimes there can be too much navel-gazing in Catholic education. We need to take all that talent and love for the Church and love for children and direct it outward to this issue.

Leaders of Catholic education at all levels — and I suppose that includes Bishops, parish priests, directors of Catholic education, universities and principals — need to encourage those in schools and classrooms; all these leaders need to 'give permission' to teachers to look creatively at our contemporary human and natural context and to focus their energies on responding to it as educators, citizens and people of faith. We have all the resources we need. We have to target them differently.

Each school has its own community. Within that community, educators can lead the community with their worldview and attitude to the world and to each other to shape their immediate environment. Each community is responsible for the way we act within the walls of that community. Each community also chooses which way the arrowheads are pointing: inwards to focus on themselves or outwards with a sense of mission to the earth and larger community. Wouldn't it be marvellous if all of our Catholic schools initiated activities and awareness which could transform their local parishes and their local communities?

Young people must be educated to an awareness of how these things affect them. This is urgent. We cannot leave it to the next decade. The curriculum of schools, including the religious education curriculum, must address these issues right now.

* * *

Catholic Earthcare Australia

Catholic Earthcare Australia (CEA) was established by the Australian Catholic Bishops Conference in May, 2002 with the mission of advising, supporting and assisting the bishops in responding to Pope John Paul 11's call to 'stimulate and sustain the ecological conversion' throughout the Catholic Church in Australia and beyond.

Catholic Earthcare Australia, inspired by the words of John Paul 11 (in his 1990 World Day of Peace Message, 'Peace with God, Peace with All of Creation' and General Audience Vatican Address of 17 January 2001) shares his vision of a world where we will:

- Stimulate and sustain the ecological conversion
- Respect the central role of humankind in safeguarding creation
- Work towards making the life of all creatures more dignified
- Protect the radical goodness of life in all manifestations, especially human life
- Work for a sustainable ecology for present and future generations
- Discover the voice of the Creator transmitted in the natural world through the life, death and resurrection of Jesus Christ
- Celebrate the community of life
- Strive for sustainable development that seeks to overcome poverty and injustice
- Prepare an environment for future generations that is closer to the plan of the Creator.

As an agency of the Catholic Bishops Commission for Justice and Service, the mission of Catholic Earthcare Australia is to help promote understanding among people that creation is sacred and endangered, and must be protected and sustained for present and future generations yet unborn.

To play its part in helping protect the integrity of creation and the health of earth's inhabitants and life supporting ecosystems, Catholic Earthcare Australia is mandated to:

- Carry out research, from the perspective of scripture and the Church's environmental and social justice teachings
- Develop national networks, with a view to initiating, linking, resourcing and supporting ecological endeavours within the Church, and extending the hand of friendship and cooperation to other like-minded groups working in the broader community
- Undertake initiatives by encouraging a reverence for creation, a responsible stewardship of Earth's natural resources and ecosystems, and providing a voice for the victims of pollution, environmental degradation and injustice
- Provide educational materials and services to Catholic schools, organisations, congregations and parishes — particularly information to assist in the carrying out of environmental audits and the implementation of more ecologically and ethically sustainable practices.

Catholic Earthcare Australia website includes valuable resources, news and links. It can be accessed on: http://www.catholicearthcareoz.net

5
Non-Catholics and Catholics in Catholic Schools in Australia

Brian Croke

Catholic schooling in Australia is a long and complex story yet to be told in all its richness. This story reflects the fortunes of the Catholic community through periods of struggle for recognition and security. It abounds in myths and tinted memories. As for all historical stories, time eventually provides a more reliable perspective on reality. Still abroad is the notion of a 'golden era' of Australian Catholic schooling, a time when Catholics were full of conviction and piety and when the inextricable bonds between school, parish and family ensured that every Catholic went to Sunday mass and every Catholic child attended a Catholic school. 'Golden eras' generally defy precise dating. This one is considered to run roughly from the 1920s to the early 1970s. Such eras also ensure that the present suffers by comparison. In this case the certainty of retrospect sometimes encourages the notions that Catholic school standards have declined, commitment has become fickle and the religious character of the school diluted.

Each element of the 'golden era' story is encrusted with its own myths which make the reality hard to recover. Surprise generally greets the discovery that during that era the attendance of Catholics at Sunday mass was only ever around 55% (early 1960s)(Mason, 2003[1]) or that in the mid-1970s only around 50% of Catholic school age children attended Catholic schools. In the first decade of the 21st century the proportion of Catholic school-age children attending Catholic schools is about the same — 43% by the latest count. What has changed significantly is the religious background of the students and teachers in Catholic schools. During the 'golden era' the students attending Catholic schools were virtually 100% Catholic as were the teachers, most of them

---

[1] My thanks to Jan Gray, RSM, for this reference.

being professed Religious — nuns, brothers and priests. Today's Catholic school is very different in terms of students and teachers.

This chapter is designed to explain the nature of such a radical change in the Australian Catholic school over the past 30 years and to explore some of its implications for the coming generation of Catholic school students, teachers, parents, principals and administrators. A new and hopeful opportunity has opened up for Catholic schools and educators.

Setting the scene, 1870s to 2007

In many ways the 'golden era' Catholic school could take itself for granted because throughout this period the Australian bishops issued only one statement or manifesto for Catholic schools – that of the NSW bishops led by the Benedictine Archbishop Roger Vaughan in 1879 which predicted famously that the new 'free, compulsory and secular' government schools would become 'seed-plots of future immorality, infidelity and lawlessness' to be avoided by Catholics (Vaughan, 1880). Local bishops generally assumed that the Catholic schools understood their purpose and possessed the capacity to keep achieving their goals. Likewise, the church at large said very little about Catholic schools except that parents required the local bishop's permission to send a child to a school which was 'non-Catholic, neutral or mixed, that is, also open to non-Catholics', lest they succumb to the 'danger of perversion' (Code of Canon Law, canon 1374).

The fears of Archbishop Vaughan and the Roman authorities responsible for the Code of Canon Law were addressed by building a separate system of Catholic schools throughout Australia from the 1880s, made possible by the efforts of religious congregations, both local (such as Mary Mackillop's Sisters of St Joseph and the Sisters of the Good Samaritan) and imported (such as the Sisters of Mercy, the Christian Brothers, De La Salle Brothers, Marist Brothers and many others) (Fogarty, 1957). By the late 1940s the preoccupation of bishops and their flock was improvement of resources so that new schools could be built to meet an expanding Catholic population, more modern facilities could be provided, large classes could be made more manageable, and teachers better qualified. Above all, from the 1940s to the 1970s the public fixation of the Australian bishops was on securing the financial future of Catholic schools through some form of government funding. The modern Australian Catholic school owes its existence and its operation to the efforts of the bishops and Catholic parents from the 1950s to the 1970s (Hogan, 1978. See also Wilkinson, Caldwell et al, 2007). Scant attention was paid to who attended Catholic schools and the religious background of those who taught in them. There were no enrolment policies, for instance, because they were simply not necessary.

By contrast, in the early 21st century Australian bishops are very interested in who attends Catholic schools and who teaches in them, particularly in their religious background. Questions have been asked, research has been undertaken and policy considerations have been addressed. In August 2007 the Bishops of NSW and ACT publicly launched *Catholic Schools at a Crossroads*, the first local episcopal statement on Catholic schools since that of 1879 (NSW/ACT Bishops, 2007). The statement had been prompted, among other things, by the realisation that in NSW and ACT the proportion of non-Catholic students in Catholic schools had reached 20% and that the time had come to take account of this new reality. Based on up-to-date and detailed data, the document represented the collective deliberations and commitment of the bishops, so it could not be ignored. While Archbishop Vaughan's 1879 statement was greeted with hostility, the 2007 bishops' statement was accorded commendatory editorials in both major Sydney newspapers and attracted serious and complimentary media coverage throughout Australia because it was addressing what is a national issue. A key theme of all the media coverage was how Catholic schools were dealing with non-Catholic students and would continue to do so. Suddenly, in Australia, Catholic schools and their non-Catholic students were an item of widespread public interest.

The new episcopal document makes clear that the Australian Catholic school has long since changed from that of the 'golden era'. The modern Catholic school is mainly funded by governments, is almost entirely staffed by highly qualified lay professionals, enjoys modern buildings and amenities, and engages in a quality teaching and learning experience comparable to all other schools. It is also widely regarded and appreciated for its ideals and values and is judged by the students it produces. That explains why it is increasingly attractive to those whose parents and grandparents would have found a Catholic school repulsive or completely undesirable for their children.

How much times have changed, even in the period between 1988 and 2006, can be summarised as follows, in terms of the religious backgrounds of Catholic school students:

- The overall increase in Catholic school enrolments between 1988 and 2006 has been almost entirely due to the increase in non-Catholic students
- In 2006 there were 1,873 fewer Catholic students in NSW Catholic Schools than there were in 1988 and 27 256 more non-Catholic students than in 1988
- In 1988 less than one in every 10 students (9%) was non-Catholic, the proportion in 2006 was one in every five students (20%)
- Non-Catholic primary school enrolments continue to increase, but there has been a 'flattening out' of the non-Catholic secondary enrolments
- Changing statewide trends in enrolment patterns mask significant diocesan and local variations across Catholic schools.

The implications of the data on non-Catholic students in NSW Catholic schools form part of a broader pastoral challenge (cf NSW/ACT Bishops, 2007), but it embraces certain definable tests:
- Maintaining Catholic schools as centres of catechesis for committed Catholic families
- Articulating and promoting the understanding of the Catholic school's role and purpose, including explaining the evangelisation of students other than Catholic as a significant part of the mission and rationale of Catholic schools
- Delineating and dealing with the internal issues, that is, issues related to enrolment policies including prescription or limits on the number/proportion of students who are not Catholic.

The bishops have set Catholic school communities the task of increasing the proportion of Catholic students in their schools, recognising that increasing numbers of Catholic families are choosing government and other non-government schools. That is because times have changed for Catholics too, so that the non-Catholic school is no longer culturally, religiously or financially alien. The bishops recognise that the number of non-Catholic students in Catholic schools is likely to keep on increasing and the school needs to reach out to them in an authentic way as part of a spectrum of belief ranging from none at all to fully committed and religiously literate Catholics. That is why Catholic school leaders, parents, priests and bishops still need to devote serious attention to this issue.

The modern Catholic school context

The Catholic community served by the modern Catholic school has itself undergone considerable change over recent decades. Although the Australian Catholic community is virtually the same proportion of the nation's population that it was in 1871, and the proportion of Catholic students attending Catholic schools is similar to 30 years ago (50%), what has changed is the more diverse ethnic composition of the Catholic community and of Australia more generally, especially in metropolitan areas. The schools now also have a more developed and supportive administrative infrastructure provided by Catholic Education/Schools Offices and other bodies including state and territory Catholic Education Commissions and the National Catholic Education Commission (Canavan, 2007).

Beyond the Catholic school, there have also been some profound changes in the educational landscape which are immediately relevant to the dynamic pattern of school choice underpinning the phenomenon of a significant proportion of non-Catholic families, unconnected to the Catholic Church, choosing Catholic schools. Again, in the past 30 years there has been a very significant growth of new non-government schools, almost all of which are religious, including a marked growth in Christian schools and schools developed by faith communities other than those associated with Christian Churches. For example, there are now 125 Christian Community schools in Australia and 69 other Christian denominational schools where there were none in 1963. There were no Steiner schools then; there are 44 now, plus 36 Montessori schools, and 30 Islamic schools. In addition, there are now twice as many Jewish schools (19) as in 1963, 58 additional Lutheran, 31 additional Anglican and 13 additional Seventh-day Adventist schools. In the 'golden era' of Catholic schools most of these schools were never an option for Catholic students.

Since then most of the longer-established non-government schools other than Catholic schools have expanded in size especially in their junior years, as have some Catholic congregational schools. The number of non-denominational independent schools, often called 'grammar schools', has also doubled (an extra 87) over the same period. At the same time, some state governments have created a more diverse government school sector with more academically selective and specialist high schools as well as an expansion of 'opportunity' or 'gifted and talented' classes in primary schools. In recent times, these options have become an increasing preference for Catholic families. An intense public debate continues about school choice and its relationship to government funding, quality and diversity of schooling and the role of the state as a provider and regulator of schooling. Schools are increasingly seen as a consumer good.

Generally speaking, compared to 30 years ago, Australia now has better educated and more affluent parents making consumer-based choices about their children's schooling (Croke, 2007). Contemporary Catholic families are, on average, no larger than other Australian families. Parents, however, are more discerning and demanding and are faced with both more diversity of school choice and more political support for the importance of their choice. Many also appear to be less motivated by adherence to a specific religion or denomination. Moreover, local perceptions of Catholic schools have been affected by factors such as the declining role of religious in Catholic schools, the end of the social isolation of the Catholic community in Australian society, and the movement of Catholic families into the mainstream of Australian social life.

One symptom of all this social, political and educational change is the increasing attractiveness of Catholic schools to families of other faith traditions. Generally, Catholic school principals admit students who are not Catholic on the understanding that the family is prepared to acknowledge and uphold the goals and values of the Catholic school. In schools, particularly in small rural towns, where the proportion of students other than Catholic is large (40% and above), such a level of non-Catholic student enrolments may/can assist with the financial viability of the school. Likewise, in some newly established areas on the metropolitan fringes a significant proportion of students other than Catholic may assist the viability of a new Catholic school. A school, which would otherwise not be available for the evangelising mission of the Church, is thereby secured. In more than half of the newest Catholic schools, (ie, under 10 years old) non-Catholic enrolments exceed 25%.

Whatever the local situation, the overall change in the religious composition of the student population of Australian Catholic schools between 1988 and 2007 gives rise to divergent responses. One view interprets the growth in students in Catholic schools who are not Catholic as a decline in the ideal of previous generations when all, or nearly all, students were Catholic. Another response evaluates the development of Australian Catholic schools from an understanding of the purpose and nature of contemporary Catholic schools as part of the overall mission of the Church. This is the road the NSW/ACT Bishops have now chosen by reaffirming their 'commitment to the essential elements of the Catholic school while recognising, and even embracing, changing enrolment patterns as 'signs of the times' and of a new mission for Catholic education' (*Catholic Schools at a Crossroads,* p.8). Accordingly, the route ahead needs to be carefully plotted out.

Non-Catholic students and teachers: the Church's understanding

The Church documents which govern the mission and operation of a Catholic school in the 21st century provide the obvious starting point for both analysis and future planning around dealing with non-Catholic students and teachers. The modern Church spends much time considering the nature and future of Catholic schooling the world over. Since Vatican Council II's *Declaration on Christian Education* (1965) official Church statements on Catholic schooling are substantial and relatively frequent. Chief among them are:

- *On Evangelisation in the Modern World* (1975)
- *The Catholic School* (1977)
- *Catechesis in Our Time* (1979)
- *Lay Catholics in Schools: Witnesses to Faith* (1982)
- *The Religious Dimension of Education in a Catholic school* (1988)
- *The General Directory for Catechesis* (1997)
- *Catholic Education on the Threshold of the Third Millennium* (1999)
- *Consecrated Persons and Their Mission in Schools* (2002)
- *Educating Together in Catholic Schools* (2007) [2]

Founded on Vatican Council II's *Declaration on Christian Education*, the proper function of the modern Catholic school is to create a community

---

[2] All these documents are conveniently available at http://www.vatican.va/roman_curia/congregations/ccatheduc/index.htm

with an atmosphere conducive to the full development of each individual student. In addition, the school has a social purpose, namely to ensure that 'the knowledge the students gradually acquire of the world, life and man is illumined by faith' (para. 8) and 'should especially care for the needs of the poor and those who are not Catholic or even religious' (para.9).

At the most basic level, in countries such as Australia with significant Catholic communities, Catholic schools exist to enable Catholic parents to fulfil their duty of 'entrusting their children to Catholic schools wherever and whenever it is possible' (*Declaration on Christian Education*, 8). Informed and conscientious parental choice of school is an important facet of the church's teaching on education. The Church documents also recognise that the Catholic school is open to all who embrace its mission (*Catholic School*, 59) and that Catholic schools are to be 'natural communities, based on a shared concept of life' (*Catholic School*, 20). In particular, the Catholic school community is 'a privileged place for the formation of young people in the construction of a world based on dialogue and the search for communion' (*Educating Together*, 53). In other words, the Catholic school is a place where students, parents and teachers come together in hope and faith.

Regarding students who are non-Catholic, the key Church statements remind us that 'the Catholic school offers itself to all, non-Christians included, with all its distinctive aims and means (*Catholic School*, 85), so that the 'only condition it would make for its continued existence would be remaining faithful to the educational aims of the Catholic school' (86). Further, the Catholic school 'is not reserved to Catholics only, but is open to all those who appreciate and share its qualified education project' (*Third Millennium*, 16). Most recently, the importance of shared values has been highlighted so that in the school setting 'the presence both of students and of teachers from different cultural and religious backgrounds requires an increased commitment of discernment and accompaniment' (*Educating Together*, 5). This means that the Church expects the multicultural and multi-faith Catholic school to respect the 'the religious freedom and personal conscience of individual students and their families' (*Religious Dimension*, 6).

The Church documents are clear that teachers have the responsibility to make their contribution to an holistic education which combines essential religious and secular goals. The Church's understanding regarding the religious background and commitment of staff is simply:

'The achievement of this specific aim of the Catholic school depends not so much on subject matter or methodology as on the people who work there' (*Catholic School*, 43). The Congregation for Catholic Education crystallises the key importance of staff when it states that it is the lay teachers 'whether believers or not' who will substantially determine whether or not a school realises its aims and objectives (*Lay Catholics*, 1).

In summary, it is the Church's understanding that non-Catholic students and teachers are welcome in Catholic schools and can contribute effectively to the essential goals of the school. The fundamental challenge – full of tension, difficulty and hope – is that of balancing this openness to those who are non-Catholic with the need for schools to remain faithful to their core values and mission. The modern Catholic school reality of an increasing number of non-Catholic students and a large number of non-practising or indifferent teachers needs to be addressed. This relatively new phenomenon for Australian Catholic schools needs to be aligned with the expectations of the parents of students who are non-Catholic, their children and the school, as well as Catholic parents and the parish communities supporting the school. In the first instance, the implications need to be specified for the Church, students, teachers and parents.

Implications for the Church

The reality of a significant proportion of Catholic students in Catholic schools who do not have any parish affiliation or commitment, together with a large number of non-Catholic students, poses a special challenge to what is normally considered the 'ecclesial identity' of the Catholic school. In other words, the ecclesial nature and purpose of the Australian Catholic school needs immediate reflection (Putney, 2005 and the first article in this book). The Catholic school is a Church school and is part of the Church's evangelising mission. Consequently, the ecclesial dimension is no appendix but needs to be recognised and fostered by the whole school community (*Third Millennium*, 11).

As a Church school, the Catholic school cannot exist or prosper in isolation, nor can it quarantine particular groups of students or teachers within it. The school needs to ensure it is always well-linked to the wider Church community through families and parishes, even though many have no parish or other Church connection. At the same time the

Catholic school constitutes its own community. Indeed it is meant to be a model functioning community characterised by collaboration among all students, parents, teachers, directors and non-teaching staff.

Implications for students

Enrolment policies and expectations

Current enrolment policies determine the priority given to non-Catholic families seeking enrolment of students in a Catholic school. Some specify proportional limits. Such policies may need review and reformulation, especially where they no longer reflect the reality of the Catholic school, or schools, for which they were designed. At the point of enrolment it is normal, and reasonable, for a principal to clarify with all parents, including parents of students other than Catholic, that the Catholic school has a religious purpose, and a religious life, for all its students. All parents should be expected to support the goals, values and shared teachings of the school as the basis of their engagement with the school's pastoral and spiritual activity.

Given the wide range of beliefs and levels of religious commitment among families of other faith traditions, and even amongst many Catholic families, the enrolment process must be handled sensitively but should not avoid clarifying and, where required, challenging the expectations of parents. Every pastoral effort, including formal programs, should be offered to parents and students to assist their initiation into school communities which have a distinctive ecclesial identity and mission.

Evangelisation

Since evangelisation is an essential goal of all Catholic schools, it needs to be clearly explained in the context of the enrolment of children not associated with the Church. In this respect, the question arises; how appropriate are existing strategies to the goal of evangelisation? Generally, it is a requirement that all students participate in the school's Religious Education program. Hence, approaches to Religious Education in a multi-faith environment require special attention and review. The extent to which a single common Religious Education program can provide for the different religious beliefs and practices of all students in a school is an immediate issue. The bishops acknowledge this reality. (NSW/ACT Bishops, 2007). A critical challenge for Catholic schools is their need to address simultaneously the differing needs of children drawn from local Catholic communities as well as those 'who are far from the faith' (*Catholic School* 59). As the *General Directory for Catechesis* notes: 'In the case of students who are non-believers, religious instruction assumes the character of a missionary proclamation of the Gospel' (75). Only with faith can catechesis follow.

Freedom of religious practice
Acknowledging and fostering the religious freedom of all its students provides a special challenge and opportunity for the Catholic school. Students seeking to publicly express and grow in their own particular faith need special assistance. This may create an opportunity to challenge Catholic students to more fully live their own faith. The participation of significant numbers of non-Catholic and non-Christian students in the prayer and liturgical life of a Catholic school, especially participation in Eucharistic celebrations, needs careful consideration.

Implications for teachers

Unlike enrolment patterns in Catholic schools in the past two decades, their leadership and staffing have been relatively stable. The teachers remain predominantly Catholic in secondary schools and almost exclusively Catholic in primary schools. In 2007 the proportion of NSW Catholic school teachers who were non-Catholic was 17%, exactly as in 1994. For primary schools, the proportion of teachers who were non-Catholic in 2007 was 6.4% compared to 5.9% in 1994, and in secondary schools in 2007 the proportion was 25% compared to 26% in 1994.

Catholic schools still have the advantage – fast receding – of a substantial core of teachers who were originally formed as Religious. There is a significant need for continued faith renewal amongst existing staff and significant formation needs for new staff. Already there are concerns about filling vacant principals' positions with candidates as qualified and committed to their faith as those being replaced. The average age of teachers is high and increasing numbers are approaching retirement age. The anticipated significant turnover of staff in all schools, including Catholic schools, in the next decade brings serious implications. Irrespective of their faith tradition and current level of religious commitment, staff members take on certain obligations and expectations by virtue of their employment in a Catholic school. Witness and personal values become relevant for all teachers, Catholic and non-Catholic. In the quest to ensure that Catholic schools remain authentic to their mission and values there are particular implications for present and future staffing practice. Critical to the future of the Catholic school are strategies to address recruitment, promotion and development of all teachers as committed Catholic school teachers. Indeed, over the coming decade or two, this may prove to be the most momentous challenge of all in keeping Catholic schools Catholic.

The criteria and protocols for sensitively assessing the faith, religious understanding and commitment of teachers and other staff, especially staff who are non-Catholic, need to be clarified. Moreover, these need to be unambiguously expressed in contractual documents. 'Conduct is always much more important than speech (*Lay Catholics*, 32). The Catholic teacher, therefore cannot be content simply to present Christian values as a set of abstract objectives to be admired ... They must be values which generate human attitudes' (30). In this context certain aspects of staff development need to be enhanced:

- Inducting and evangelising new staff, Catholic and non-Catholic, into the values and mission of the Catholic school within the Church
- Expectations and provision for ongoing faith formation and professional development in keeping with the recent exhortation that staff should naturally be 'open also to spiritual and religious formation and sharing' (*Educating Together*, 20)
- Whole of staff formation to ensure alignment between teachings and values, remembering that while teachers educate 'they can also dis-educate, with their verbal and non-verbal behaviour' (*Educating Together*, 38)
- Challenging staff to give witness to Christian values and Church teachings in a more diverse and pluralistic environment.

Implications for parents

The proper functioning of the Catholic school is predicated on the support it derives from parents (*Declaration on Christian Education* 3, 6). Therefore, Catholic schools need the confidence of parents. Likewise, all parents also have duties, one being to support the purpose and mission of the Catholic school to 'the best of their ability' and to cooperate in their children's education (para. 8). By way of reciprocation, the Catholic school has an obligation to accommodate the needs of parents and students. This is best expressed in *Third Millennium* as a 'constant aim' for contact and dialogue with the pupils' families, which should also be encouraged through the promotion of parents' associations, in order to clarify with their indispensable collaboration that personalised approach 'which is needed for an educational project to be efficacious' (20).

The most recent Church document goes further, encouraging schools to more actively support all families, both Catholic and non-Catholic, in their responsibilities, especially 'to develop an increasingly closer bond between the values proposed by the school and those proposed by the family' (*Educating Together*, 48). Dealing with parental issues, including the implications of increasing numbers of non-Catholic students in Catholic schools, is therefore appropriate for organisations representing the interests of Catholic school parents.

The signs of hope

In recent years most Australian Catholic schools have had little difficulty in accommodating non-Catholic students and their parents on the expectation that they support the religious goals and integrity of the Catholic school. Nonetheless, the NSW/ACT bishops' recent document proposes that it is timely to identify and re-examine some of the implications involved. For many non-Catholic families who choose Catholic schools, the religious nature of the Catholic school is an attraction. However, the bishops' *Crossroads* document is not focused on the needs of non-Catholic students. Rather it advocates a process of re-evangelisation of all those involved in Catholic schools as parents, teachers and students. It highlights the particular challenges posed by increasing numbers of Catholic families choosing government and other non-Catholic schools for their children, plus the overriding challenge of making Catholic schools more accessible to poorer families, Catholic and non-Catholic. Those are significant questions in their own right but still require far more detailed research and sophisticated analysis before firm policy guidelines can emerge.

Meanwhile, the reality remains that the religious backgrounds of students in Catholic schools has changed considerably over the past 20 years. It is now well documented and appreciated that a significant proportion of non-Catholic students is a natural and integral element of the modern Australian Catholic school. At the same time, the proportion of non-Catholic teachers has also begun to rise although much more slowly. This may increase more rapidly as the teaching force renews itself over the next few years. Future parents, teachers and leaders have the benefit of better understanding and responding to these particular challenges. They also have the assurance of knowing that the bishops acknowledge the reality of this development, and its evangelical and pastoral potential. Historically, services provided by Catholic hospitals and social welfare agencies such as the St Vincent de Paul Society and Centacare have been seen as a gift to all Australians, regardless of their religion. They deliver a faith-inspired service to society as a whole but to the poorer in particular. In some respects at least, in the early 21st century Catholic schools are only now catching up.

References

Bishops of NSW/ACT(2007), *Catholic Schools at a Crossroads*, Sydney, accessible at http://www.cecnsw.catholic.edu.au/

Canavan, K. (2007*) The Development of the Catholic Education Office and a System of Schools in Sydney since 1965*, Sydney. (cf Ch 6 in this volume.)

Church Documents. All these documents are conveniently available at http://www.vatican.va/roman_curia/congregations/ccatheduc/index.htm

Croke, B. (2007) Australian Catholic Schools in a Changing Political and Religious Landscape. In G. Grace and J. O'Keeffe, *International Handbook of Catholic Education,* Dordrecht, pp. 811 33.

Daily Telegraph, (2007) Protecting and raising a flock, 8 August, p.24.

Fogarty, R. (1957) *Catholic Education in Australia 1806-1950*, 2 vols. Melbourne.

Hogan, M. (1978) *The Catholic Campaign for State Aid* ,Sydney.

Mason, M. (2003)'Challenges of engagement with the Community', Catholic Health Australia National Conference Address (Hobart, 2-4 June, 2003), p.1, available at http://dlibrary.acu.edu.au/research/ccls/Otherpap/Mason_presentation_at_CHA_National_conference_2-6-03.doc

Putney, M. (2005) The Catholic School of the Future, *Australasian Catholic Record* 28 pp. 387-98.

The Sydney Morning Herald , (2007) Keeping faith at a crossroads, 9 August, p.12.

Vaughan, Archbishop (1880) Catholic Education: Pastoral Letter of the Archbishop and Bishops exercising jurisdiction in NSW (Sydney 1879), p.11, reprinted in Archbishop Vaughan, *Pastorals and Speeches on Education* (Sydney 1880).

Wilkinson, I.R, Caldwell, B.J, Selleck, R J W, Harris, J , Dettman P, (2007) *A History of State Aid in Australia,* Canberra.

6
The Development of Catholic School Systems[1]

Kelvin Canavan

Until the early 1960s Australian Catholic schools were relatively autonomous and any links to a diocesan Catholic Education Office (CEO) were tenuous. Deprived of any financial assistance from government, they struggled to accommodate all those seeking places in a Catholic school. But, within the space of 40 years, these parish primary and regional secondary schools were transformed and became partners in flourishing diocesan systems of schools, managed by CEOs as enrolments rose to record levels.

This chapter identifies the factors contributing to the development of the CEO, of the Archdiocese of Sydney and provides an overview of its contribution to the educational mission of the Church. In the years ahead CEOs will face a new set of challenges as they help schools respond to a weakening of the Catholic culture and religious practices symptomatic of a more secular society. Diocesan CEOs are unique to Australia, and their story needs to be told.

The growth of large and influential CEOs during the past 40 years has had a significant impact on almost every aspect of Catholic education in Australia. During this period the structure and character of Catholic schooling underwent permanent change. What had once been a loose network of self-supporting, relatively autonomous schools, under the control of parish priests and religious institutes, was gradually transformed into centralised systems that took different forms in different dioceses.

---

[1] An extended version of this chapter may be found in 'The development of the Catholic Education Office and a system of schools in Sydney since 1965' published by the Catholic Education Office Sydney, (*Bulletin* 93) in September 2007.

Historical overview

The development of CEOs in the late 1960s came at a time when Catholic schools were struggling with enrolment pressure, large classes, a reduced ability to build and staff new schools, rising costs, and negligible government assistance. The Religious Sisters and Brothers, who for the past 80 years had done most of the teaching and all of the administration, were thinly spread and seeking some relief. Bishops turned increasingly to their Directors of Schools for assistance with planning and the allocation of scarce resources. In many dioceses finances were centralised, staffing levels and diocesan school fees schedules were established, and responsibility for the payment of teachers' salaries was transferred from schools to CEOs. For the first time, Catholic communities began dealing with diocesan education offices.

For almost a century Catholic schools had struggled on without any government financial assistance, apart from some Commonwealth support for secondary school science laboratories and libraries and, in New South Wales (NSW), an interest subsidy scheme for loans on school buildings. The breakthrough for Catholic schools in NSW came in 1968, when the NSW State Government introduced grants of $12 for each primary school student and $18 for each secondary school student attending a non-government school. At about the same time the other Australian States and Territories began to provide some financial assistance to students in all non-government schools. Initially the grants were modest, but they were sufficient to keep the schools open. In 1970 the Commonwealth Government also began to pay grants to assist with the ongoing recurrent funding of all non-government schools in Australia.

The functions of CEOs were gradually expanded, and by the early 1970s Catholic schooling in the various dioceses began to take on some of the early characteristics of a 'system'. The move towards more structured diocesan administration was assisted by the deliberations at the National Conference on Catholic Education in Armidale in 1972. This conference crystallised a considerable volume of earlier debate on the administrative needs of Catholic education. The Australian Episcopal Conference then established an expert committee which held its first meeting on 27 April 1973. This committee met on five occasions and its report 'The Organisation of Australian Catholic Education' was released four months later. The major recommendations were quickly adopted and diocesan, State and national administrative structures were put into place without much delay. These new structures were required if Catholic schools were to maximise the emerging opportunities flowing from the education policies of the Whitlam Government.

True to pre-election undertakings, the Whitlam Government lost no time implementing the directions in the 'Karmel Report' and immediately CEOs were required to manage new programs, including general recurrent resources, school buildings, primary and secondary libraries, disadvantaged schools, Special Education, teacher development and innovation. The establishment of the Australian Schools Commission in 1973 had immediate implications for Catholic schools, and served both as a catalyst and an incentive to hasten the development of suitable organisational arrangements. The Commonwealth Government declined to deal with individual schools, leaving the various State and diocesan education authorities to assume responsibility for the distribution of government per capita grants to individual schools, according to need.

To access these new Commonwealth programs, those responsible for diocesan systems of schools were required to have in place administrative procedures that satisfied the program guidelines and accountability demands of the Government. Given the ready availability of considerable funds for immediate expenditure, the CEOs quickly gathered staff to manage the new programs. Many of these staff had little previous administrative experience, and considerable on-the-job training was required.

The above arrangements, while restricting the direct administrative involvement of the Commonwealth Government in individual schools, significantly increased the responsibilities and spheres of influences of the CEOs. In the Archdiocese of Sydney, for example, the CEO in 1969 had a total staff of about 15 people, predominantly priests and Religious, most of whom were part-time due to other responsibilities. By 1979 the staff in the CEO had increased to about 80, with some salaries paid from Commonwealth Special Purpose programs.

By the end of the 1970s, Catholic schooling in Australia had a very different appearance from a decade earlier. School communities and parishes continued to be highly committed but, for the first time, the schools had the resources that allowed them to respond more appropriately to the needs of students. There was a new confidence in the future of Catholic schooling and increasingly CEOs were giving some shape to this new environment. This growth of CEOs was to continue and, over the next 25 years, the various CEOs became involved in the delivery to systemic schools of an increasing number of State and Commonwealth Government policies and programs. This period was marked by increased government accountability and compliance requirements, as a condition of funding.

This confidence was a tribute to the religious institutes, the bishops and clergy, principals and teachers, parents and students, and the wider community who set aside established traditions and practices to reposition their Catholic schools for the decades ahead. They had responded pragmatically to new opportunities in a changed environment. The pace of this reshaping was breathtaking.

Diocesan CEOs are unique to Australia and their history needs to be told. What follows is a very broad overview of the development of one of these CEOs, told by someone personally involved in the administration of the Sydney Catholic school system since January 1968.

The beginning of the system in Sydney: 1965-1986

Prior to 1965, Catholic schools in Sydney were relatively independent. Each school raised its own funds, and the principal or the parish priest paid any lay teachers employed. As a response to a financial crisis, a decision was taken in 1965 by Cardinal Norman Gilroy, Archbishop of Sydney, to pool all financial resources and liabilities from parish primary and regional secondary schools, and to pay teachers' salaries and stipends for Religious from a common fund. A scale of tuition fees for these schools was introduced, and all proposals for additional buildings would require approval. Expenditure was tightly controlled as archdiocesan accountants negotiated overdrafts with the Commonwealth Bank to keep paying salaries and stipends. The Catholic Building and Finance Commission (CBFC) was established as the principal decision-making body and Cardinal Gilroy chaired the monthly meetings. The Catholic Education Office (CEO) was a link between the CBFC and the schools and became progressively responsible for the management of this new 'system' of schools. At this stage the CEO occupied four rooms at the end of the Housie Hall in Cusa House, 175 Elizabeth Street, Sydney.

The 1965 decision to begin to centralise and co-ordinate what had previously been a loose network of self-supporting, relatively independent parish primary and regional secondary schools was to change permanently the structure and character of Catholic education in Sydney. In the early 1970s the CEO, Sydney and the CBFC had quickly to assemble staff to manage the emerging system and to allocate government funds to systemic schools according to need. This was a difficult task, as the earlier model of Catholic schooling had not prepared people for these new responsibilities. Bishops, the Diocesan Director of Schools (Mgr John Slowey), priests, Religious and lay employees found themselves assessing needs and managing programs that only a few years earlier could not have been imagined. Their roles required them to work with experienced public servants. Some recently retired Catholics from the NSW Department of Education also played important roles in this transition period.

In 1973 a lay principal was appointed to De La Salle College, Ashfield and the Diocesan Director of Schools assumed responsibility for his employment. With the coming of the first Industrial Award in 1970 for teachers in Catholic schools in NSW, the CEO, Sydney assumed responsibility for a range of employment-related functions. In a few dioceses, the parish priest emerged as the employer of staff working in Catholic schools. The 1970 Award was significant as it provided Catholic school teachers for the first time with salaries comparable to teachers in government schools. The introduction of a superannuation scheme in 1981 and the first Award for Catholic school principals in 1989 completed the remuneration arrangements that allowed lay employees to opt for a long-term career in Catholic education.

The rapid withdrawal of Religious principals, particularly from parish primary schools, had an immediate impact on the development of the 'systematisation' of Catholic schooling in Sydney. Between 1975 and 1977 a total of 44 lay principals were required to replace Religious who had been withdrawn by the leaders of their Institutes. This took the small CEO, Sydney and the Catholic community generally by surprise. It demanded a concerted effort to find sufficient lay leaders and to put in place conditions of employment and contract arrangements. This gradual replacement of Religious principals continued and progressively the CEO, Sydney accepted a variety of management responsibilities that had previously been undertaken by Religious Institutes. The need for the professional development of the new primary lay principals – and the continuing Religious principals – became an immediate priority for the fledgling CEO, Sydney.

During the early 1980s the roles and responsibility of the CEO, Sydney continued to grow in response to an expansion of Commonwealth Schools Commission initiatives including a Participation and Equity program, an English as a Second Language program, a Multicultural Education program, an Ethnic Schools program, a Country Areas program and a Professional Development program. The rapid growth in the roles, services, and structures of the CEO, Sydney and the transfer of considerable authority and responsibility from the priests and Religious to the CEO and CBFC were characterised by tension and ambiguity, as those in positions of responsibility struggled to clarify lines of authority and responsibility in the developing system of schools.

Over the years the archdiocesan authorities attempted to address these tensions and ambiguities in a series of reviews. As early as 1970 the representatives of the leaders of Religious Institutes, Sr Philomena Ryman, rsm and Br Othmar Weldon, fms – both members of the CBFC – were proposing changes to the organisational arrangements introduced by Cardinal Gilroy in 1965. They argued for a coming together of the separate educational and financial departments under a single Catholic Education Board. A number of other studies were commissioned but the various reports had limited impact on the administrative structures of the Sydney Catholic school system. Change would have to await the arrival of the next Archbishop of Sydney.

While the tensions and role conflict that gave rise to these reports continued at the system level, Catholic schools were already showing the effects of additional government funding. By the mid-1980s schools were enjoying the benefits of the steadily increasing government financial assistance: class sizes continued to fall, the Commonwealth's Special Purpose Programs were assisting students with particular needs, and teachers were benefiting from professional development programs. Principals had access to substantial leadership courses, were supported by school secretaries, and had considerable relief from day-to-day classroom teaching. Some new schools had opened and others had been refurbished, some courtesy of the Commonwealth Capital Grants Program. Lay principals for the most part were accepted by the Catholic community and provided strong leadership in changing times.

Archbishop Edward Clancy was appointed Archbishop of Sydney in 1983, and early in 1985 authorised 'a wide-ranging review of the structures and procedures within the archdiocesan system of schools' to be undertaken by Victor Couch. In May 1985, in a preliminary report,

Couch restated the organisational weaknesses identified in previous reviews. Concurrently, a doctoral study of perceptions and expectations surveyed all 256 systemic school principals in the archdiocese and all 124 CEO professional staff in October 1985. The interplay between people, organisational structures, services and goals to be achieved was examined. The study found:

> The system is characterised by a confusion resulting from an uncertainty of roles and mutual expectations of principals, priests, the CEO, the Catholic Schools Finance Office and the Sydney Archdiocesan Catholic Schools Board, by discontinuity in structure and goal setting, by tension and by dissatisfaction (Canavan, 1986, p.28).

The conditions found in the various reports could be readily explained, given the existing network of schools prior to centralisation: the rapid rate of change; the transference of power and responsibility from Parish Priests and principals to the CEO, Sydney; the appointment of lay principals, and the retirement of many Religious principals and teachers.

The first 20 years (1965-1986) of the expanded CEO, Sydney were characterised by efforts to facilitate new administrative and organisational arrangements to allow systemic schools initially to survive, and then to readjust and begin to flourish in a changed education environment. The next phase (1987-2007) would see the schools benefiting from a more stable and mature organisation.

Consolidation of the system in Sydney: 1987-2007

In April 1986 a decision was made to establish two dioceses from what was previously the large Archdiocese of Sydney. The new bishops of Broken Bay and Parramatta appointed Directors of Schools and established separate CEOs in January 1987. At the same time Archbishop Clancy responded to the calls for changes by restructuring the Sydney Archdiocesan Catholic Schools (SACS) Board, and incorporating the financial arm of the school system, the Catholic Schools Finance Office (formerly the Catholic Building and Finance Commission) into a restructured Catholic Education Office. The separation of financial from educational responsibilities by Cardinal Gilroy in 1965 had initially served the struggling system of schools well, but in the following years this separation had become dysfunctional and a cause of considerable tension.

The leadership of the CEO capitalised on the more settled administrative environment by gradually focusing the attention of both school principals and CEO staff on the improvement of classroom practice and student learning. This shift of culture was faster in primary schools than in the larger, more complex secondary schools. Increasingly, the agenda of the CEO moved from administrative and organisational issues to improved educational outcomes. The new leadership team at the CEO, Sydney, moved quickly to provide clear strategic direction for the school system. Priorities were established. Principals responded to this lead from the CEO and progressively became more strategic in their own leadership. By 1993 most schools had adopted a cyclic approach to planning and school review. School strategic management plans began appearing and in 1995 a new ten-year strategic plan: *Sydney Catholic Schools: Towards 2005* was launched at the Darling Harbour Convention Centre.

In the 1986 study principals had been ambivalent in their perception of the influence of the CEO, Sydney on classroom instruction. By 2004 the perceptions were different. A doctoral study by Mark Turkington carried out in 2002-2003 reported that principals and senior CEO personnel perceived the CEO as a learning organisation having a positive impact on standards in Religious Education, literacy, and numeracy.

The initial factors contributing to this change of perception included:
- System-wide priority for improvement in teaching and learning
- Focus on data analysis and reporting school achievement
- Target-setting at school and system level
- Tracking individual student performance
- Student academic achievement in NSW Basic Skills Tests and in the Higher Schools Certificate
- Targeted intervention to improve student performance in particular schools
- Reporting achievement against published Key Performance Indicators and targets
- Principals responding to the challenge from the Executive Director of Schools and CEO staff to provide strong instructional leadership and to be personally involved in teaching and learning.

In 2004 a panel of four distinguished educators, including two from the

UK, was engaged to evaluate the implementation of the *Towards 2005* plan and to report on the effectiveness of the CEO and the system of schools. The *Report from the External Review Panel* stated:

> Overall the CEO, Sydney is a highly effective and well-led organisation, characterised by the high commitment of staff at all levels. Its strong Catholic and educational mission adds significantly to the work of systemic schools and to the educational experiences and learning of young people (Gamble, Stannard, Benjamin, Burke, 2004, p.vii).

Throughout the periods of change outlined above the Religious Education and formation of students continued as 'core business' for the CEO, Sydney. New K-12 Religious Education curriculum documents were developed between 1989 and 1996. This Religious Education curriculum was revitalised by CEO staff and re-launched by Cardinal George Pell in St Mary's Cathedral in December 2003. CEO staff had worked closely with colleagues in the Archdiocese of Melbourne in the production of a revised edition of the *To Know, Worship and Love* student textbooks, which was launched on the same day. The new curriculum and student textbooks were well received by principals who indicated that the revitalised curriculum was strengthening the teaching and learning of Religious Education across all years from Kindergarten to Year 10. They also said that the new textbooks had been well received by students and parents.

Between 1976 and 2006 the region encompassing the Archdiocese of Sydney had experienced a steady decline of 42 300 (or 10.5%) in school-age population and a shift of young families to the south west of the Archdiocese. Many Catholic schools in the Eastern suburbs and the inner west were only half full, while families in the new growth areas could not be accommodated. Working with the clergy and parish communities, the archdiocese closed or amalgamated 66 schools between 1980 and 2006. In the same period 13 new schools were established in growth areas. Without a strong and well-resourced CEO this shift of resources would not have been possible, and enrolments in the school system would have declined significantly, rather than increasing by 4900 (or 6.5%) between 1976 and 2006. There is now a significant Catholic education presence in the developing areas of the archdiocese and land has been acquired for further development.

By the late 1970s the CEO, Sydney, in association with the NSW Catholic Education Commission and the National Catholic Education

Commission, had become involved in the politics of government funding for Catholic schools. Initially this involved the protection of funding levels from those opposed, including the NSW Teachers Federation. The education of the broader electorate was essential, and the misinformation provided by opponents of Catholic schools needed to be corrected. The CEO, Sydney regularly prepared print and electronic materials to ensure that the facts about government funding of schools were clearly explained. The CEO involved school principals in this campaign, and relationships with members of Parliament were fostered.

Catholic schools have progressively become more dependent on government funding as illustrated by Table 1.

TABLE 1 Combined Australian Government and State Annual Grants for Students in Catholic Systemic Schools in NSW 1967-2006

	K-6 Student	7-12 Student
1967	$0	$0
1968	$12	$18
1969	$27	$36
1989	$1,568	$2,390
1999	$3358	$4,631
2005	$5261	$7,056
2006	$5580	$7,312
2007	$6,212	$7.947

Source: Catholic Education office, Sydney archives

Nevertheless, the cost to parents of Catholic education continues to rise, and there is a renewed awareness that costs must be controlled if Catholic schools are to be accessible to less affluent Catholic families.

In NSW, each of the 11 CEOs relates to the Catholic Education Commission (CEC), and to the Catholic Commission for Employment Relations (CCER). These two organisations were established by the hierarchy of NSW to co-ordinate aspects of Catholic education which have

State-wide implications. They have authority and exercise considerable influence on the CEOs and the schools. In turn, the CEC, NSW, relates to the National Catholic Education Commission (NCEC), based in Canberra. The NCEC works closely with the eight CECs and provides a single voice on matters of national significance. The CCER relates to the Australian Catholic Commission for Employment Relations.

A consequence of these new administrative arrangements was a new political strength that allowed Catholic authorities to lobby effectively on behalf of all schools and to ameliorate the impact of legislation on schools. Successive Commonwealth and State governments used these new structures to consult with the Catholic sector. The relationships between leaders of Catholic education and successive Commonwealth and State Ministers and their senior staff have been of enormous benefit to the students in Catholic schools. Those who prepared the 1973 report 'The Organisation of Australian Catholic Education', and the bishops that accepted it, have every reason to be very satisfied with the effectiveness of the organisational arrangements they put into place 35 years ago.

The effectiveness of the CEO, Sydney that was recognised by both the 2004 External Review Panel and the 2007 Australian Business Excellence Award, can be partly explained by the emergence of a shared culture, characterised by good relationships and consistent approaches to school management and leadership. In the development of this culture the personal and professional support for leaders was a priority, and system processes were complemented by opportunities to gather, to pray and to celebrate. The strength of this school system was greater than the sum of the parts.

In 2007, the geographical area that until 1986 was the Archdiocese of Sydney is served by three dioceses which employ more than 500 persons in their education offices and have responsibility for annual recurrent budgets totalling about $1 billion. The NSW Catholic Education Commission and the NSW Catholic Commission which have a combined staff of about 50 persons, support the three CEOs for Employment Relations. Forty years earlier, schools in this same geographical area were supported by a CEO staff of about 15, most of whom were part-time, and who shared four small offices in Cusa House in the Sydney CBD.

The years ahead

The initial development of Catholic education systems in Australia administered by CEOs was clearly a consequence of the reintroduction of government financial assistance and the early decision by the Commonwealth not to become involved with individual schools, but rather to have the Catholic authorities distribute recurrent funding to schools according to need. This development was accelerated by the acceptance by CEOs of leadership and administrative responsibilities for more and more schools as Religious Institutes no longer had Sisters and Brothers available to lead systemic schools.

The continuing growth of these CEOs is also directly related to increasing government intervention in education. As a condition of funding, the Commonwealth government now demands compliance on an ever-widening range of matters, and the CEOs and the CEC need to ensure that all schools are compliant. As a consequence of the *NSW Education Act 1990* (part 7:39-40) the eleven CEOs in NSW are the approved authorities for systems of non-government schools and have responsibility for monitoring compliance of systemic schools with the Act.

A continuing challenge for leaders of school systems is to ensure that systemic schools remain connected to local parish communities. The long-term future of these schools is dependent on their continuing connection with the parishes. School and system leaders must resist any moves that would weaken this relationship. The use of the term 'CEO schools' is not helpful, as it can convey the notion that the CEO is a Catholic equivalent of the NSW Department of Education. Rather, parish and regional schools are partners in diocesan systems that continue to be the principal agents for the evangelisation and education of young Catholics in Australia. These systems are able to harvest resources that are then allocated according to need. Schools in need are supported and new communities assisted with the provision of school facilities. CEOs need to provide support and service without stifling initiative or weakening local ownership of the schools. Considerable wisdom and sensitivity is required to achieve the appropriate balance between local and system responsibilities.

Catholic schools in Australia have changed dramatically in the past four decades. The transition from Religious Sisters and Brothers to lay teachers, the reintroduction of government financial assistance, the steady increase in enrolments, and the emergence of strong CEOs and their systems of schools have all had a profound impact on the shape of Catholic education.

Catholic schools are well regarded. There is considerable community confidence in their effectiveness, and demand for places is strong. Paradoxically, the same 40 years have seen a weakening of the Catholic culture and a creeping secularism. Many traditional Catholic beliefs and practices are less obvious, and fewer students and parents attend Mass. Some commentators blame Catholic schools for failure to maintain a vibrant Catholic culture and Catholic practices, while others are of the view that the ability of schools to withstand the secularisation of Australian society is limited. The entire Catholic community is challenged by many complex social factors that make Catholicism less cultural than it used to be. World Youth Day 2008 provided parishes, families, schools and CEOs with a unique opportunity to deepen the engagement of young people with Jesus Christ and the Church he founded.

This chapter has given a very brief overview of the development of one CEO in Australia and how it has supported the schools through a prolonged period of transition and transformation. This writer believes that the CEO, Sydney has done this well. In the years ahead CEOs in Australia will be called upon to support schools to manage a different set of challenges in an increasingly secular and technologically-shaped society.

References

Bourke, J. et al. (1973) *The Organisation of Australian Catholic Education: Report of a Committee.* Canberra: Commissioned by Australian Episcopal Conference.

Canavan, K. (1986) *Perceptions and Expectations of Roles, Services, Structures and Goals of the Sydney Catholic Education Office Held by Principals and CEO Staff.* Ed.D Thesis. University of San Francisco.

Canavan, K (2007) *The Development of the Catholic Education Office and a System of Schools in Sydney Since 1965.* Bulletin 93 Catholic Education Office, Sydney.

Couch, V. (1985) *Review of Structures and Procedures, within the Archdiocesan System of Schools.* Sydney: Commissioned by Archbishop E B Clancy.

Gamble, I., Stannard, O., Benjamin, A., Burke, T. (2004) *Report to the Archdiocese of Sydney on the Catholic Education Office, Sydney and the Sydney Archdiocesan Catholic Schools Board.* Sydney: Catholic Education Office, Sydney.

Gleeson, G. (circa 1973) *Report on the Administration of Catholic School Education,*

Sydney Archdiocese. Sydney: Commissioned by Archbishop James Carroll.

Payne, A. (1981) *The Catholic Education Office, Sydney and Regionalisation: Report of a Survey*. Sydney: Commissioned by the Archdiocesan Council.

Turkington, M. (2004) *The Catholic Education Office Sydney as a Learning Organisation and its Perceived Impact on Standards.* PhEd.D Thesis. Australian Catholic University, Strathfield.

PART TWO
Learning from Broader Perspectives

7
Responding to Leadership Challenges in American Catholic Schools

Timothy J Cook

Our experiences in the American context are greatly affected by the larger American society and Church. We have a long-standing tradition of strict separation of church and state. Certain 'ism's'- consumerism, materialism, and individualism, secularism, pluralism- are prevalent values in American society. In *A People Adrift*, Peter Steinfels (2003) describes the American Catholic Church as experiencing a crisis of identity and leadership brought about by the generational mainstreaming of Catholics into society, the decline of religious vocations, and the sexual abuse scandal.

This chapter describes the top three challenges facing Catholic school leaders in the American context and explains how leaders have responded to these challenges thus far. It concludes with reflections about moving forward with hope in uncertain times.

Leadership challenges and responses

The most pressing challenges Catholic school leaders face can be grouped into three categories: Funding, Catholic Identity, and Leadership.

Funding

Funding is the most urgent issue. One in four United States' Catholic primary schools is considered financially unstable or unviable (Dwyer, 2005). Because Catholic schools in America receive very little government funding, schools are forced to fund themselves primarily through parish subsidies, tuition, and fundraising (Harris, 2000). As school costs escalate, this funding formula makes the following three financial challenges more acute:

Recruiting and retaining teachers

Catholic schools are only as good as their teachers, but it is increasingly difficult to find and keep quality teachers when the average Catholic primary school teacher makes only 54% of a public school salary and a secondary teacher makes 73% (Schaub, 2000). Teachers often teach for a few years in Catholic schools and then move to public schools out of necessity. Salaries also vary among Catholic schools, which make them compete with each other for teachers. These teacher salary inequities seem contradictory to Catholic social teaching.

Balancing affordability with quality

As educational costs rise each year, so does the tuition. The average primary school tuition is $3008 AUD and the average secondary tuition is $7970 AUD (McDonald, 2007). Most schools set their own tuition depending on what the market will bear. The challenge leaders face is to provide schools of excellence that are faithful to their mission without pricing themselves out of the market. As tuition increases, Catholic education becomes less affordable for the poor and middle class. Some call this the "eliting" of American Catholic schools. Moreover, school quality has become a function of affluence. Affluent parishes have better funded schools that often result in higher quality facilities and programs.

Justifying worth

The more costly Catholic schools become, the more people question whether they are worth the sacrifice. Less than 20% of U.S. Catholic children attend Catholic schools. Parish principals must defend the school's budget to the pastor and finance committee, especially if the school subsidy eats up much of the parish budget and/or the majority of parish children attend public schools. Also, school leaders are dealing with Catholic families today who are less willing to make sacrifices to send their children to Catholic schools, especially if there is a good public school nearby.

Responses

To meet the funding challenges, those involved in Catholic education have continued to fight for government funding. Parent advocacy groups have been formed in many states to fight for vouchers and other forms of government assistance that will enable them to exercise the right to choose a religious education for their children.

We have stepped up marketing and public relations efforts through the annual National Catholic Education Association (NCEA)-sponsored National Marketing Campaign and Catholic Schools Week as well as through national and local publications and media releases that keep schools in the public eye. We must continue to convince people that a Catholic school education is a valuable investment.

The most common longstanding vehicle Catholic schools have used to supplement parish subsidies and tuition is fund raising. However, fund raising, tuition, and parish subsidies are short-term strategies for a long term problem. They merely balance the yearly budget. This is no longer a good funding model, yet it is all too prevalent.

More sophisticated dioceses and schools, especially larger high schools, have followed the lead of Catholic universities in their approach to financial well-being. They have established development or institutional advancement offices with personnel designated to spearhead and coordinate public relations, recruitment, fund raising efforts, and periodic capital campaigns. The most forward thinking operations concentrate on building a multi-million endowment that will ensure long-term viability. This is done through planned giving or estate planning and is sometimes a goal for a capital campaign. The majority of Americans die without a will, which makes personal bequests a huge untapped financial resource for Catholic schools.

Entirely new models of school are emerging as well. For example, Cristo Rey high schools are an exciting new venture. Designed to serve financially disadvantaged urban youth, these schools fund their tuition by sending their students on internships to local businesses one day a week. In 2007, seven new schools opened, bringing the total of Cristo Rey schools nationwide to 19 (www.cristoreynetwork.org).

Looking ahead, we need to take a more system wide approach to funding schools through strategic planning. The parish funding model is no longer viable (Dwyer, 2005). Right now we operate on an 'every school for itself' mentality. We also need to focus our efforts on planned giving. The greatest amount of money in American history will pass from one generation to the next in the coming years, which will be a source for much money in the future. We must also continue to fight for the share of public funding to which we are entitled.

Catholic identity

Financial struggles have forced us to attend to our Catholic identity in order to justify our worth to parents and church officials. Parents still consider religious mission to be a key reason for choosing Catholic schools (CARA, 2006). Gone are the days when Catholic identity can be assumed. Today we have to be intentional about our mission, and there are four challenges associated with this mission. First of all, Catholic schools must be good schools before they can be good *Catholic* schools. 'Catholic' is not the noun, it is the adjective. Academic excellence is a reflection of the Catholic intellectual tradition. According to canon law, academic excellence is a constitutive element of Catholic school identity. Furthermore, the Catholic community will not financially support mediocre schools. *So the first challenge for leaders is to use limited resources to operate excellent schools.*

Building a better academic mousetrap is not enough. The American bishops state in *To Teach As Jesus Did*, 'integration of religious truth and values with life distinguishes the Catholic school from other schools' (National Conference of Catholic Bishops, 1972, #105). *Therefore, the second challenge for the Catholic school leader is to ensure that the Christian message and Catholic vision permeate the school curriculum and culture.*

School leaders are being more intentional about cultivating their Catholic ethos and culture (Cook, 2001). Miller (2006) believes that schools need to provide quality assurance that they are fulfilling their religious mission. Some schools and systems are putting structures and processes in place to assess their Catholic identity in order to prevent them from becoming a private school with a cross on top (Cook and Ostrowski, 2007). For example, *Validating the Vision*, which is published by the NCEA, is a protocol that can be used in conjunction with required state and regional accreditation to assess mission effectiveness. Religious order networks are beginning accreditation processes of their own. It is common for a school board to have a mission and identity committee. Some larger Catholic high schools now have a second tier administrator called Vice President for Mission Effectiveness, and some diocesan Catholic Education Offices have a designated person who fulfills this role.

School leaders cannot ensure Catholic identity themselves. Catholic schools will achieve their religious mission to the degree that all teachers, or at least a critical mass of them, participate. Even secular subject teachers and coaches have significant influence on student spiritual formation. *The leader's third challenge then is to recruit and retain teachers who 'get it'.* This was a no-brainer when Catholic universities were the natural supplier of Catholic school teachers. This is no longer the case for two reasons. First, many Catholic university teacher preparation programs emphasize public education. Second, many graduates who paid expensive Catholic university tuition cannot afford to teach in Catholic schools. Additionally, since religious education is not taught in the public schools, finding qualified religious education teachers is next to impossible. No state save Nebraska recognises religious education as a teaching field (2003). Retaining such teachers is also a serious problem that contributes to shortages (Cook and Engel, 2006).

To address recruitment and formation issues, leaders are being more intentional about hiring for mission. Principals are also devoting more time and energy forming teachers for mission, especially on the elementary level when all teachers teach religion. Leaders are beginning to design teacher evaluation instruments and processes that include mission-related items.

One of the exciting responses to the shortage of faith-filled and qualified teachers for under resourced urban and rural schools is the Catholic teacher corps. Initiated by the University of Notre Dame in 1994, the teacher corps idea has spread to other Catholic universities. Today 14 American Catholic universities comprise the University Consortium for Catholic Education (http://www.ucceconnect.com). Students in these teacher corps spend two years of service teaching in a Catholic school. They live in community and earn their master's degree and teaching credential over the two-year period. These are reincarnations of religious community. When a teacher corps begins service in an area, we refer to it as 'opening a house' just as religious orders did in the past. Each year these programs supply over 400 teachers to Catholic schools.

The leader's fourth challenge is to reconcile the tensions between Catholic school vision and 21st century reality. How do you teach Catholic values when the Church lacks credibility? How do you satisfy both liberal and conservative Catholics in a polarised Church? How do you balance market with mission in a secular society, finding the middle ground between being 'too Catholic' and 'not Catholic enough' (Cook and Davies, 2008)? How do you emphasise school faith community without building a parallel parish? Do Muslim headscarves violate the uniform code? One girls' high school principal I talked to asked, 'How do you explain to young women, especially in a girls' school, why they cannot take their full place at the table in the Catholic Church?'

Although we live in a global society, Americans are very self-focused. Moving ahead, if we as Catholic educators really want to make a unique and invaluable contribution to American society, we need to accentuate the global and international aspect of our Catholic school identity. Because we belong to a universal church that operates a worldwide system of schools, American Catholic schools should be leading the country in global and international education. Yet, we have not capitalised on this inherent part of our identity. If we really want to distinguish ourselves from public and other private schools, and fulfill a need in our country, American Catholic schools should promote global awareness and solidarity, multicultural perspectives, and international relationships. We should produce graduates who think of themselves as both American citizens and citizens of the world.

Leadership

Leadership itself is the third critical issue today because we need strong and visionary leaders to address the funding and identity issues. National leadership should start with the bishops but a challenge for them will be to re-establish their credibility while the American Church continues to suffer the fallout of the sexual abuse scandal (D'Antonio, Davidson, Hoge, and Gautier, 2007). Furthermore, at the school level, one-half of the nation's dioceses opened the school year without at least one principal (Schuttloffel, 2003). The following are three specific educational leadership challenges.

The overwhelming job description

Catholic school principals are overwhelmed with an ever-expanding list of duties and expectations. They are asked to do the equivalent job of a public school district superintendent, only without the large support staff. High school principals usually receive assistance from one or more deputy heads, but most of the primary schools do not even have a deputy head (Schuttloffel, 2003). One primary principal describes the situation this way:

> My peers in public schools need only concern themselves with students, discipline, and parents. Everything else is done for them at the

district level. I, on the other hand, take care of budgeting, personnel, curriculum, grant writing, school calendar, school maintenance, student recruitment, and the list goes on.

All of this is very difficult to do when you are in survival mode. The job requires principals to walk on water, yet most times they can barely tread water.

To respond to the complex nature of Catholic school leadership, a growing number of high schools have adopted a two-person president /principal leadership model. The president is the chief executive officer whose responsibilities include Catholic identity and mission, finance and development, public relations, strategic planning, and the Board of Trustees. The principal is the chief academic officer who runs the school day-to-day. The principal's responsibilities include faculty formation and supervision, curriculum, discipline, athletic teams, and pastoral care of students. Elementary schools are sorely in need of new school leadership models, and some have explored the concept of co-principals, but this model is still very rare.

The lack of system support and collaboration

Catholic educational leaders at all levels feel isolated and unsupported. They feel like they are in this alone. Using a metaphor from American Westerns, I characterise them as Lone Rangers. Educational leaders feel ambivalence from Church leadership. Parish principals often feel unsupported by the parish pastor, who is either disinterested or overburdened. Most new principals are told to pick their position based on the pastor.

The Catholic school system operates more like a system of independent schools. Superintendents usually function with a bare bones staff and lack authority with pastors who run their parishes like fiefdoms. Catholic schools operate autonomously. One superintendent likened her role to herding cats. Because schools stand alone, competition between them for students and resources can be fierce.

While school autonomy is good, the 'every school for itself' mentality that prevails is not. For instance, in my hometown there is a fierce rivalry among the three Catholic high schools. As the number of Catholic children in the region continues to drop, the rivalry between schools no longer makes sense. These schools are beating each other into the ground when the real threats to their existence are new public charter and magnet schools.

In an attempt to foster collaboration and coordination among schools, some dioceses have created regional school systems within the diocese that have their own superintendent or president. Religious order schools have formed national networks to increase collaboration among member schools with a distinctive heritage, charism, and mission.

As we move ahead, we must create new governance and leadership models to replace the outmoded pastor as Chief Executive Officer model. Many priests do not want to be assigned to a parish with a school because they consider schools a burden. Who can blame them since priests face more duties and fewer brother priests? We must unburden priests of a duty for which they have little interest and training. Furthermore, no one person should have the power to determine the fate of a school. One principal commented, 'The pastor can make or break the existence of a parish school'. We need to increase the role of school boards and system-wide leadership structures.

Inadequate preparation and succession

Principals in Catholic schools wear many hats. Unlike their public school counterparts, they must be astute in managerial, educational, and faith leadership. Unfortunately, too many newcomers to Catholic leadership are inadequately prepared. Because schools are so fragile, an unskilled principal can do a lot of damage quickly. We therefore need each principal to be creative, talented, and faith-filled.

Of particular concern is the principal's preparation for faith leadership. Schuttloffel's (2003) survey indicates that over half of novice principals lack the necessary theological or spiritual knowledge to be faith leaders. It rises to 95% for novice leaders who come from public schools. In another study of Catholic secondary school principals, 70% responded that their formal coursework did not adequately prepare them to be faith leaders (Joseph, 2002). This stands to reason since the overwhelming majority of leaders earn their credentials at secular institutions. Even if they attended a Catholic university, there is no guarantee that Catholic school issues were addressed.

In response, the Association of Catholic Leadership Programs (ACLP) was formed in 1983 to promote degree and licensure programs specifically designed for Catholic school leaders. There are currently 30 member institutions (http://aclp.ncea.org/). The majority of super-intendents believe that these Catholic leadership programs offer the most effective preparation for principals. Yet, at present, these programs only prepare 25% of school leaders (Schuttloffel, 2003). In the future, ACLP institutions need to aggressively pursue distance learning options to make specialised leadership preparation more accessible and affordable to today's aspiring leaders.

Leadership succession is a related challenge. Some scholars believe we do not have our best people in leadership. Many dioceses have created succession programs, but there are still dioceses that do not have leadership succession plans in place. Finding qualified lay leaders has intensified in recent years as Catholic educational leadership continues to transition from religious to lay. From 2004 to 2007, the percentage of vowed religious or clergy leaders fell significantly among elementary principals (33% to 21%), secondary principals (46% to 35%), and diocesan superintendents (63% to 36%).

The way ahead in uncertain times

There is no doubt that we are experiencing a crossroads, even a crisis, in American Catholic school education. As I conclude this chapter, I offer these reflections about the way forward for American Catholic schools.

How to move ahead?
The psalmist writes, 'Unless the Lord builds the house, they labor in vain who build it' (Psalm 127:1). We must continue to keep God at the centre of our enterprise as we move forward.

We must ask fundamental questions like 'How can we provide the best faith-based education to the most students using limited resources' and 'What unique contributions can Catholic schools provide families, American society, and the Catholic Church in the 21st century?'

We must be bold and creative. We must think in new ways and be less parochial in our thinking. This includes looking beyond our own country's borders for new ideas. We must think and act more like a system and end our 'every school for itself' approach. We must engage in strategic planning processes at the school, diocesan, and national level.

It appears the traditional self-supporting parish elementary school model of Catholic education with pastor as Chief Executive Officer is obsolete. We must adopt funding, governance, and administration models that lessen the burden of both pastor and principal and maximise the benefits of being part of a Catholic school system. While continuing to fight for our just share of tax dollars and government funding, we must also aggressively pursue private citizen bequests through planned giving.

We must be more intentional about leadership succession and we must add new flexible pathways to school leadership. We must recognise that parents are new colleagues in leadership and in turn strengthen their capacity to lobby and advocate for Catholic schools. We must internationalise and globalise American Catholic education to be a more authentic expression of our Catholic identity and to distinguish ourselves among American schools.

Why move ahead?

One of my favorite quotes is from St. Irenaeus, 'the glory of God is the human person fully alive.' God wants us to become who we were born to become. Unlike public schools, Catholic schools can provide an environment of Catholic humanism five days a week that helps students become fully alive by helping them become fully human – mind, heart, *and* soul.

The day before giving a talk to the Catholic principals in Columbus, Ohio, I was at a restaurant. I asked a mother who was sitting with her two daughters in the booth next to me why she sends her children to Catholic schools. She told the story of her son's letters from boot camp in which he thanked his parents for instilling religious faith in him and for sending him to Catholic schools. He wrote in one letter, 'If it weren't for my religion, I'd be lost.' The mother told me, 'People ask us why we spend $14 000 on tuition a year for our children; this is why.' And this is why we should move ahead: because we are effective in our religious mission and we make a difference in the lives of young people.

Recent world and Church events have given Catholic schools new opportunities to make significant contributions to the nation and Church in this new century. In a world and society fraught with division, fractured relationships, and fragmentation, the unique gift that contemporary American Catholic schools can offer the nation and Church are graduates who understand and nurture cross-cultural, international, human, divine, and conceptual relationships. Building a culture of relationships is the charism of American Catholic schools in this new century.

'Why do I work in Catholic education?' Each of us has asked that question at one time or another. I do so because we make a difference in the lives of young people. As a professor, I have the opportunity to observe student teachers in both public and Catholic high schools. When I'm in a

Catholic high school Religious Education class witnessing students talk about God and faith, I often ask myself, 'What parent wouldn't want this for their child?'

To be honest, I work in Catholic education for selfish reasons as well. My work allows me to live my faith freely in my professional life, and it allows me to participate in the faith development of young people. For instance, as a principal giving communion at school masses, I experienced many moments of grace. Students coming to me for communion were students I had just disciplined or students who I knew were dealing with heavy issues in their personal and family life. What moments of sublime spiritual intimacy, integrating faith and life for me and the students!

One year my school hosted an exchange student from Brazil. Midyear his mother in Brazil was killed in a car accident. The student was distraught and numb. To make sure he made his international flight connection home, I flew with him from Rhode Island to New York City. When his flight to Brazil was called, I remember instinctively taking the cross I wear around my neck and putting it around his neck. The look in his eyes melted my heart. Surprisingly, he came back and finished the school year. At a pool party after the school prom, I noticed him in the pool still wearing the cross. That is why I do what I do!

What gives me hope?

I have hope because one-third of American Catholic schools have waiting lists. I have hope because recently the United States bishops published a document renewing their commitment to Catholic schools and outlining recommendations to strengthen them (United States Conference of Catholic Bishops, 2005). As a result, some dioceses are holding summits and creating action plans. Some Catholic universities have responded in concrete ways as well (University of Notre Dame, 2006; Cook and Durow, 2008).

I have hope because we continue to create innovative responses to our challenges such as Cristo Rey schools and Catholic teacher corps programs. Furthermore, we are achieving new levels of collaboration. In addition to the examples mentioned throughout this chapter, another unique and promising venture incorporated in 2006 is the Mid-Atlantic Catholic Schools Consortium. This new association comprised of six dioceses provides an administrative structure to collectively and strategically address challenges shared by all in the region (www.midatlanticcsc.org).

I have hope because I know this is not the first time Catholic schools in the United States have struggled. I know that my forebears were victims of riots and the burning of schools. I know they built schools by hand, brick by brick. One principal at a Sisters of Mercy high school told me jokingly that she can relate to Mercy Foundress, Catherine McAuley, and how she responded to her struggles because Catherine's famous 'comfortable cup of tea' probably had more than a teabag in it.

I have hope because I know that we are standing on the shoulders of giants – our forebears who built the schools by the sweat of their brow and the scores of selfless vowed Religious who educated generations of American Catholics like me.

I have hope because I have faith in those who will come after me. Master's level students in a course I taught wrote in their course evaluations that they are 'on fire for Catholic education'.

I have hope because renewal has been a theme in Church documents related to Catholic education (Congregation for Catholic Education, 1982, 1997). 'It must never be forgotten that the school itself is always in the process of being created …' (1982, #69). I love how the documents refer to Catholic education as an 'educational project' (1997, #4) because the term speaks to the idea that Catholic schools are not 'finished projects' but 'works in progress' that are always 'under construction'.

I have hope because I have faith in the Resurrection. Our entire faith is built on the cycle of renewal and redemption and new life. All of life imitates the paschal mystery. There must be Good Friday before Easter Sunday. Without a cross, there is no crown. Judging from our current cross, ours will be a mighty big crown.

I have hope because when Jesus sent his disciples to go and teach, he assured them saying, 'And behold, I will be with you always…'(Matt 28:20).

Finally, I have hope because I feel solidarity with people in other nations who have responded to leadership challenges in their own corner of the vineyard.

References

Center for Applied Research in the Apostolate. (2006) *Primary trends, challenges, and outlook: A special report on U.S. Catholic elementary schools, 2000-2005.* Washington, DC: Author.

Congregation for Catholic Education. (1982) *Lay Catholics in schools: Witnesses to faith*. Boston: Daughters of St. Paul.

Congregation for Catholic Education. (1997*) The Catholic school on the threshold of the third millennium*. Rome: Libreria Editrice Vaticana.

Cook, T.J. (2001) *Architects of Catholic culture: Designing and building Catholic culture in Catholic schools*. Washington, DC: National Catholic Educational Association.

Cook, T. J. (2003) Professional qualifications of religion teachers in Catholic high schools in the United States. *International Journal of Education and Religion, 4*(2), pp.128-144.

Cook, T.J., and Davies, M.F. (2008) Small "c," big "C": Religious diversity and Catholic identity. In E.F. Litton and S.P. Martin (Eds.), *Justice, care, and diversity: Research and best practices in Catholic secondary schools*. Washington, DC: National Catholic Educational Association.

Cook, T. J., and Durow, W. P. (2008) The upper room: A university and diocese partner to develop leaders for Catholic schools. *Catholic Education: A Journal of Inquiry and Practice,* 11(3).

Cook, T.J. and Engel, M.T. (2006) Predicting retention of Catholic high school religion teachers in the United States. *Journal of Empirical Theology,* 19(2), pp.163-181.

Cook, T.J., and Ostrowski, D.A. (2007) Measuring religious mission effectiveness in the United States: Are Catholic schools making a difference? In T. d'Arbon (Ed.), *Directions for Catholic Educational Leadership in the 21st Century: The Vision, Challenges and Reality*. Proceedings of the 2007 International Conference on Catholic Education Leadership (ISBN: 0 949233 27 7). Sydney: Australian Catholic University.

D'Antonio, W. V., Davidson, J. D., Hoge, D. R., and Gautier, M. L. (2007) *American Catholics today: New realities of their faith and their church*. Lanham, MD: Rowman and Littlefield.

Dwyer, T. W. (2005) *Stable but fragile: Assessing the quality and scope of diocesan policies, procedures and expectations for Catholic school financial management*. Washington, DC: National Catholic Educational Association.

Harris, J.C. (2000) The funding dilemma facing Catholic elementary and secondary schools. In J. Youniss and J.J. Convey (Eds.), *Catholic schools at the crossroads: Survival and transformation* (pp. 55-71). New York: Teachers College Press.

Joseph, E.A. (2002) Faith leadership. In T.C. Hunt, R.J. Nuzzi, and E.A. Joseph (Eds.), *Catholic schools* still *make a difference: Ten years of research 1991-2000,* pp. 3-8. Washington, DC: National Catholic Educational Association.

McDonald, D. (2007) *United States Catholic elementary and secondary schools 2006 -2007*. Washington, DC: National Catholic Educational Association.

Miller, J. M. (2006) *The Holy See's teaching on Catholic schools*. Atlanta, GA: Solidarity Association.

National Conference of Catholic Bishops. (1972) *To teach as Jesus did.* Washington, DC: United States Catholic Conference.

Schaub, M. (2000). A faculty at a crossroads: A profile of American Catholic school teachers. In J. Youniss and J.J. Convey (Eds.), *Catholic schools at the crossroads: Survival and transformation* (pp. 72-86). New York: Teachers College Press.

Schuttloffel, M.J. (2003) *Report on the future of Catholic school leadership.* Washington, DC: National Catholic Educational Association.

Steinfels, P. (2003) *A people adrift: The crisis of the Roman Catholic Church in America.* New York: Simon and Schuster.

United States Conference of Catholic Bishops. (2005). *Renewing our commitment to Catholic elementary and secondary schools in the third millennium.* Washington, DC: Author.

University of Notre Dame (2006) *Making God known, loved, and served: The future of Catholic primary and secondary schools in the United States.* Available online:http://president.nd.edu/activities-and-initiatives/catholicschools/files/task_force_final_report.pdf

8
Challenges to Faith Schools in the United Kingdom

Oona Stannard

England and Wales have, arguably, enjoyed the best position internationally in terms of funded provision for Catholic schools. Around 2300 Catholic schools, generally known as Catholic voluntary aided schools (VA), enjoy significant levels of public funding and statutory protection regarding levels of independence in relation to matters of governance and other arrangements that ensure their Catholic distinctiveness. These schools are undoubtedly very popular with parents, both Catholics and other alike. Many Catholic schools are oversubscribed by Catholics and competition for places is particularly stiff in London and the South East. Nationally, approximately 28% of pupils across the Catholic school population of England and Wales are other than Catholic. In many cases these pupils will be from families who value the opportunity to have the distinctive education offered by a Catholic school where an emphasis on respecting faith, learning about faith and living within a faith framework receives due emphasis. Unsurprisingly therefore, places have often been taken up, where available, by Muslim families and others. Catholic schools remain the recipients of high levels of recent Catholic migration from countries including those in Eastern Europe, Southern India, Africa, South America and elsewhere. Against falling rolls in many community schools (the most prevalent type of maintained school in England), Catholic schools in many areas are experiencing an increase in applications.

Church schools: the right to exist

Despite this evident popularity and the acknowledged high standards of education provided in Catholic schools (CES, 2006), there is much public debate about the existence of church schools of any type, and within this, Catholic schools appear to draw unfair criticism. This is happening despite a Government that supports schools with a religious character through extensive funding and which has also recently acknowledged the contribution that such schools make to the education system. In its recent publication *Faith in the System*, the Government Department for Children, Schools and Families (DCSF, 2007) stated:

> We are taking the opportunity to highlight the very positive contribution which schools with a religious character make as valuable, engaged partners in the school system and in their local communities and beyond.

They continued:

> Faith organisations have a long and noble tradition in education in this country... From 1852 the Catholic bishops have worked to make available, wherever possible, schools for all Catholic children regardless of their parents' ability to pay .(DCSF, 2007).

Very significantly in echoing the collaboration that had taken place between the DCSF and those who provide schools with a religious character to produce *Faith in the System*, DCSF wrote:

> This dual system of voluntary schools supported by faith organisations and schools without a religious character is therefore at the heart of the school system in England. The Government continues to support the benefits to society that this system brings for parental choice and diversity and we recognise that with the changes in society, it is only fair that pupils of all faiths and none have the opportunity to be educated in accordance with the wishes of their parents. Our unequivocal purpose in agreeing to this document is for other parties to appreciate the contribution of faith schools.

Catholic schools in partnership with Government

As a statutory partner in the provision of schools, the Catholic Church has a unique relationship with Government at this interface and the Church takes this responsibility very seriously. This was notable, for example, during the passage of the *Education and Inspections Act 2007* when Government sought to introduce quotas for places in new Catholic schools. This would have reserved 20% of places to be allocated without reference to faith and was strongly opposed by the Church. Explicit in the move to introduce such places was the Government's argument that it would make places available for local children without reference to faith. In rebutting this attempt the Catholic Education Service for England and Wales (CES) argued that it would do little to promote community cohesion if Catholic pupils watched others walk past them to places that had been denied to them despite their Catholic baptism and the Catholic community's financial contribution to building the school. It was also argued that it would be flawed to designate a Catholic school as the local school for any other pupil without the parental wish to choose this type of school. Finally, it was agreed that in building any new Catholic school extra places, beyond those needed to meet Catholic demand, may be added to provide community places, subject to local agreement. The negotiations to reach this change in the proposed legislation were complex and not without tension at times. Letters were provided via the bishops to every parish to explain the situation and to seek support for the Catholic position. However, throughout this process, those negotiating on behalf of the Church always sought to work as partners with Government, looking for solutions and accommodation that would meet the needs of one another. Media portrayals of Government's 'climb down' or 'U-turns' were inaccurate; partnership working across the Church and with Government enabled a mutually satisfactory solution to be found.

The attack on church schools

Given the context of *Faith in the System* and the history of a long partnership with Government, why do schools with a religious character or as they are more colloquially termed 'faith schools' feel so under attack? The attacks are there in such eye catching media headlines as 'Religious Schools Show Bias for Rich' (*The Observer*, 2/3/08). Many other media reports could be cited to illustrate other allegations concerning schools with a religious character. Even Government seems to want to distance itself from direct support for schools with a religious character. A spokesman for the Department for Children, Schools and Families recently said:

> There is no policy to increase the number of faith schools – it is up to

local communities to decide the kind of schools they want. (Mail on Sunday, 23/3/08)

Most recently, a pilot exercise by Government into the conduct of admissions arrangements to all maintained schools has led to reports focusing on the alleged shortcomings in the admissions arrangements of schools with a religious character. (*The Guardian, Financial Times, The Times & Independent,* 12/3/08.)

That the Chairman of the House of Commons Select Committee for Children, Schools and Families makes spurious remarks about schools with a religious character may also be taken as an indication of the current climate. He is reported as having said :

> It seems to me that faith education works alright as long as people are not that serious about their faith.(Asthana, 2007)

The same Select Committee recently invited Catholic bishops and representatives of the Catholic Education Service to be witnesses interviewed by the Committee (Select Committee for Children, Schools and Families, 2008). The witnesses called to give evidence were advised by the Secretariat of the Committee to expect the following broad areas of questioning:

- The principle of faith schools – their distinctiveness and the issue of whether they should be publicly funded.
- Faith school performance and pupil intakes – the implications of voluntary aided faith schools being their own admissions authorities and the impact of the new Schools Admissions Code.
- Faith schools and community cohesion — how faith schools can balance building a strong religious identity among their pupils and promoting tolerance; preparing pupils for living in a multicultural society; and recognising different aspects of pupils' identity as well as their faith.

This briefing hints at two issues which are at the heart of the public challenge to schools with a religious character. They are firstly the issue of admissions and who has access to education in a Catholic school, and secondly, the promotion of community cohesion.

Admissions: A climate of envy

In the case of admissions, a short hand way of describing this might be a *climate of envy*, or to put it another way, 'if I cannot have a place that I want in a school with a religious character, irrespective of my own religious affiliation, then I object to anyone else having access to a place in such a school'. By extension this may be less about the desire to be in a Catholic school or another faith school than the understandable wish to secure a good education; an education with recognisable successful outcomes. Catholic schools certainly achieve this not only in terms of academic results but also in terms of young people whose education is about more than exams; an education that is about the formation of the whole person. (CES, 2006). Whilst some of our critics may not recognise this in such words, it is this that parents, Catholics and others, seek. It is not an attack on what is provided in Catholic schools but rather an obtuse acknowledgement of, or yearning for, the education that Catholic schools provide. Arguably, every parent wants a good school for their child and many would contend that this is not comprehensively available in England and Wales at present. Each March the details of the outcomes of the applications for secondary schools are released and parents know whether or not their child has been successful in obtaining a place of their preference. These announcements attract much publicity and a good deal of social and political rhetoric, as well as anguish for parents.

In a March 2008 statement ('School Admissions and Parental Preferences for 2008') issued by Jim Knight, Minister of State for Schools and 14-19 Learners, it was announced that only 64% of parents in Greater London had been offered a place at their first preference secondary school. Across the whole of England this figure was 81.6%. Some sceptics have suggested that it was to divert attention from such figures that ministers simultaneously announced that they had undertaken an analysis of the published admission arrangements in three local authority areas and found that 'a significant minority' of schools in their sample appeared not to be compliant with the School Admissions Code and that a disproportionate number of these were voluntary aided or foundation schools. (Department for Children, Schools and Families, 2008). This was a very provocative statement given that it was the result of a desk exercise using unverified material. Unsurprisingly, it drew opprobrium from within the Catholic sector. It has been called, for example, 'an act of betrayal on the part of a Government increasingly in thrall to an anti-faith-school lobby' (*The Tablet*, 2008). One Catholic headteacher asked (ibid):

Are we the enemy? We are in a situation where many MPs are frightened of religion — for them religion equals extremism. We are not trusted and it's a difficult climate to work in when the teaching of the faith is regarded as indoctrination.

Community cohesion: a lack of understanding

This statement is the harbinger of a concern felt amongst some in the Catholic community that our schools are under attack because of a lack of understanding about community cohesion and the role that our schools play in helping to build community cohesion.

By statute, the Office for Standards in Education, Children's Services and Skills (Ofsted) now has a duty to inspect whether schools are promoting community cohesion (Education and Inspections Act, 2007). During the passage of the Education Bill which led to the 2007 Education and Inspections Act, the CES called for this requirement upon all schools. Whilst this may not have won friends amongst head teachers and their colleagues because of the additional bureaucratic burdens, the CES was confident that Catholic schools make a very significant contribution to educating for community cohesion (CES, 2008). We wanted this to be transparent to all, both to reinforce good practice but also to make clear to any detractors that we take the promotion of community cohesion very seriously. We also suspected that Government might have introduced a duty for the inspection of community cohesion in schools with a religious character only, whilst leaving it uninspected in community schools. This would have been grossly unfair both in terms of prejudice and also in terms of collecting a sound evidence base on which to promote good practice nationally and advice on areas for development. It was already the case that the separate inspections of religious education, worship and the Catholic life of the school, carried out on behalf of the diocesan bishop, reported on aspects of community cohesion.

Whilst the matter of admissions to schools with a religious character is probably one which predominantly exercises parents and also politicians (because they must face the questions about what this says about standards across all schools and Government's meeting of its various targets), the matter of promoting community cohesion in schools is likely to resonate not only with parents and politicians but also 'the citizen on the street'. Whilst it is seldom stated in these bald terms, their concerns can often be tracked to residual perceptions following the 9/11 attacks on the World Trade Centre and the more recent bomb attacks on the London Underground Network, 7 July 2005. These events have left a legacy of wariness amongst some, generally based on ignorance, as to the desirability of schools with a religious character. Some of their ignorance will be based on a lack of knowledge about who attends schools with a religious character, what the requirements are and other factors associated with a lack of first-hand experience, and a degree of scaremongering. In particular, some of their opposition to schools with a religious character may lie in the fact that the last ten years has seen the introduction of maintained Muslim schools into the English education system whilst many more small Muslim schools function independently. Since the Education and Skills Act 2007 there are also more opportunities for anyone to propose and promote a new school accompanied by significant public funding. This can be observed in the growth of 'academies' with charitable, businesses and even church sponsorship. Whilst maintained Muslim schools are few in number there is no reason why legally, and on issues of demand and numbers, there could not be a very significant growth in such schools. To judge from the reaction to the existence and potential growth of Muslim schools (Jonathan Dimbleby Big Debate, 2008) there are those who must previously have been relatively unworried by the existence of schools with a Christian character but who do find the notion of Muslim schools unacceptable. Rather than have an informed discourse on Muslim schools, the critics make an assault on any school with a religious character and Catholic schools seem to come into the firing line for reasons that can only be speculated upon but as has already been indicated, are likely to do with envy and unnecessary fears.

Any such attacks, whether about maintained Muslim schools or Catholic schools, are woefully misplaced. Both history and legislative safeguards uphold this point. When in the second half of the 19th century the bishops of England and Wales gave priority to setting up Catholic schools, even before churches, they were serving the needs of largely impoverished displaced Irish Catholic immigrants. The descendants of that Irish community and the many other immigrants that followed are now to be seen flourishing in every echelon of professional, civic, public and community life, contributing inestimably to the common good, in the service of society. To use a current Government education policy term *Every Child Matters (DCSF, 2004)*. Thanks to the Church this maximum was lived out. By providing Catholic schools, immigrants and other Catholics were able to grow in their faith, know that their faith was respected, and to live life according to their faith, all in the context of an excellent education. This must have made an immensely positive impact on their self-esteem and sense of identity and belonging. It is this which can also be nurtured by enabling those of other faiths to have their own schools too. Done well, schooling with a religious character helps people to confidently look outwards and ultimately to feel more secure and valued in society and better able to contribute to that society. Being within the fold of maintained schools, whether VA or other, also offers those involved the mutual support of belonging to a broader network of schools. It also gives access to their experience and expertise, e.g. specialist schools sharing some of their facilities or human resources.

Catholic schools are fortunate to have over 150 years of running schools within the maintained sector. Our Muslim brothers and sisters, amongst others, do not have this tradition. The CES has therefore, proposed to Government that we be resourced to work with other faith school providers to explore and share expertise in implementing the commitments that we all made in *Faith in the System.* (DCSF, 2007). These are:

    a. Promote community cohesion. In this context, the providers of faith schools and their faith communities welcome the duty imposed on the governing bodies of all maintained schools in the Education and Inspections Act 2006 to promote community cohesion and for Ofsted to report on community cohesion in its inspection reports of maintained schools and Academies. The duty on schools to promote community cohesion came into force in September 2007 (cf Guidance, 2007)

    b. Work in a spirit of partnership with the local authority and the Learning and Skills Council (LSC) as commissioners of education. In this context, the providers of maintained faith schools and Academies welcome the involvement of local authority governors as members of their governing bodies

    c. Endeavour to meet the needs of all their pupils whether they are of the faith or not

    d. Offer high standards of education

    e. Work in partnership with other schools and organisations from the voluntary and statutory sectors and play a full role in the local Admissions Forum and Schools Forum

    f. Safeguard and promote the welfare of all the pupils and, like all schools, link with the Local Safeguarding Children Board

    g. Respect and dignity of the human person within each individual

- including pupils and staff – of all faiths and none; and additionally
h. (in the case of faith schools), nurture young people in the faith of their family.

The accountability of religious schools

It is right that there are checks and balances in education and that schools with a religious character must also be accountable to both Church and State as appropriate. In England and Wales schools are required to be inspected and publically reported upon by Ofsted and Estyn[2] respectively. Much regulation surrounds this with the most typical, statutory inspection in England being referred to as 'Section 5' inspection (Education Act, 2005). These make public the school's attainment and amongst other things, the extent to which the school is meeting other statutory duties, e.g. to hold a daily act of collective worship, to report to parents, to promote community cohesion, to fulfil national curriculum requirements. This external inspection brings a level of transparency and accountability that should help allay fears of non-compliance or, at worst, extremism. If inspection reveals concerns about a school there are both support mechanisms and sanctions to be put in place. The most severe of these is putting a school into 'special measures'. During this time it is subject to targets and careful scrutiny and, ultimately, a new interim governing body may be stipulated or the school closed. Voluntary aided schools also experience separate inspection (Section 48) of religious education, worship and the faith life of the school. These inspections are publicly funded but carried out by the 'faith provider' of the school. In the case of Catholic schools, these inspections fulfil the canonical requirements of the diocesan bishops and are organised by the diocese working collaboratively with the National Board of Religious Inspectors and Advisers (NBRIA), and with the CES. Given their centrality to the school, the CES has been keen to make these reports as widely accessible to the public as possible. Accordingly, they are published on the CES website. It should be noted that the Catholic Church was a signatory to Religious Education; Non Statutory National Framework (QCA & DfES, 2004). This counteracts those who suggest that education in a school with a religious character means that you do

2 Office of Her Majesty's Chief Inspector of Education and Training in Wales.

not learn about other faiths. Overall, society should feel satisfied that any type of faith school has a high degree of public accountability and transparency. Equally, such schools should feel well able to teach their religion and to make it a lived experience for pupils and staff whilst also learning about other major world religions.

Whilst envy of some schools with a religious character and fear at the prospect of Muslim schools may be the two main reasons for opposition to schools with a religious character, a third reason may be found in the lobby for a secularised British society. Both the British Humanist Association (BHA) and the National Secular Society (NSS) call for the abolition of schools with a religious character. The BHA (cf BHA website) describes faith based schools as divisive, discriminatory and unnecessary. They propose 'the inclusive, accommodating community school'. They ignore the fact that this term could as easily refer to the inclusive, accommodating Catholic school. The NSS (cf NSS website) is similarly against faith schools, calling for their eventual elimination 'in order to create a fairer and safer school system in Britain'. In castigating Tony Blair, ex Prime Minister, the NSS speak of his legacy as a 'religious time bomb' and they assert that he has appeased and bolstered religious leaders;

> 'By consulting religious leaders he has emboldened them', states Keith Porteous Wood. (NSS Website) 'They now regularly use their new found power to seek to thwart socially progressive legislation and make self-serving demands, including for the suppression of freedom of expression and the restriction of the human rights of others.'

This statement is both outrageously wrong but also very revealing. It exemplifies the hostility that lurks amongst those who fear religious freedom and religious voice in the public space. Schools with a religious character are a very strong, undeniable presence representing religion in the public space. As such they make an easy first point for verbal attack on religion.

Freedom of expression: the Catholic Church and the individual

Religious leaders of the Catholic Church call for freedom of expression and seek to protect human rights including being able to choose an education in line with parents' religious beliefs (European Convention of Human Rights, 1950). Undoubtedly the Catholic Church can be a very unwelcome voice in such matters for those for whom individualism is the guiding principle. Archbishop Vincent Nichols, Chairman of the CES in addressing a National Conference of Catholic Secondary Headteachers (Archdiocese of Birmingham, 2006), spoke of a strong and proud tradition of respect for the individual and a desire to enhance personal autonomy but he cautioned against the cause of the individual and of personal autonomy as the central values on which to build. Instead, he emphasised the relational aspects of the human person. He suggests that society does not have a true understanding of the human person and has lost its nerve when it comes to the reality of religious belief.

> There will never be a truly cohesive society that does not take seriously the spiritual quest of its people, in all the forms of that quest, and which does not give a space in its public culture for the religious beliefs of its people. The rigorously secular, liberal project of social cohesion is mistaken in its fundamental view of the human person and simply will not work. Is this why much public discourse, on the one hand, belittles faith schools and the contribution they can make, whilst on the other, our schools are popular among so many people? Is this why those who espouse the secular liberal view of society speak out so vehemently against faith schools, not simply because they are opposed to religious faith, but because all that a faith centred education stands for exposes the fallacies of their position? Is this why the driving force for social cohesion has become the elimination of all difference, or at least the elimination of the appearance of all differences, when the true richness of life lives in appreciation and critically evaluating, by reasoned discourse, the values held in differences?

Conclusion

To a person of faith their religion is not a bolt-on activity or something just to be attended to on Sunday, Friday or at some other prescribed time. It is something to be actively lived; something that informs all of life, the person's thinking and their actions. For such a person faith is at the heart of their being, an intrinsic part of their identity and who they are. We would never relegate disability, gender or any other issue of identity or equality to the margins and ask that it be kept hidden and only observed in private space. And so it should be with faith and the availability of Catholic schools. The undermining of faith in the public space works against mutual understanding, harmony in society and community cohesion. Transparency and a better appreciation of one another's positions are needed throughout society. Catholic schools, in their rich diversity, are well placed to help to bring this about.

Catholic schools in England and Wales account for 10% of the schools in these countries. They have a history of welcoming the disadvantaged and the poor. Today, they continue to be the places where many migrants find comfort and familiarity because of the recognition, respect and support for their faith. Catholic schools remain places where the intrinsic humanity of each member of the school community is cherished. The universal meaning of the term 'Catholic' is well evidenced in Catholic schools which are, typically, ethnically very diverse (CES, 2006). Too often, the critics of Catholic schools forget that religion, ethnicity and culture are not synonymous. Catholic schools are not ghettos but places that work in partnerships with many others, both within and beyond the Catholic sector. Pupils will learn about other world faiths and will also almost certainly learn about, learn from and with people beyond the Catholic community.

A 14-year-old Muslim boy in a West London Catholic school captured the essence of his school when he said, 'I get respect here, we all get respect – we're all equal anyway, that's how God made us.' Equality, however, does not mean sameness. If you strip out the characteristics of a Catholic school or remove the features that enable it to offer a distinctive education it will no longer be a Catholic school. In the continuing public debate about the existence of schools with a religious character there are those who say 'Let Catholic schools continue but they must accept anyone who applies and there must be no restrictions on who may be employed in the school or the behaviour expected of them.' To do this would simply be to leave the school with a 'Catholic' cipher whilst making it in reality a community school like any other. A Catholic school needs, for example, Catholic leadership and the Catholic vision must inform all its policies and practices. It must be able to have a lived Catholic character, evident in the thousands of daily interactions of the school. Cardinal Cormac Murphy-O'Connor said that you cannot have fruits without roots. This is well exemplified in Catholic schools.

One of the great characteristics of England and Wales is that they are pluralist societies where people experience high levels of freedom and choice. These choices extend to schooling where the range of provision available is constantly growing, for example, technology colleges, specialist schools, foundation schools, academies and independent schools. Schools with a religious character are part of this rich diversity enjoyed by parents, pupils and teachers alike. Taxpayers are not being asked to unfairly pay for schools with a religious character as is sometimes asserted. Faith communities are made up of parents, teachers and members of parish communities, all paying taxes in the same way as their neighbours. If there were not Catholic schools, places would be needed in other schools to provide for these children. Indeed, the Catholic community pays more for the education of its children (and the 30% of young people in our schools who are not Catholic) because we pay 10% of the capital costs of our schools, amounting to well in excess of £20 million per year. Catholic schools therefore save other tax payers money!

The Catholic school has been described as 'a service to society' (Congregation for Catholic Education,1997). This is achieved by our schools continuing , through the Beatitudes , to depict the countenance of Jesus Christ and portray his charity (*The Catechism of the Catholic Church*, 1994). This is no easy feat in the face of many pressures, not least those of secularisation. This is happening against a societal backdrop of educational policies that all too often seem to focus on the functional, and which have a preoccupation with goals of economic prosperity and a view of Human Rights which actually often undermines the sanctity of human life. Perhaps, therefore, Catholic schools are of the greatest service to society because they are countercultural. They are places of real freedom experienced in the values of faithfulness and integrity, dignity and compassion, humility and gentleness, truth and justice, forgiveness and mercy, purity and holiness, tolerance and peace, service and sacrifice (Archdiocese of Birmingham Diocesan Schools' Commission, 2005) Long may Catholic schools be able to continue to make this contribution to the good of humankind.

References

Archdiocese of Birmingham Diocesan Schools' Commission, (2005) *Christ at the Centre. Summary of Why the Church Provides Catholic Schools*. Archdiocese of Birmingham.

Archdiocese of Birmingham, (2006) 'Archbishop Nichols, Speeches and Talks', www.birminghamdiocese.org.uk.

Asthana, Anushka, (2007) *The Observer*, Education Correspondent, 30th December.

BHA Website, British Humanist Association, www.humanism.org.uk.

Catechism of the Catholic Church, (1994) London, Geoffrey Chapman.

CES, (2006) *Quality and Performance: A Survey of Education in Catholic Schools*, London, Catholic Education Service for England and Wales.

CES, (2008) *Catholic Schools and Community Cohesion: CES Guidance,* London, Catholic Education Service for England and Wales.

CES Website, Catholic Education Service for England and Wales, www.cesew.org.uk .

Congregation for Catholic Education, (1997) *The Catholic School on the Threshold of the Third Millennium*. www.vatican.va/roman_curia/congregations/ccatholic.

DCSF (2007) Guidance on duty to promote community cohesion, www.teachernet.gov.uk/wholeschool/communitycohesion.

DCSF, (2004) *Every Child Matters- Change for Children,* Department for Children, Schools and Families.

DCSF, (2007) *Faith in the System- The role of schools with a religious character in English education and society*, Department for Children, Schools and Families.

DCSF, (2008) *Strengthening the School Admissions System*, Department for Children, Schools and Families, March.

European Convention of Human Rights, (1950), Articles 2 and 9. Rome.

House of Commons Children, Schools and Families Committee, 12th March 2008.

NSS Website, National Secular Society, www.secularism.org.uk.

Ofsted, (2005) 'Section 5*', Education and Inspections Act,* Office for Standards in Education, Children's Services and Skills.

Ofsted, (2007) *Education and Inspections Act,* Office for Standards in Education, Children's Services and Skills.

QCA & DfES (2004) *Religious Education; The Non-Statutory National Framework* Qualifications and Curriculum Authority (QCA) and Department for Education and Skills (DfES).

The Jonathan Dimbleby Big Debate, (2008) 'Religion in Schools,' accessed 16th January, www.teachers.tv/video/24057 .

The Tablet, (2008), 'Heads accuse Minister of 'Betrayal'', London, 22nd March.

9
Fostering a *Globo Sapiens* Attitude amongst Students as the World Becomes More Interdependent

Patrick J Lynch

People's humanity is greatly enhanced when they have a life mission bigger than themselves. With such a driving force, individuals are better able to navigate their lives in circumstances where dramatic global external challenges occur, as is becoming daily apparent. Despite these problems, there is much room for hope since the human spirit is resilient and human talent and creativity are abundant. Fundamentally history teaches us to hope and hope is fundamental to the Christian way of viewing life.

Facing the future

Our New Zealand Catholic schools, which teach about 9% of the total number of school students of New Zealand are part of a strong international network of 50 million students. They have a wonderful opportunity to provide an education which will enable them to take a leading part in seeking out solutions to many of these highly significant issues which humanity has never faced before. Life and death issues always focus the mind. Attitudes that seek out alliances with others in regional and international settings will be crucial to successfully navigate the challenges we face.

The Church as the People of God has much to say to the world and to contribute to the world's development. However, in order to positively influence the world, it will need to be more creative in getting alongside people, in order to do its work of preaching the Good News. Simply castigating the world's negative behaviour is not productive; positively engaging the world is a much surer option if it's evangelising mission is to be more effective.

When Vaclav Havel (past and first President of the Czech Republic) addressed the Congress of The United States of America a few years ago, he said that the world needs a story that will help humanity 'to be a people with an elementary sense of justice, the ability to see things as others do, a sense of transcendental responsibility, archetypal wisdom, good taste, courage, compassion and faith.' These are prophetic words which could provide a blue print for Catholic school leaders to emulate as they face the future. Our 'story' will need more, however. Leaders will need to develop the capacity to think over the horizon and systematically plan for the future.

Dr Jonathan Sacks, the Chief Rabbi of the Commonwealth of Nations, is right when he asserts that you defend a country with defence forces but you defend a civilisation with schools. We can draw from the wisdom of Sacks and Havel a vital sense of inspiration and enthusiasm for life, and the need for education in spirituality and values.

Education is fundamentally a moral endeavour where young people are encouraged to be virtuous, while interacting with other virtuous people and being taught about virtue and its acquisition. While the acquisition of both knowledge and skills is vital for any young person's education, what is even more important is to nurture their spirituality, their values, their philosophical and faith dimensions, which in turn will strengthen their spirits in facing the inevitable complex decisions they will have to make as the 21st century progresses.

History and contemporary experience teach us that anarchy readily emerges in states that lose their moral vision and moral purpose. When the social virtues of self-control, politeness, decency and the pursuit of human ideals are not taught and practised, a rapid dilution of social cohesion and disorder occurs in any society.

The 1996 UNESCO Report 'Learning the Treasure Within – education for the twenty-first century', was direct when it proclaimed that if mass education systems did not start actively addressing the civic, spiritual and moral dimensions of young people's education, democracies might not survive in the 21st century and humanity itself could well be in jeopardy. Fast forward twelve years to 2008, and the observation takes on more poignancy given what is happening in the world today.

Catholic schools

It is against these broad considerations that Catholic schools operate. The

Church's strong tradition of establishing and developing high quality education in its schools is predicated on proclaiming the Gospel, which in turn is pivotally focused on the well being of human beings. After all, Jesus' life purpose was, 'I have come that they may have life, life to the full' (John 10:10). Our schools in the future will need to be even more outward looking in their orientation than they have been in the past, owing to the taxing geopolitical and geostrategic issues the world faces.

Nearly 20% of the world's population professes Catholicism. The Catholic Church has established itself as a respected moral voice on the international stage over two millennia. The fundamental values of the western world owe their origins to Catholic values and insights. In turn, Catholic schools deliver a highly visible, internationally recognised brand of education which has quality, excellence and faith as its foundations.

In positioning themselves in the market place to address the inexorably changing geopolitical circumstances, Catholic schools will constantly need to transform themselves so they become fundamentally global in their outlook, accepting that their students are in fact international citizens with responsibilities to their fellow global citizens, wherever they happen to be living on the planet. Schools will need to enable their students to become 'critically reflective, responsible, wise global citizens – *Globo sapiens*' (Kelly, 2006).

A pro-active agenda

Today's world population is 6.8 billion individuals, with 10 billion expected by mid-century. This inexorable growth is the major driver humanity has to face, if it is to not only to survive, but to flourish.

The year 2007 marked the first time 50% of the world's population has become urbanised, a trend that will accelerate. Pressures on resources of fresh air, soil, water, rivers, fish stocks, energy fuels, minerals, forests and climate environmental issues are all significant, with any one of them likely to create an ongoing crisis in various parts of the world. Add to this the issue of the rich – poor divide and one can readily conclude humanity is going to need concerted brain power concentration and strong collaboration in order to work out ongoing practical solutions, which mitigate the negative dimensions of these emerging issues. Isolationism and hiding away from them has no place in any Catholic education setting. Being pro-active in forming young people to mount strategies to solve these issues is vital, if schools are going to serve their families and their students well. After all, most of the world's problems are man-made. Therefore the solutions to these issues can also be found.

The adage, 'one of us is never as strong as all of us', will have to be the guiding principle, if the world is to strengthen the idealistic, yet practical, 'community of nations' construct. This construct has to become the lens through which our young people learn to view the world and their place in it.

The establishment of a well-thought-out philosophy and theology of education which is fundamentally Catholic, has to be the framework for a Catholic school of the future. Concepts such as, 'we are a caring community', are simply not good enough in a mission statement since by themselves they are more reflective of a humanistic philosophy than a religious one, which emphatically has to be the foundation of a Catholic school.

The leaders of schools ought to have on the tips of their tongues just what this statement is for their school. If they don't, it is not a good sign. However, having worked out why they are doing what they are doing, leaders will then be focused on the way they deliver the outcomes that are expected of them by their stakeholders. Having clearly thought out their own philosophy of education, so it is not just theoretical, but also has 'landing gear', they will be able to practically implement it. This process is incumbent on any successful leader of a school.

Because Catholic schools have a range of stakeholders, from church authorities and governmental authorities, through to families and students themselves, it is important that principals and school boards define and publish the following so they are put themselves on the line with all those they serve:

- a clearly articulated mission statement and charter
- a statement of the religious mission of the school
- a definition of graduate outcomes, outlining what graduates look like when they leave the school, both in the qualitative and quantitative dimensions.

From an accountability point of view, schools will, like any other professional service, have to progressively develop their systems for ensuring that what they say they are doing, actually occurs in practice. When this happens stakeholders will be able to have assurances that their investments of various kinds are being delivered.

Fear can be paralysing. As the President of the United States of America Franklin D Roosevelt, said when taking office in 1933 during the Great Depression, 'We have nothing to fear but fear itself' (Roosevelt,

1933). The world of the future is, unfortunately, likely to be a scary place for our young people, given the massive challenges it faces on several fronts, including implications of climate change. Our schools will need to deliberately build enough confidence in their students so each has these character dimensions: resilient personalities, audacious thinkers, imaginative dreamers, critical questioners, innovative inventors, enthusiastic experimenters, faith filled leaders, strong willed individuals in the face of adversity and committed collaborators. If leaders of schools and their staff do not think through these requirements and plan for them to become part of what their school delivers, they will not lead cutting edge institutions, which their stakeholders legitimately expect them to be.

Many schools remain in the 'average' category or 'could do better' category, because the leadership of the school has not put enough thought or reflection into determining the school's actual philosophy as well as its operational dimensions.

A philosophy of education has to be unique to a particular school. This then enables clarity in all aspects of the school's documentation and makes a statement about what it stands for. No school can any more get away with the statement, 'you can sense the difference', and then struggle to describe what the difference is when asked. A school's philosophy needs to describe all of the following and much more: a clear focus on Catholic teaching and values, commitment to high standards and the achievement of excellence across a spectrum of activities; effective personalised learning programmes for students; staff development; innovation; creativity; community service focus; relationship with the wider Church community; relationship with families, along with relationships with the civic, national and international communities; discipline systems; extra-curricular activities; leadership development openings; support for the weak, the fragile and the poor; social skill development, specialised attention to developing talent wherever it is found; emotional quotient and spiritual intelligence development; openness to society and the myriad of diverse religious communities within it; commitment to sustainable development in all of its dimensions – and the list goes on!

Catholic schools are unabashedly religious schools, not indoctrinating institutions, but schools that are worthy of the best Catholic education traditions, which go way back to the monasteries and the first university traditions. One of the Church's greatest gifts to humanity is education. In Europe it was the Church which pioneered education for the masses four centuries ago. Likewise, the Church's missionary activity has helped to raise countless millions of people out of poverty and hopelessness – this of course continues and will continue in the future. It is of more than passing interest that the Catholic Church cares for just on 70% of AIDs sufferers around the world.

International best practice

A leading edge Catholic school benchmarks itself against leading international best practice both in its Catholic culture and its education delivery.

One of the major difficulties school boards, their principals and teachers have is to find ways to learn what school 'international best practice' looks like within a Catholic context. While much is to be learned and emulated from local and national jurisdictions, it is also incumbent on principals, school boards and Catholic administrative leaders to seek out from international sources just what contemporary quality standards look like in running a benchmarking Catholic school. It is so easy not to know what one does not know. However, information and ideas can be found by targeting relevant journals, and publications, as well as seeking out information via international Catholic school conferences and internet information exploration. The challenge to find out what best practice looks like is always with us. This can only be addressed by actively seeking out descriptions of what superior education standards for students and teachers look like. Maybe there is a need for groups of principals and teachers, along with Catholic administrative authorities, to set up think tanks, national and international alliances and exploratory groupings to distil this information. In the commercial world and in tertiary education institutions this kind of dynamic structure is now a fact of life and is a systematised construct.

The internationally acclaimed network of 21 leading universities, Universitas 21, which includes Australian and New Zealand members, is a model worth looking at closely, and emulating. These universities benchmark their standards against one another in a range of ways which include: achievement standards, research standards, procedural and administration systems, course content, pastoral care of students, the exchange of staff and students and simply sharing what works for them to deliver a top quality education for students in an increasingly competitive world.

Global citizenship

Geopolitical realities are such that relationships, which meet the needs of the world's 197 nations are fundamental. Kofi Anan, the former United Nations Secretary General, just prior to his departure from his role in late 2006, said 'Our biggest challenge in this new century is to take an idea that seems abstract (sustainable development) and turn it into reality for the world's population.' Sustainable development is not just environmental protection. It includes ecological, social and economic dimensions. It encourages people to adopt transformational attitudes to ensure that our grandchildren will be able to enjoy lives where the good and positive aspects of them, which we enjoy, are able to last and to be enjoyed by billions more people. At rock bottom, much of what is encompassed in the international understanding of sustainability involves spiritual values, as much as anything else, since a peaceful world is predicated on individuals having a significant sense of spirituality and its central place in a person's life.

When the peoples of the world become less suspicious of one another and see each other as fellow global citizens, we will have a greater chance of living together harmoniously, rather than ring-fencing ourselves in isolationism and fear. Alliances and collaborative relationships, if well-constructed and nurtured, will have a significant role in creating a sustainable peaceful world.

In facing the challenges of creating global citizenship Catholic educators have a sacred responsibility to mould and challenge the minds and spirits of their students so they become committed to becoming proactive global citizens with a *globo sapiens* mindset. This also means that students are exposed to the fundamentals of economic, technological, business and entrepreneurial literacy. Without this literacy they will not be able to influence the world for good since they will not know how to do so in a concrete way. Essentially, a Catholic school community is called upon, in the words of the late Pope John Paul II, 'to be people who live with gratitude for the past, enthusiasm for the present and hope for the future' — a simple passport for a peaceful future in a world that looks after all its people. Our schools are also called upon to enable their students to become active citizens who contribute to the wellbeing of their community, their nation and the international community and not to demonise others who are different. Equally they are also called upon to be magnanimous in their attitudes, because peace emerges through a generosity of spirit. All of this can become a reality when individuals are confident in their abilities to engage in dialogue with others whom they do not know.

The Catholic Church, along with its schools, will become more influential and effective as a force for good when it seeks to engage the world. It is important that if we are going to properly prepare students for their 21st century adult lives, they will be educated about the world, its people, its geography, its history, its cultures, its economics and most importantly its geopolitical issues and issues of wealth distribution and health standards.

Educating for social justice and hope

There is a pressing need to strengthen bonds between the peoples of the world, and between poor and rich nations. Catholic school students can be influential in this if they are thoroughly familiar with the Church's social teachings which are generally well regarded by the world's law makers. The Church's social vision is consistent and secure in times of doubt and distress. There is an unwavering commitment to human dignity, just labour practices, distribution of wealth, superior relationships between peoples and the identification of and rectification of causes of poverty, discrimination and oppression. The documents outlining the teachings, which encompass this treasure of ideas, start with the encyclical *Rerum Novarum* of 1878 through eight other landmark documents to *Centesimus Annus* of 1991. These succinct volumes are used by many politicians and think-tanks to formulate legislative policy and are widely accepted political blueprints.

While this may seem a tall order we need always remember that nothing we do in this life is complete; we simply do our bit to make the world a better place and sow ideas which others reap. This is another way of saying that the Kingdom always lies beyond us, which is another reason for hope in our lives and the lives of young people. Saul Alinsky was right on the button when he asserted, 'We will see it when we believe it.' Hope is always the foundation of everything a Christian does, where one believes tomorrow can be better than today.

For students to grow into being people of hope they must be given opportunities to make the world they know a better place through initiatives they are able to identify and connect with. Since personal values are more caught than taught, a school culture and a program which provides opportunities for students to serve others, is indispensable for a 21st century Catholic school. Also, Religious Education programs and the other ethos dimensions of schools will need to better address the spiritual development of students and to do so in a more intellectually engaging way. This will include education in the dimensions of Emotional Quotient and Spiritual Intelligence development, which are now being recognised in a wide range of settings as being vitally important to life success. Spiritual and Emotional Intelligences empower individuals to be happy in spite of their circumstances and not because of them. Both of these give people the vision to see something positive in every problem they face and the wisdom to handle them to advantage. They also help individuals to attain their highest potential, since they are free from the limitations of the immediate, the material and the obvious. All of this recognises that education is in fact a moral enterprise — and Catholic education is fundamentally, just that.

The religious response

Albert Einsten's recently published biography by Walter isaacson quotes his response to the question whether he was religious. His reply was:

> The most beautiful emotion is the mysterious. It is the fundamental emotion that stands at the cradle of all true art and science. He to whom this emotion is a stranger, who can no longer wonder and stand rapt in awe is as good as dead, a snuffed out candle. To sense that behind anything that can be experienced there is something that minds cannot grasp, whose beauty and sublimity reaches us only indirectly: this is religiousness. In this sense and in this sense only, I am a deeply religious man. (Quoted in *Time Magazine* April 16th 2007.)

One of the ways our schools are able to entice young people into an in-depth appreciation of the divine and to develop their relationship with the designer of the universe is through experiences which elicit the 'wow' factor. Given modern technology and the raft of opportunities it opens to all sorts of scientific and cosmic worlds, this is another wonderful way to engender faith development in terms young people appreciate and can understand.

Our students are citizens of the 21st century at a time when, in the developed world at least, relativism and individualism are rampant. Truth is created by individuals themselves. Whatever 'floats their boat', is acceptable to large numbers of people who do not seem to worry about asserting what they believe is correct even though reality does not support their assertion. Unfortunately, institutions are regarded skeptically by large numbers of people, mainly because they do not always deliver what people legitimately require.

The challenge as educators is to recognise the cultural and religious realities of the world and seek to persuade students to accept that absolute truth does exist and that Catholicism does have deep wisdom about life, about who we are, why we are here and where we are going. While nobody has a monopoly on enlightenment, our Catholic worldview does bring a humane view of human nature and recognises that reasonableness is the basis of our faith.

The cluster of seemingly insoluble issues facing the world is, in the words of John Gardner, the founder of Common Cause, 'a series of great opportunities disguised as insoluble problems.' Our schools will need to boldly promote the ethic of stewardship, stewardship that thinks over the horizon, so that all people in the world can have a better future which is free and secure. Such a mindset will help inoculate them against the siren calls of those who preach doom and gloom and black and white answers to complex problems.

Leadership

As the world becomes more complex the exercise of leadership at all levels of human interaction is becoming more difficult, yet without it, organisations including schools, and nations, go nowhere. Leadership is an imperative for productive change and development. The contemporary experience of today's leaders is teaching us that leadership is not so much a position as a way of doing things. To be successful, leaders have to be able to show there are better ways of doing things and then seek to convince those they are leading that they have the vision, optimism, honesty, expertise and flair to deliver on the challenges that are being faced.

Fundamental to leadership that delivers is inspiration and the infusion of hope into an organisation. Hope is the vital ingredient in any situation which requires change and challenge.

Hope enables people to see that change is possible and that they can engage in the change process. Hope is strong in a group when the individuals are affirmed, when openness is apparent and when they feel they are engaged with what is happening. Hope is much more deeply rooted than simple optimism. It normally taps into an individual's faith and spirituality and therefore is much more robust.

Of necessity, a leader has to be a champion of hope, since talent in students and staff blossoms when this potent force provides the inspiration and energy to enable individuals to grow and develop. However, if hope is not visible in the leader, the organisation will only limp along.

Conclusion

It is unrealistic to expect quantum leaps in addressing societal and global challenges, but we must be committed to constant ongoing incremental change which progressively makes life more sustainable and enduring.

'Building a new social order' was a phrase first coined in 1932 by Columbia University professor George S. Counts. Many political leaders have used it countless times in the intervening years to help inspire people to change their ways of doing things in order to improve their lives and the lives of those about them. Building a new order where long-term stewardship is the lens through which we view the earth is today's clarion call to action, which is rising in volume.

The need for a new order is not because the earth is going to implode or fall apart. Man-made problems have man-made solutions. Historically, new orders have delivered positive change, as the history of many countries attests. However, they only succeed when leaders lead boldly and those who follow realise that doing nothing is not an option.

Today's world, despite all its difficulties, requires more understanding than condemnation. It is too easy to focus on war, terrorism, violence, selfishness, greed and so on, which are all tragic manifestations of our fallen nature. Rather, we are better off to embrace the scriptural injunction 'Do not be afraid. I am with you, I have called you by name, you are mine' (Isaiah 43:1). One of Catholicism's great imperatives is the vital importance of life and light – life which is a God-given reality, reflecting divine life and light. Our task is to place a light on the hill top and not hide it under a cover.

Catholic schools are authentic when they live by the vision and the injunctions of the Gospels. God's presence shines through the lives of those who know him and follow him. There is a nobility about Catholic education since it seeks to nurture the totality of an individual's human potential – a potential the world needs, more than ever.

By emphasising the importance of the God-given sacredness represented in each human being, Catholic schools will continue to be a force for good in the world. There is no reason not to believe the world cannot be a better place – we must believe this, if we believe in the Kingdom Jesus proclaimed. Our schools are able to actively contribute to delivering the great gift of hope to our own communities and to humanity itself.

Clearly school leavers will need to continue to be purveyors of hope, optimism, resilience and enthusiasm, all undergirded by their faith which is the motivating dynamo. Our school leavers will then be able to go into the world with strength and courage to make the bold decisions that will be needed from them.

References

Kelly, Patricia, Learning for Sustainable Futures: One Intervention, *Journal of Futures Studies, Feb 2006* (Original term Malaska, Pentii: *Sustainable Development as Post-Modern Culture* 1997, FUTU).

Roosevelt, Franklin Delano, Inaugural Presidential Address, 1933.

10
A Shared Hope in Catholic Schools of the South Pacific

KALO SIKIMETI

The story of Christ's call to Peter teaches about hope. When Peter and his cousins brought their boats to the shore, they left everything and followed Jesus. Jesus said to them, 'From now onwards you will be catching people alive' (Luke 5:10). Jesus invites Peter to embark on a journey to the future. There is a similarity between the call of Peter and the call of the leaders, teachers and parents to accept and fulfill our new pastoral role in the Catholic schools in the South Pacific. In doing so, Catholic schools in the area have become a source of shared hope and joy in sharp contrast to the climate of fear and anxiety besetting many of the South Pacific communities they serve.

The call to partnership

Vatican II is clear about the responsibility of teachers in Catholic schools:

> But let teachers realise that to the greatest possible extent they determine whether the Catholic School can bring its goals and undertakings to fruition ... Above all let them perform their services as partners of the parents (*Declaration on Christian Education* (1966)).

In a survey conducted at the beginning of 2007 on the current situation of the South Pacific nations, leaders, teachers and parents of Catholic schools from 20 Pacific nations were invited to respond to the following questions:
- How do Catholic schools accommodate for family diversity and support parents as first educators in the current situation?

- What are the issues that hinder parents and students from learning in an interconnected world?
- How do Catholic schools address issues to help educating towards hope in an age of fear?

There were 57 Pacific leaders, teachers and parents who responded to the survey and the results suggested that:
- Schools listen to concerns of parents and try to address any issues. Schools are open to talk with parents about students' concerns. Schools and parents are working in partnerships.

Most Catholic schools have limited resources. Teachers are trained to a minimum standard. Many Catholic education systems employ graduates who have no formal teacher training. Many children come from broken homes and those experiencing domestic violence. Parents have a fear of their children not being successful, not getting a job, going to jail and getting pregnant.

The results also showed that:
- Catholic schools are communities of hope, peace, justice, compassion, joy and love, living the teaching of Christ Jesus.

Furthermore, the results showed that there are more people now in the South Pacific who are aware of their dignity and their Christian calling to contribute to the coming of God's Kingdom in the society.

The need for common vision

There has been an extremely fast pace of change in the last 20 years. New technologies and instant communication seem to be the order of the day and they impact upon the well-being of Catholic schools. Leaders, teachers and parents need to stand together and try to develop a common vision about education. The atmosphere and discipline are different from that experienced by most previous leaders, teachers and parents. Many of the young children now come from broken homes, or have one or both parents overseas. However, there is far greater social communication within the school and between schools through sports and other social/cultural activities. Far greater freedom and responsibility is given to the young children. And there is much more opportunity for leisure time. A culture of fear and uncertainty, caused from riots and violence, has emerged in some of the South Pacific nations. For example, in Tonga, it is evident that as the country tries to move towards democracy, people are still confused because of the injustices, riots and unrest. These are the realities faced by Catholic schools in the South Pacific. However, there are important Catholic church documents that are enlightening when we think about our own local situation. Some of these documents are Vatican II's *Decree on Christian Education*, *The Catholic School*, *Lay Catholics in Schools: Witness to Faith*.

Our schools are working under conditions that are new to most leaders, teachers and parents. While there is goodwill between these parties, there is a need for all to realise that working together, planning together and having common vision is an imperative, not an option!

The Church's concern

Vatican Council ll's *Decree on Christian Education* has some clear things to say regarding families and parents in relation to schools:

> The operation and the progress of the schools deserve to engage the joint participation of families and teachers.
>
> Parents must be acknowledged as the first and foremost educators of their children. Their role as educators is so decisive that scarcely anything can compensate for their failure in it. Parents need to create a family atmosphere so animated with love and reverence for God and people that a well-rounded personal and social development will be fostered among the children. (*Declaration on Christian Education*, 1966).

Catholic schools in the South Pacific are marked by their diversity. The church, communities, families and nations have benefited greatly from the services of their past students. As well as giving their students an excellent all-round education to prepare them to be good leaders and citizens, they also lead an intensive prayer life, and develop faith in supportive Christian communities based on religious and pastoral roles. An holistic education in all aspects was very much to the fore in the pastoral concern of the leaders of the Catholic schools. However, the background of the current situation calls for a special commitment to their pastoral roles from leaders, teachers and parents to the young people, focusing on the aspects of Christian community and prayer.

The pastoral role of the Catholic schools

The call to Catholic schools in the South Pacific nations to play a strong pastoral role is similar to the call to Peter (Luke 5:10-11). Peter's faith was challenged and compared to the strength of the rock as a cornerstone of the Church. The Catholic schools too, are challenged to have strong faith and to be a pillar of strength to young people and the people in their communities. The role is demanding but also important, and carries a wonderful challenge to discover signs of hope. In a world that is tempted to despair in these uncertain times, Catholic schools are an expression of hope for humanity, families, communities and the South Pacific societies. The Catholic school is called to equip children for independence of thought by forming in them the habit of critical reflection (Laffan, 2004). Families in the South Pacific nations engaged in learning accept responsibilities to integrate themselves into the pastoral role of the Catholic schools by working in partnerships with the schools through their ex-students and parent-teachers associations. Ex-students help the schools in paying school fees of children whose parents cannot afford to pay, the homework projects and needs like textbooks. Parents support the schools in their efforts to discipline the children, visiting families who may need extra support in any kind, and helping the community leaders to support schools in workshops and seminars to enliven the spirit and character of the Catholic school. The pastoral role has to be integrated in a formative way with surrounding culture by listening and identifying with the community, the needs of their leaders, parents, students and the teachers. We are called in our pastoral role to work in partnership, following Christ's mission and commitment to Christian community and prayer.

Christian community

Catholic schools seek to infuse a Catholic worldview into all their activities, integrating faith and culture (The Congregation for Catholic Education, 1998). As it is for any faith tradition, the nature of belonging to the Catholic school has variety of aspects (Noseda, 2006) that could support South Pacific families. A Catholic school emphasises expressive symbols of the school and caring for the physical environment of the school, Christian community and development of the whole person through relationships. Furthermore, as already noted, Catholic schools recognise parents as having the first responsibility for the education of their children, and emphasise the partnership of the parents with the school in its pastoral role. The contemporary social context in which any Catholic school functions has a significant impact upon the ways it operates and upon the ways its goals may be redirected to cater for the current needs of the wider society it serves. These changes are experienced in the relationship of the school with the students and their families who form the meeting point with the culture in which it ministers (Mellor, 2005).

Research on effective schools by Bryk and Driscoll, 1988 (cited in Flynn & Mok, 2002) in the United States confirmed that good schools foster a sense of community and that this has a pervasive effect on the achievement of students and teachers and they and the children have great hope for the children's future. An important component of the culture of the Catholic schools is the sense of community and belonging which they nurture in students, teachers and parents. For St Paul, the unity or communion between followers of Jesus, expressed the essence of what is meant to be Christian. Writing to the Philippians he insisted on the need for community: 'Be united in your convictions and united in your love, with common purpose and a common mind.' (Philippians 2:2).

Professor L F Neal, 1971 (cited in Flynn & Mok, 2002) also shared his experience of Catholic schools:

> Whenever I am invited to a Catholic school … I feel that I have been invited as a friend into the bosom of a warm and intimate family … This family quality is a uniqueness which Catholic schools could, I believe, develop … Their great success in making the school a natural part of the home and the Church – an undivided Trinity – is an educational gift which Catholics have to offer the rest of us.

What Professor Neal referred to as 'the essence of their existence' and an 'educational gift to the nation', is the experience of Christian community:

> which bonds together leaders, teachers, students and parents in Catholic schools. In doing so, Neal was drawing attention to the unique contribution of these schools in Australia. However, his insight could also apply to the Catholic schools in the South Pacific nations, namely, that they stand as communities founded on belief in God and faith in Jesus Christ which are dedicated to the full personal growth

and development of young children, creating in them love and faith with great hope for themselves and for those around them (Flynn & Mok, 2002).

Our educational mission

As Christian educators we are called to show what it means to live with hope, to open our schools and hearts to all people, inspired by being loved by God and our loved ones. We are also called to stand strongly without waver, for justice, peace and the rights of the children. The Catholic schools of the South Pacific can give families, children and Pacific people the choice to do well, to enter the kingdom of God and to have a good education. 'The worst poverty in the world is those who do not have education' (Mandela, 1994).

> The joy and hope, the grief and anguish of men and women of our time, especially of those who are poor or afflicted in any way, are the joy and hope, the grief and anguish of the followers of Christ as well (*Pastoral Constitution on the Church in the Modern World*, Vatican Council 11, p. 903).

We are called to be followers of Christ, to prepare young children for life and assure them that there is hope now and the future. We have the responsibility and opportunity to hope now and in the future. We have the responsibility and opportunity to engage in this pastoral role in all our Catholic schools as teachers in our Christian communities. One of the features of the story of the educational mission of the Catholic Church is a traditional belief that teaching is a free response to serve with love from within oneself. Teaching is one of the first ministries named by Paul to the church of Corinth (1 Corinthians 12:8). For over 2000 years the church community has held in high esteem the vocation of teaching. In the gospels, Jesus is addressed as a teacher (John 8:2). The title 'teacher' appears 48 times in the four gospels. The teaching mission of Jesus is situated within the context of the Hebrew tradition of Wisdom. The wisdom teacher not only imparts knowledge but shows the true way of justice and integrity (Proverbs 3:6, and 8:6).

The late Bishop Patelisio Finau, dearly loved leader of Tonga and the South Pacific and known as a man of the poor, called on leaders, parents and teachers in a 'Share Jesus' mission with all the young children in caring, serving and providing them with love, faith and hope' (Finau, 1993).

Flynn (1993), quoting the Congregation for Catholic Education, states that 'the specific mission of the Catholic school is a critical systematic transmission of culture in the light of faith, and the integration of culture with faith and of faith with living out love with great hope'. (Flynn, 1993, p. 21). This integration of life and love, faith and hope means that we do not separate our lives into secular and religious moments; rather the two dimensions co-exist as we make meaning of all learning opportunities' to the community. We are called, to have courage, a strong faith to take the risk and not to be afraid to be consistent in sharing our gifts and strengths with our young children despite the fact of knowing that we are not perfect. 'Our deepest fear is not that we are inadequate. Our deepest fear is that we are powerful beyond measure. It is our light, not our darkness, that most frightens us' (Williamson, 1992). When human weaknesses fail to fulfill our responsibilities to give love, faith and hope to our children, God is always there to give us the courage and strength not to give up. We communicate and relate to God in our journey constantly through prayer.

Prayer

The message of the following lines (adapted from the United Nations, in their presentation of a declaration of children's rights, 1995) speaks of the needs of many young children in the South Pacific nations:

MY DREAM SCHOOL

My dream is to be in a special school, a school where I can feel safe, where I am treated the same as every other child, where I am treated with respect and dignity, a place where I feel that I belong, where I feel free to explore myself and my environment, a place where I find love, peace and security, where I have nutritious food to eat when I am hungry, where I can turn on the tap and drink, fresh, cool, clean water when I am thirsty, where I have a shade tree to sit under when the sun is too hot, where the grass is green and I have a place to play, a place where I find lots of friends, where my teachers are caring and always on time and be in the classroom to make sure we are all there, and my parents are supportive. A place where I am excited to go each day, a place where I am not abused or harassed. A place free of drugs and full of fun, and lots of beautiful flowers, red, yellow, white and all sorts of colors. My special school is a place where I am free to love, to learn and to grow in every way. A place where I am protected from the wind, the sun, the rain and cold. Regardless of my race, my religion, my culture, or where I come from, I am nurtured as a very, very special person.

Leaders, teachers and parents of Catholic schools are persistently challenged by the message of this statement. The needs of the young children and the needs of the societies are so complex that we are painfully aware that this is not an easy time. Many adults feel less secure about the future for themselves and their children than they did just one year ago in the South Pacific nations. While we may feel we have no control over the situation we are now in, we still have to be active where we can, and do it well. This chapter would like to highlight 'prayer' as one activity that we can initiate to involve every single person in our school communities and the whole society to give a sense of connectedness, a feeling of commitment and purpose to one another and to our children. Prayer is very powerful and it is a pillar of hope to the young children. In our prayer we pray that every child will receive an education.

We educate ourselves and our young children to pray for 'forgiveness' and wisdom to know and to understand that it is alright to be imperfect, as long as we keep on trying. 'The greatest glory in living lies not in never falling, but in rising every time we fall' (Mandela, 1994). If all or at least some of us can develop the great gift of enthusing young people, of providing an environment of love, understanding, joy and hope, where they have the means of earning a positive reputation, where everyone can be someone, the rewards in the creation of a better school, a better family, a better community, and a better society are boundless. Our Catholic schools will give joy to the anguish and worries of the people of the South Pacific. The nations of the South Pacific are scattered and prayer is one simple powerful and practical way to use to give hope to our children who pray constantly for hope for our generation now and in the future. It is wonderful to know that we are not depending on the leaders and politicians of the governments to change our lives and the situation of the South Pacific. In prayer we have an opportunity for each person to own the responsibility to make a difference to the lives of the young children in this time of uncertainty.

Prayer through communities of the Catholic schools in the South Pacific nations can be very powerful during this time. Jim Wallis, one of the prophets of hope in today's world, has a wonderful way of illustrating this. He used the example of the dismantling of apartheid in South Africa. Wallis (1994) proclaimed that apartheid in South Africa was not brought down by guns, violence or even by changing the politicians, but it was by the hope of people who had great faith and courage despite experiencing racial injustice. The people, families and children in South Africa began to pray together for the day apartheid would come to an end. They lit candles and placed them in their windows so that their neighbours, the government and the whole world would see their belief. The government did see and they passed a law that it would be illegal to light a candle and put in the window. It was seen as a crime, as serious as owning and flaunting a gun. The government of South Africa had reason to be concerned because eventually those burning candles, and the prayer and hope behind them changed South Africa (Wallis, 1994).

We all need to pray and act in a mission of conviction to ourselves, our schools, our communities, the South Pacific nations and the whole world, to convince them that there is hope. God says, 'I will protect those who trust in my name. When they call upon me, I will answer, I will be with them in trouble. I will rescue them and honour them' (Psalm 91:14-16). When accompanied by a prayer or a rainbow symbol, the three words 'there is hope' can communicate so much into the lives of despairing children who read them on a leaflet, landing on a doormat, or on the side of a bus, or on a church or school notice board, or on the internet. As leaders, parents and teachers we cannot leave it up to the politicians and other people to create hope and offer peace to our children.

Conclusion

The pastoral role of Catholic schools has revealed that a new cultural educational, spiritual and religious landscape is emerging in the nations of the South Pacific. The Catholic school is no longer only an educational institution that has the responsibility to dispense mono-dimensional Catholic truth. The curriculum now has to be integrated into a formative way with the surrounding culture and the life of the people it serves (Congregation for Catholic Education, 1998). The attitudes, values and behavior of the family, and the community within (Fraser & Gorinski, 2006). It is paramount then, that leaders, teachers and parents at homes and in the Catholic schools of the South Pacific work together to meet these new pastoral demands in educating children in an holistic way. Furthermore, every single person should be encouraged to pray, for peace and have conviction that there is hope now and in the future for the young children. The following statement from Kofi Annan, former secretary general of the United Nations, sums up the challenge:

> Much of the next millennium can be seen in how we care for our children today. Tomorrow's world may be influenced by science and technology, but more than anything, it is already taking shape in the bodies and minds of our children.

11
Islamic Schools :
Another faith perspective

Silma Ihram

Muslim schools, one of the newest additions to the independent school sector in Australia, face many of the same problems of other faith-based schools in a secular, modern and liberal society. They also face a greater accountability, difficulty in obtaining approval through local councils, and a range of student or cultural identity and faith-related problems. The Muslim community is continually portrayed in mainstream media as a violent and intolerant religion closely identified with political liberation causes, violent international struggles and threats to 'liberal democracy'. The United State's war on terror and the Australian government's anti-terror laws along with its support for United States' international policy decisions, have created complicated loyalties in relation to religion and country for much of the multi-ethnic community in Australia which identifies with Islam. Often forced into a defensive position when outspoken or non-English speaking Imams attract negative publicity, the attitude of Muslim parents is ambivalent towards what a Muslim school should be offering their children. For the most part, Muslim schools have opted for the easier solution by focussing on high academic achievement, engaging heavily in interfaith and interschool activities while struggling to establish high quality competitive facilities for their low socio-economic families. School administrators continue to struggle with how to assist their students in resolving their identity issues, instil faith in a spiritual non-politicised religion while preparing them for life in a secular, liberal even permissive post-school environment.

The history of Muslim schools in Australia

Muslim schools are a relatively recent addition to the private schooling sector in Australia. The first two Muslim schools to appear in Australia were established in 1983 by very different organisational entities, the first a grassroots small association of women with very limited funds, the other by the national body, the Australian Federation of Islamic Councils with substantial funding from Saudi Arabia. Al Noori Muslim Primary School began out of one woman's frustration with the prevailing attitude of both private and public schools and depended on only five women – two of them Muslim converts – in Sydney in 1983 (Buckley 1991). King Khaled Islamic College opened in Melbourne following the purchase of the partially burnt premises of a former Catholic School by the Australian Federation of Islamic Councils (Saeed 2003). Since that time 29 Muslim schools have been established but two closed because of inability to maintain sustainable enrolments. The total population of Muslim students currently stands at 15 000 students, represented nationally by two organisations, the Australian Council for Islamic Education in Schools (ACIES) and the Australian Federation of Islamic Councils (AFIC). The challenges faced by these schools in the intervening years have changed substantially, initially being matters of survival and currently more matters of the ultimate goal of education particularly in relation to the twin priorities of academic achievement and development of faith.

The current status of Muslim schools

While new or significantly expanding Muslim schools still continue to struggle with local councils and adjoining residents, Muslim schools have now become a significant and established contributor to private education. Able to access Federal and State funding, due to their low socio-economic status, Muslim schools have generally been able to build substantially and most have more than adequate facilities allowing them to compete favourably with the local government schools for students. Those that have the space and a supportive Board of Governance, currently offer high school, with the focus of development shifting from an establishment mode of operation to providing a competitive academic education. While parents seem to value school facilities, high academic achievement appears to be the chief deciding factor amongst parents in choosing a Muslim school. This is indicated by public comparisons of final year results and consequent increases in enrolment for schools with high results. Schools that engage in a wide variety of extra curricular activities, or support students that may be struggling academically, do not have the same enrolment attraction as schools which are sometimes ruthless in allowing only those with academic prowess to progress from year to year.

This competitive demand for academic excellence places a huge burden particularly on the student. Enrolment in outside tutorial classes, often from the early primary years is a standard if not compulsory practice for students in the more academically competitive schools. Students who are not successful in meeting the required pass mark and consequently lose their position in the school often display extreme behaviour at the school where they are eventually enrolled, usually public schools, due to the loss of self-esteem that results from being forced to leave such academically competitive schools. The damage can be long lasting, affecting the student's overall morale, and ability to cope in the new environment which is often less demanding academically, and less restrictive in its behaviour management systems.

Schools as caring communities

The role of the school in nurturing individuals cannot be underestimated in the development of the child. The school is second only to the family in its long term influence over children. Where schools are warm and caring, with teachers who show care and compassion along with firm discipline, students are most likely to excel. According to Bill Rogers, a specialist in behaviour management, 'Teachers are key caregivers in the lives of children. They provide significant emotional and social security, especially for students with emotional, behavioural disorders'(Rogers 2003).

This aspect of school community life is critical especially for Muslim students who already feel alienated and marginalised by the media and occasionally by personal experience. As Muslim schools usually have a higher proportion of Muslim teachers, there is a greater capacity to understand this sense of alienation than in a public school which may have a minority of Muslim students in its multi-ethnic population.

While individual teachers reach out to students and develop mentoring relationships with their pupils in the playground and through extra-curricular activities, there has been little training to support Muslim teachers who are themselves struggling with identity issues and feelings of alienation. A limited number of interfaith programs such as the Affinity Youth Encounters Leadership Program currently provide training for selected students, and most of the Muslim schools offer a variety of leadership programs, debating and extra curricular activities to develop confidence and self-esteem (Year Book 2006). However training must also be provided for the teachers themselves, who often hold similar feelings of inadequacy in dealing with the media, and struggle on a daily basis with the ongoing war on terror, anti-terrorism laws and inflammatory media comments.

Federal challenges to Muslim schools
In 2004 the Association of Independent Schools (AIS) in New South Wales prepared a booklet for public distribution which celebrated the background and achievement of its member Muslim schools (AIS 2005). This followed a number of crisis meetings between Muslim school leaders and members of the executive of the AIS. The AIS includes in its membership all non-government Muslim campuses in NSW. Muslim schools appeared to be targeted by the Federal government at that time, which was in the process of establishing the Muslim Community Reference Group as a consultative forum. Frequent statements had appeared in the media questioning the loyalty of the Muslim community in general and the intent of Muslim school curricula. The then Federal Education Minister, Brendan Nelson stated that he had received letters about the curriculum and teaching goals of Muslim schools (*Sydney Morning Herald* 2003). The letters expressed concern that Muslim schools were teaching anti-Christian and anti-Western sentiments.

Brendan Nelson developed a Values Education policy listing nine basic values that were required to be taught in every school. This was at the time of the arrest on terrorism charges of a group of Sydney and later Melbourne Muslims, concurrent with the widespread reporting of comments by Imams in national papers. In the aftermath of September 11 Muslim schools took the initiative, with the support of the ACIES, to develop a Muslim School's Charter. The Charter was adopted by all member schools as a requirement of entry to the organisation. The Charter had been officially recognised by Minister Nelson (at that time not Education Minister) and widely published. The Charter stated clearly where Muslim schools stood in relation to the teaching of values, attitudes towards terrorism, violence and Australian values.

The publication of the values policy and subsequent comments by Minister Nelson were therefore seen by Muslim schools and the Muslim community as effectively targeting their community. Kim Beazley joined in the criticism of Muslim schools demanding that the Government force them to enshrine Australian values of tolerance, respect and mateship in order to 'stamp out any extremism in Islamic schools' (Fewster & McPhedran 2005). In Sydney, the Noor Al Houda Islamic College was visited by three different television camera crews within the space of 24 hours to investigate the allegations of Minister Nelson, on each occasion reporting back to the Minister that the school was complying with all requirements. Following each visit, the minister made ever more detailed allegations about the specific content of the school curriculum and the knowledge of the students in regard to details of the poster which carried the specified nine values. Needless to say, the school not only displayed the required poster throughout the school, but the students also successfully responded to queries on specifics of Simpson and his donkey, who were displayed in the background.

These events were followed by the engagement of Erebus International consultants to establish a National Showcase Seminar (ASCA 2006). This was organised in conjunction with the Muslim Community Reference Group and was designed to specifically investigate what values were being taught in targeted Muslim schools, particularly in Melbourne and Sydney. The Erubus investigation included visits to the schools and a meeting with the ACIES, inspection of curriculum related documents, and a presentation by selected Muslim schools at Parliament House, where they were to demonstrate the values included in their curriculum.

Many of the ACIES schools had also adopted a theme based document prepared by the Perth Australian Islamic College which celebrated 40 values throughout the 40 weeks of the school year, each of these values being supported by religious texts and class activities across the school (Theme of the Week). In comparison the seven prescribed Federal values did not include what were considered by the ACIES as critical values of honesty, justice and good manners. Each of the schools that ultimately presented in the Erebus Showcase demonstrated clearly how they interacted with other local schools on environmental, interfaith, and joint academic projects, including a strong moral basis, all of which exceeded the apparently ambiguous values of the Federal Government's policy.

After the ACIES voiced strong complaints that the Muslim community alone was being singled out, schools from other faiths were also included in the investigation. However, the overall impression was that Muslim schools faced a particular political challenge. It was seen that there existed strong suspicions in relation to Muslim loyalty to

Australia and the convergence between Islamic values as espoused in their teaching, and what were considered to be standard Australian values. The same accountability did not appear to exist for other private schools which belonged to a different faith.

Community and media challenges to Muslim schools

Over the past few years a variety of educational administrators and public education supporters have expressed concerns that Muslim schools will encourage the isolation of Muslim children from the mainstream society, teach them cultural norms which will further alienate them from Australian society, and ultimately encourage a fundamental view of Islam which could jeopardise the safety and security of Australia's diverse community with a terrorist agenda (Steketee 2007).

The concern with alienation or isolation is also expressed as a form of ghettoisation of the Muslim community, an allegation which Islamic schools would reject in the same manner as their Jewish or Christian peers. Muslim schools are engaged constantly in a proactive manner with inter-school supports, debating contests and interfaith activities. Recent funding under the Federal Values Education Program has seen a drilling down of prescribed values and how they are taught through projects involving the interaction of a cluster of Muslim schools and public schools from the Shire. Projects such as this are in response to concerns that Muslim youth were 'suffering tremendous pressures and the main pressure is one of alienation' (Harris 2005).

Facilities of Muslim schools
Muslim schools vary considerably throughout Australia in their religious facilities, but they are generally characterised by an ability to cater for the immediate religious needs of Muslim students. This includes offering daily prayers, uniforms which include the hijab, halal food, support during the fasting of Ramadan, the teaching of the Quran, Arabic and Islamic Studies, and in most cases Muslim teachers as role models and mentors. Most schools have attracted sufficient funding to build substantial halls or prayer facilities, although smaller schools; Arkana and the former Noor Al Houda Islamic College, still struggle to provide a large enough prayer area to meet the needs of all students simultaneously. Muslim high schools provide the obligatory Friday prayer, occasionally encouraging students to prepare the sermon.

While permission to wear the hijab as part of the uniform is evident in all Muslim schools throughout Australia, its status as part of a compulsory uniform varies. In most schools the male students have uniforms that are indistinguishable from their independent Christian peers, while Muslim girls with their characteristic hijabs, often worn from the early primary years, cause them to be immediately identifiable, occasionally suffering discrimination and harassment from members of the public as a result. This has in some ways facilitated the determination and resolve of female students, and encouraged high academic results from previously traditional families where women were not always encouraged to access higher education. Girls in Muslim schools often achieve a higher rate of continuing tertiary education than their male associates.

Faith-based challenges

In 1977 at the First World Conference on Islamic Education the following primary aim was listed:

> Education should aim at a balanced growth of the total personality of man through training of the spirit, the intellect, the rational self, feelings and the senses. Faith is to be infused in the pupil to create an emotional attachment to Islam to enable him to follow the Qur'an and the Sunnah and to be governed by the Islamic system of values, willingly and joyfully, so that he may proceed to the realisation of his status as Khalifatullah (Vice Regent) to whom Allah has promised the authority of the Universe (Erfan & Avlie 1995, pp.3-4).

This emphasis on morals and values, the mind and the spirit are infused into every Muslim school's mission statement and charter. The role of the Muslim as a responsible agent of God, is still a central aim in some Muslim schools, notably the Australian Islamic College. Its website is replete with Islamic source material, video clips, links to international and local information about Islam, and whose welcome webpage clearly spells out the role of the school in assisting students mentally, spiritually and finally academically to grasp the importance of a being an active, engaged Muslim. In recent years however, this emphasis on producing a spiritual faithful Muslim has been largely supplanted with an emphasis on a faithful citizen, or a Muslim Australian, who is able to meet the needs of the nation. Statements such as 'education which will equip them with virtue, and the academic and social skills necessary for effective participation as Muslims in Australia' (Al Zahra website) or 'to achieve Islamic educational goals harmoniously with the Australian community in which we live' (Arkana website) are commonly seen. This is most apparent in one of the most successful and large Muslim schools in Australia. The Australian International Academy (AIA), which no longer has any reference to Islam in its name, has relegated any reference to Islam to a sixth point in its aims and objectives as follows: 'To build in students the Muslim character that exemplifies Islamic manners and shows respect and tolerance to other opinions and appreciation to differing cultures' (AIA website). Previously the AIA was known as the King Khalid Islamic College and included in its aims the following encouragement in relation to Islamic identity, 'students are taught to be proud of their Islamic identity and of being Australian Muslims' (Saeed 2003).

Muslim schools have been forced to be on the defensive, seeking to justify their teaching of Islam, and constantly feeling under pressure to respond to challenges about their worthiness in comparison to other faith based schools. The challenge for Muslim schools in the future must be to truly value the historical and spiritual contribution that association with Islam can bring. The risk that is run by Muslim schools in their defensive attitude of Islam is that Islamic schools may not truly value their heritage, and may eventually become nominally Islamic schools, focussing on a compatibility and assimilation of Islam, and Islamic knowledge and history to Australian history.

In his recent address to the University of Western Sydney Access and Inclusion Conference in 2007 the former Chair of the Council for Aboriginal Reconciliation, Patrick Dodson encouraged Muslims to truly value their heritage, the contribution of their engineers, philosophers, scientists and spiritual leaders to the history of civilisation (Dodson 2007). In 2007 an Iranian Jewish collector of Islamic art whose avowed intention was to improve the relationship between Jewish and Muslim communities, offered to Edmund Capon from the NSW Art Gallery the opportunity to display hundreds of items of his collection of Islamic antiquities. In his introduction at the opening of the exhibition he espoused the desire to bring to the world a greater understanding of the contribution of Islamic civilisation. The exhibition was almost fully booked from the day it opened, with many Muslim students discovering sometimes for the first time the extent of their civilisation and history.

This proactive stance that has been taken by Aboriginal and Jewish leaders must be foremost in the aims and objectives of Muslim schools.

By recognising the extent of Muslim history and civilisation, the achievements of Muslim civilisation and the broad range of achievement in literary, artistic, architectural, social, legal and above all spiritual areas, Muslim schools can assist their students to overcome the feelings of humiliation or low self-esteem that are the result of the negative media to which they are continually subjected.

Unfortunately in recent centuries there has been an overwhelming trend, borne out of the increasing influence of fundamentalist Salafi and Wahhabi teachings, to ignore or even reject the significant developments that occurred during the centuries of Islamic progress and to return to the initial sources of Islam without regard for the vast body of scholarly development that has occurred since the 'Golden Era', represented by the first four Caliphs of Islam. There is little reference to the centuries of Islamic civilisation which were categorised by differing scholarship and widely different cultures existing for centuries across the continents of Europe, South Asia, South East Asia, the Middle East and North Africa. To demonstrate this fear of being overtly Islamic, there is little information or recognition of Rumi by any of the Muslim schools either on their websites or in their 2007 activities, despite 2007 being the UNESCO year of Rumi.

Teaching faith in school

As with all faiths the believing Muslim engages in religious rituals, has texts to study for religious guidance and instruction, and abides by a variety of essential ethical principles. Separate and underlying all of these more practical issues is the matter of faith. While rituals, ethics and texts can be taught, ultimately faith is a personal journey into a spiritual dimension which can only be mentored but not directly taught.

In most schools however, there is an assumption that Muslim students have already acquired such faith. 'How do we enter Islam completely? There are several ways – one of them is to gain the (sic.) Islamic education to improve the faith' states one religious teacher in a school 2006 year book. The original experience of faith however is assumed.

In my experience as a Muslim school principal it has become apparent that faith is ultimately a matter of personal experience, but is frequently associated with cultural practice. Parents have often expressed that they wish their children to study in an 'Islamic environment', presuming that having facilities to support the teaching and practice of Islam, and a majority student community of Muslims will necessarily develop an

'Islamic environment'. They are occasionally shocked to find that students in Muslim schools also commit the same offences of swearing, behaving badly, thieving and bullying that exist in secular public schools.

The challenge for Muslim schools is to develop programs that specifically highlight the benefits of a spiritual encounter with God, a discipline more akin to Sufism than with traditional teaching of Islam. Islamic textbooks that are generally available within Muslim schools tend to emphasise the rituals and texts of Islam, rather than developing a spiritual and reflective awareness. This is partly due to the international movement which has been variously described as 'fundamentalist', a term characterised by Waleed Aly as an inappropriate description of the current phenomenon in the Muslim world (Aly 2007). Such influence has generally seen Sufism and active spiritual contemplation as a private matter and discouraged the active teaching of prominent Sufis who wrote extensively throughout the Islamic civilisation. Combined with traditional cultural Islam as practised by Muslim migrants who have often had limited Islamic scholarship themselves, the active acquisition or encouragement to acquire faith is often not addressed due to the drive for curriculum development and preparation of teaching materials. In my own experience the greatest assistance to acquisition of faith in Muslim schools is through the personal interaction of sharing of faith by caring teachers, rather than any specific school program or instruction. This is a vital challenge for Muslim schools into the future that has received scant attention by scholars or practising educational administrators.

Succession

Many of the original founders of Islamic schools in Australia still remain in key positions. The schools established largely due to the driving influence of strong individuals have often demonstrated greater success than those established by community organisations dominated often by ethnic politics and volunteer boards. The Australian Islamic College of Perth for example was established in 1986 by Hajj Abdullah Magar, an Egyptian migrant who believed that the 'only way to stop Muslim youth from losing their Islamic identity was to have a comprehensive Islamic education system with an Islamic environment' (Jones 2004), an aim he has single-mindedly and successfully pursued, with his college having one of the largest enrolments of any school in Australia.

A major challenge facing Muslim schools within the next decade will be the preparation of a new generation of Australian educated leaders who will either take over the running of existing organisations through the careful mentoring of their current leaders, or challenge the existing systems which have entrenched positions of authority. Despite the proliferation of leadership programs throughout the Muslim community for Muslim youth, there is a virtual absence of similar programs mentoring young people into the more significant positions of leadership. A rare exception to this situation has been the democratic election of Australian educated representatives to the Victorian Islamic Council, representing a genuine grass roots movement for leadership change. The recognition of the skills and expertise of aspiring Australian born Muslims into the educational leadership of Muslim schools is an urgent priority which has yet to be tackled.

Identity and culture issues

The Muslim community is often referred to as a monolithic entity in Government policy, community attitude and the Australian press. The reality however, is that the Muslim community comes from a multitude of different countries and cultural variations. While many of the Muslim schools existing in Australia today were established by ethnic associations and were designed to ensure the transmission of particular cultures, Muslim students today identify strongly with the prevailing Australian culture, are often not fluent in the language of their parents, and have no personal recollection of the land of their parents. Instead they are sometimes tempted to respond to a discourse which relates to a global Ummah - an idealised space where there is no marginalisation, religious discrimination or cultural confusion. Muslim schools find difficulty in meeting such contrasting expectations of parents who want maintenance of the existing culture, of students who are struggling with issues of cultural identity and of the Australian community which demands social inclusion. The outdated Arabic curriculum used in most Muslim schools and student reluctance to study Arabic is just one symptom of this dilemma.

Conclusion

In many ways Muslim schools are still in their infancy. Having generally established quality facilities for the provision of teaching, they are still to develop organisations, networks and the required mentoring to ensure that the vision of Muslim education will continue into the future in a specifically Australian oriented manner. With an emphasis on academic results rather than on spirituality, Muslim schools have responded to tradition rather than the deeper side of faith in providing solutions for a traumatised young Muslim community living through an era of the war on terror. Those students who have not managed to maintain their studies due to personal problems, self-esteem or academic difficulty are not yet catered for in the competitive drive to maintain enrolments through the high grades of graduating students. The challenges facing Muslim schools are many and include not only the development of more Australian based religious and Arabic teaching programs but also a vision which will adequately serve the needs of the Muslim community into a diverse and tolerant society into the future.

References

Affinity Youth Encounters Leadership Program at http://www.affinity.org.au/html/youth/interfaith/Year2007/YEShore2007.php accessed 27th March 2008

Al Zahra website at http://www.azc.nsw.edu.au/ourvision.php accessed 27th March 2008

Aly, W. (2007) *People Like Us – How Arrogance Is Dividing Islam and the West* Sydney, Pan Macmillan.

Arkana website at www.arkana.nsw.edu.au accessed 27th March 2008

ASCA, DEST (2006) Report on National Showcase Seminar: Encouraging Tolerance and Social Cohesion Through School Education, 25 May.

Association of Independent Schools of NSW (2005) *Islamic Schools in NSW*, Sydney.

Australian Islamic College at www.aic.wa.edu.au/website/welcome.htm accessed 27th March 2008.

Buckley, Silma (1991) *Bridges of Light – The Struggle of an Islamic Private School in Australia*. Sydney, Muslim Service Association.

Dodson, P. (2007) Keynote Speech Access, Inclusion and Success Conference Proceedings, University of Western Sydney.

Erfan, N and Valie, Z.A (editors) (1995) *Education and the Muslim World: Challenge and Response*. Recommendations of the Four World Conferences on Islamic Education, Islamic Foundation, Leicester pp.3-4.

Fewster, S & McPhedran, I (2005) Hard Line Islamic School Hits Back at ALP, *The Advertiser,* 2 August, We Are Australian Through and Through, Adelaide.

Harris, T. (2005) Get out of Ghettoes, Young Muslims Told, *The Australian,* 15 August, Canberra.

Rogers, B. (2003) *Behaviour Recovery*. Melbourne, ACER.

Saeed, B. (2003) *Islam in Australia*. Sydney, Allen & Unwin.

Steketee, M. (2007) Muslim Integration Still A Simmering Discontent, *The Australian* 20 September.

Sydney Morning Herald (2003) Unity, Diversity and Religious Schools, 1 April.

Year Book (2006) *The Australian Islamic College*.

12
A School Generation Facing the World's End-Time

Hedley Beare

The decade 2005-2015 is mooted as being critical to life on Earth as we know it. Our students need to be nurtured with constructive approaches while they are still at school as they are instructed in just how dire the situation is with regard to climate change, population explosion and limited resources. These issues will affect their lives daily in the 21st century. They are, more than ever, the future.

This article gives a brief up-to-date summary of the most urgent problems into which our youth have been born, followed by five insights into featuring a positive curriculum in the 21st century.

The state of the world

Climate change
The United Nations 1200-page assessment of climate change containing contributions from 2500 scientists, 6000 reports cited and reviews by 750 experts, concluded that:
- We can expect global temperatures to rise by 2 to 4.5 degrees Celsius in this century
- The planet cannot absorb rising levels of carbon dioxide
- Sea levels could rise 20 to 60 cms this century
- Snow will vanish from all but the highest peaks, and
- There will be an increasing incidence of extreme and violent weather (Chandler, 2007, p.1).

> The human and economic costs of climate change are likely to be highest in poor countries, which have typically contributed least because of their much lower greenhouse gas emissions' (Minchin, 2007, p.1).

Severe drought, intense bushfires, salination of river basins, floods, freak weather and diminishing supplies of fresh water all interlock. Damage to the earth's ozone layer is already causing ice to melt from high peaks and from polar icecaps. When pack ice disappears, polar bears die from habitat destruction. Earth's warming alters where rain falls, making formerly arable land unfit for cropping, and affecting world food bowls. Rising sea levels affect the height of tides, with some low-lying land on which people now live being permanently flooded. The circulation of ocean currents changes the weather patterns in the land-masses they wash against.

The alarms have been triggered because although these issues have been discussed for decades, they have now arrived on our doorsteps simultaneously and interactively. So in 2000, the President of the Worldwatch Institute wrote (Brown, 2000):

> There is no middle path. The challenge is to build [a world community] that is sustainable or to stay with our (present) unsustainable economy until it declines. One way or another, the choice will be made by (this) generation.

Heeding the warnings fast enough

In 1968 Aurelio Peccei, head of Fiat, convened a group of the world's most eminent thinkers later known as the Club of Rome. United by an 'overwhelming conviction that the major problems facing mankind are of such complexity and are so interrelated that traditional institutions and policies are no longer able to cope with them' (Meadows et al, 1972, pp.9-10), they commissioned a study, whose findings, published in *The Limits to Growth* (1972), startled the world community. Using five key indicators, the study team devised a computer model of the earth which showed where the trends were pointing, establishing that there were tangible limits beyond which life on the planet became unsustainable. They named the decade when we would overshoot the planet's ability to survive, warning, 'Every day of continued exponential growth brings the world closer to the ultimate limits to that growth. A decision to do nothing is a decision to increase the risk of collapse' (Meadows et al, 1972, p.183). The time they prophesied about is now.

An update in 2002 showed that the team's predictions had been almost pin-point accurate. In 1972 they had speculated the end-date for growth to be around 2015. There was then still time to consider some options. 'Humanity has largely squandered the past 30 years…(We) do not have another 30 years to dither…The collapse will arrive very suddenly, much to everyone's surprise' (Meadows et al, 2005, pp.xi-xvi, xxi).

For similar reasons, Ervin Laszlo founded the Club of Budapest in 1993. In *The Chaos Point* (2006, ch.7) he lists the issues with which we now grapple, and a list of constructive actions we can take. The decisional window is still open, he says, and it is not yet too late to act (Laszlo, 2006, p.85). But business as usual is not a survival option. Laszlo warns that collapse occurs when the stable cycles and processes of a system 'give way to complex, seemingly unordered behaviour,' and we reach:

> (A) crucial tipping point in the evolution of a system in which trends that have brought the system to its present state break down and it can no longer return to its prior states of behaviour. It is launched irreversibly on a new trajectory that leads either to breakdown or to breakthrough to a new structure and a new mode of operation.

By any measure, he argues, earth is at the tipping point now and our window of decision is 2005-2012. The chaos point is likely to be reached in 2012. (Laszlo, 2006, pp.3, vii, 84, 13-14).

Characteristically when confronted by an 'uncomfortable truth', people pass through three stages: 1. denial, when they try to carry on as though nothing is wrong. 2. fervent use of technology (a quick fix, a miracle cure, a new invention) to solve the problem. 3. finally, acceptance, and the adjustment of behaviour, life-style, and beliefs. Is there enough lead time left for the world community to work through these stages?

In his Gaia hypothesis developed in 1972, scientist James Lovelock used an earth model which demonstrated that the planet itself is behaving like a single living system regulating its own conditions of life. What threatens Gaia as a whole, Gaia rejects as a cancer in the body. 'The great Earth system, Gaia, behaves…like a mother who is nurturing but ruthlessly cruel towards transgressors, even when they are her progeny' (Lovelock, 1988, p.147). In *The Revenge of Gaia* (2006), Lovelock argues that the earth community is currently suffering 'the fever brought on by a plague of people'. He too bewails the wasted lead time, believing we have no option now but to prepare for the worst' (Lovelock, 2006, pp.3, 152-153).

George Monbiot proposes that we may already have started the chain-reaction which could incinerate many life-forms, including human beings. It is still possible to decarbonize a country's economy without wrecking it, and he too offers some creative solutions (Monbiot, 2006).

Lord Rees speculated whether the human species will be able to survive beyond the end of this century. It is now possible for technologies to get out of hand; 'multiplier' infections can be set off unwittingly, especially in the 'congested megacities of the developing world'; disasters can occur through human incompetence as easily as through malice; there are 'disruptive capabilities' available now to individuals skilled in genetics, bacteriology, and computers; and the 'disaffected fringe' has the power to inflict awesome terror on the rest of us (Rees, 2003, pp.8, 52, 61, 62, 131).

The people of the 21st century

Neilsen (2005, p.1) points to the wildfire escalation in the world's population as the driving force behind all critical global trends. Until 1804, the world's population remained below one billion. Two billion was passed in 1930; 6.1 billion by 2000, and by 2007 6.4 billion. Put baldly, it took over 200,000 years for the human race to reach one billion; just 130 years to add a second billion; and adding the most recent billion took just 12years! By the year 2050, the planet's human population could be over ten billion and on an exponential curve skywards. When the children now in kindergarten leave high school, there will be a billion more people on earth than when they started school.

If, as one study predicts, world populations are unlikely to decline before 2070 (Fannin 2001, pp.1-2), this generation of students will live their whole lives with a world population at least two and a half billion in excess of what we have at present. Can the planet support this population, and who makes the decision? What happens — not least to our own children — if the escalation cannot be arrested (Neilsen, 2005, pp.1-13)?

Because affluent developed countries have limited the number of births, the poorest developing countries contribute close to 99 per cent of the annual increase in global population (Neilsen, 2005, p.17). Consequently, an overwhelming proportion of children born this year will live in communities which lack essential services, are disease-ridden (e.g. AIDS), are under-educated and lack any new learning technologies.

Davis (2006) shows that the growth of cities poses most of the world's human problems. In 1950, there were 86 cities in the world with populations above a million; by 2015, the number will be at least 550. There are now around 22 megacities (15 of them in Asia) with more than ten million people, featuring huge slums where nearly a billion people live.

Age distributions

Half the world's people are under 25; one third are of school-age (Saltau, 1999, p.3). A billion of the world's population in 2007 are between 14 and 25 – of child-bearing age and the parents of the generation who should now be at school ('Six billion and more' 1999, pp.48-49). They are about to produce what has been called a 'youthquake', a global baby boom. They co-habit the society Australian students will enter as young adults.

They are also competitive. We simply cannot overlook the hopes and aspirations of half the world's people who are under 25. They will be very aggressive in a number of ways over the next few decades. A Hong Kong bank recently advertised, 'There are three billion people in Asia. Half of them are under 25. Consider it a growing market'. Certainly, they will have a huge, collective impact on the economic patterns of the world.

If the world's population is to stabilise at a sustainable level, a much larger proportion of that population (about 34%) will be over sixty years of age, with higher proportions in developed countries – 49% in the Pacific (including Australia); 45% in Western Europe; 40% in North America (Fannin 2001, p.2). The UN estimates that by 2050 a quarter of the populations of North America, Europe and Japan will be over the age of 65, and there could be 2.2 million over 100 (Kluger, 2000, p.49). If the present trendline persists, two thirds of those now in their forties will live to be over ninety; students now in school can expect to live into the 2080s.

And that is a dilemma, for the aging, not the young, dominate public policy and political economies, and tend to determine where the tax-dollars are spent. Already in many Western countries, public health (the priority of the aging) has crowded out education from its position on the political agenda. We must therefore consider what schooling and education will be like in this scenario.

Ethnic distribution

National distributions are changing with astonishing rapidity. The world community's age profile means that the world's cultural and geopolitical centre of gravity will inevitably move in the next decades away from Europe and North America and towards Asia, Africa, and South America. Our students and their teachers must confront this re-distribution.

Between 1950 (when it had 358 million people) and 2000, India's population tripled. When today's school children are 50 years old, India (with a population by then of 1.529 billion) will have displaced China (1.478 billion) as the world's most populous country. Asia and Africa will account for 80% of the people in the world in which today's school-children will live as adults. By 2050, Pakistan's population will be 345 million, greater than that of the entire North American continent combined — USA, Canada, Mexico, Central America (Brown 2000, p.7). There will be more people in the one Asian city of Shanghai than the entire population of the South Pacific (including Australia, New Zealand, and Papua New Guinea). On the other hand, Europe and North America will be home to only 11% of the world's people. The contemporaries of the children now in school, therefore, will be dominantly non-Caucasian and non-Eurocentric.

Birth rate patterns
Around the world, homes with high incomes average less than one child per household; whereas low-income households have nearly three times as many children as the rich do.

> In 2002, 61 developed countries had cut their birthrates to below 'replacement levels'. Another 34 in Asia and Latin America were approaching that level (Bone, 2002, p.11). In the last few years, Japan became the first modern economy to have more people over 65 than under 15 (Backman, 2000, p.1), a birthrate so low that 'childlessness' is almost out of hand (Sayles 1998, p.13).

Marriage patterns are changing everywhere. There is a forty per cent chance – and rising – that the parents of any student now at school will divorce and remarry while she is still at school. Many students will not grow up with their natural brothers or sisters or with both natural parents; or get much support from grandparents or extended family because nuclear families move home so often. Many children grow up in one-parent families.

Languages

If this generation of school students wants to be able to talk to their peers across the world, they will have to consider what languages they can speak. Mandarin Chinese is already the mother tongue of a sixth of the world's people. Nearly three times as many people speak Chinese as speak English, and the number keeps growing. Our students will *have* to speak more than one language, and preferably more than two. Language learning will be a necessary part of their schooling.

Although 80 % of the world's websites are in English, fewer than one person in ten speaks English. English, being the language of Internet, disenfranchises 95% (900 million people!) of the Indian population who do not speak English. On the other hand, Asian countries like India and China are rapidly moving onto the information superhighway, and much of the information they will trade is likely to be in an indigenous language, from which monolingual English speakers and readers will be automatically excluded.

The world's living space and resources

If everyone had the present lifestyle of middle-class Europeans, North Americans, and Australians, an area equivalent to almost *three planets* would be required to support the world population (Rees, 2003). The present inequalities are so gross that, if unaddressed, they will become explosive, fuelling the blind striking-out against perceived, entrenched privilege. Already, the richest billion people on earth own 80 % of the world's wealth, and the way they use it is often selfish and morally indefensible.

Environmentally, what happens within the borders of one country is no longer solely that country's business. By the time contemporary school children start to work, environmental responsibilities will be enforced internationally, and the world could be threatened by 'green wars'. The consumption and distribution of water, food, fish, and forests will be in constant dispute through the 21st Century. Pollution of the atmosphere, climate change, and the use of energy (and how it is generated and shared) will be international issues. Human and genetic engineering, access to health services, and the use and occupation of space colonies will be major political items.

Some specific natural resources cause concern:

The sea. More than half the world's people live within 160 kilometres of a seacoast. The community cannot continue to allow sewage, acid sediment, chemicals, fertilizers and toxic spills to pollute the oceans and to poison the sea's creatures.

Farming the sea and fish. Worldwatch estimates that a third of all fish species are in danger of extinction (Brown, 2000, p.9). The sea has been called one of the 'global commons', a sort of park area available for everyone, but we need to be more responsible about how the park is cared for.

Water. Since 1950, the world's water usage has tripled. Around the world watertables are getting lower, and even the great artesian basins which keep the inland of Australia alive are affected. Destroying the aquifers creates salty soil in which nothing will grow. Yet diesel pumps can be bought for about US$350, are available across the world, and enable millions of people to lift water out of rivers, lakes, and wells, without giving the water tables time to replenish.

Forests. About 42 % of the wood harvested in the world for industrial purposes (that is, all wood except firewood) goes into paper production (Abramovitz and Mattoon, 2000, pp. 105, 107). About two-fifths of rubbish collected in USA is paper, called now 'the urban forest'. The World Trade Organisation (WTO), set up in 1994 after the Uruguay Round of talks, produced an agreement which ran into an astonishing 26 000 pages of paper! Chris Bright (2000, p.24) writes of 'Earth's tattered cloak of natural forests'.

Local eco-systems. As the world economy expands, we now understand three principles about collapsing *local eco-systems*. (1) Nature is incredibly complex; the earth is an awesomely interlocking, interdependent living system. (2) 'Nature gives nothing away for free'; everything has its trade-offs and its penalties. And (3) 'Nature has no reset button'; you cannot put things back the way they were once you have tampered with them (Bright, 2000, p.37).

What must teachers and school leaders do?

'What we need,' Lovelock pleads in his most recent book, 'is a book of knowledge written so well as to constitute literature in its own right', a 'manual for living well and for survival', the quality of its writing such that 'it would serve for pleasure, for devotional reading, as a source of facts, and even as a primary school text.' We need, he says, some agency that does for the present century what the monasteries did for the Middle

Ages (Lovelock, 2006, pp.157-159). Could 21st century schools do the job?

Indeed, they may, because:

1. The educator profession is by nature future-oriented and almost incurably hopeful — from being daily with the rising generation and responsible for preparing them for their futures. When teachers hear new ideas or outlooks which will enhance their programs and help their students, they introduce those elements into their lessons immediately, like tomorrow!

2. Children do bring about change in the wider community, for no one is more effective at educating parents than children. Promulgating new and creative ideas about the world is a task which children do well!

Furthermore, detailed data is readily at hand for teachers to use. In *The Little Green Handbook* (2005) nuclear physicist Ron Neilsen gives a coolly mathematical, dispassionate assessment of where we sit on each of the major trend lines. A most useful resource book for teachers is James Martin's *The Meaning of the 21st Century* (2006). In this and earlier works (1981, 1995) he has been largely right in his predictions, and he gives illuminating details. Teachers could build a curriculum using his most recent book as their base.

Five positive suggestions

There are many implications here for schools, for patterns of schooling, for the world-wide teaching service, for learning technologies, for the shape and content of the curriculum, for what make up the most efficient learning modes. Since we began by speculating on the factors and content which need to be built into the education of the children now in school, somewhat idiosyncratically let me illustrate the kinds of ways we might respond to these new demands.

1. Make sure our students become truly global citizens

A section of the world's population is already both 'global' and 'borderless'. They are by and large drawn from among the affluent, they work in internationalized firms, are at ease in a globalised environment; they are multi-ethnic, multi-lingual, and behave as though the nation-state is of diminishing importance.

The international analyst who invented the term 'the borderless world' (Ohmae, 1990) has suggested that there now exists an 'invisible continent' (Ohmae, 2001). Without land, it is a huge economic presence, with awesome political clout; it has some binding laws; many internationals identify with its culture and feel as though they are its citizens; its governance structure is only half-formed but yet it is quite real, 'as palpable and vital, as tangible and solid, as if you could find it on a map' (Ohmae). It operates through technology.

The breeding grounds for the world's economic powerlifters are in this borderless world. Zachary (2000) discovered that the nation-states' influence is being supplanted by regional trade centres like Silicon Valley in California, and Singapore. Employed in these centres is 'a new breed of talented people' whom no one knows how to categorise and whose nationality is irrelevant. Because they are by nature rule breakers, defy ethnic purity, and challenge chauvinism, Zachary calls them 'global hybrids' and the process of their formulation 'mongrelisation' – indicating they are multicultural with a touch of the rebel about them. Nations that welcome the contributions of outsiders and natives with different values are prospering; while those who resist this trend are stagnating (Zachary, 2000, pp.57, 59). Welcoming nations deal in 'the economics of ideas', and they are at the heart of the so-called new economy, where 'open systems outmatch closed ones'. To succeed in this newly internationalised, borderless, post-national arena, one must 'mongrelise or die'. The most creative cities in the world are cosmopolitan, he points out, and there is not a 'brain drain' so much as a 'brain circulation' (Zachary, 2000: ch 3).

2. Reduce the gap between rich and poor

It is already a lopsided, unfair world in which 1.6 billion people live in absolute poverty; and only one billion can be confident of having three meals a day. In 1996 the richest fifth of the world's people were better off than the poorest fifth by a multiple of 30 (Brittain and Elliott, 1996, p.1). Developed countries contain only a fifth of the world's population, yet they consume about three quarters of the world's energy, three quarters of the world's metal production, and 85 % of the world's wood. What would happen if the entire world demanded what your family and mine takes for granted as its right?

The students in the 21st century school will live all of their lives with this problem. The 'basic human needs' for everyone on the planet, already enunciated, include: access to at least primary schooling; access to health care; clean drinking water; satisfactory sanitation; immunisation of all children; access to family planning services; universal adult literacy; elimination of severe malnutrition; and radical reductions of death in child-birth.

3. Develop a framework with which to respond to and decode the world community

The terrorist attack which demolished the World Trade Centre Towers in New York on 11 September 2001 brought home graphically that the world is deeply interconnected, that technology makes anyone vulnerable anywhere, that isolationism of any kind is deeply dangerous, that the divide between rich and poor in the world is offensive, that greed over the use of earth's resources is fundamentally unacceptable, and that religious fixities can be literally destructive (Brittain and Elliott, 1996).

According to Samuel Huntington (1997), there are five ways to regard the world community: (1) treat it as though we are a single human race sharing the same aspirations and holding to a set of universal values; (2) consider the world as two blocs – those who share our worldview and those who do not; (3) consider the world a disparate group of nation-states of varying sizes and kinds, all pursuing their own interests in a kind of international bazaar; (4) regard world affairs as 'sheer chaos' and on the path to planetary destruction.

Huntington's fifth mode (5), however, provides a useful framework for the curriculum of 21st century schools, especially for those whose charters are overtly religious or cultural. 'People define themselves', he says, 'in terms of ancestry, religion, history, values, customs and institutions' (Huntington, 1997, p.21). On the basis of these six dimensions, there are about eight major cultural groupings in the world, which he calls 'civilisations' - Chinese (or 'Sinic'), Japanese, Hindu, Islamic, Orthodox, Western European/American, Latin American, and African. Some have already modernised, and all the rest are trying to do so but without necessarily 'westernising'. 'In fundamental ways' he says, 'the world is becoming more modern and less Western' (ibid, p.78).

Each civilisation-group, Huntington observes, tends to have a dominant religion at its foundation. If a country's traditional religion cannot adapt to modernisation, it tends to open the way either for Western Christianity or for Islam. 'In the long run, however', he says, 'Mohammed wins out. Christianity spreads primarily by conversion, Islam by conversion and reproduction'. In years to come, Muslim populations will be escalating, disproportionately young, and skewed towards teenagers and people in their twenties, the years of protest and revolution. Each of these civilisations 'sees itself as the centre of the world and writes its history as the central drama of human history' (Huntington, 1997, pp. 117, 55).

4. Develop a genuine love of the earth community
The obscure Provencal hermit Giles (d.710 CE) lived a simplified life with the animals in the woods where he had his cell. Legend has it that a hind, pursued by hounds and horsemen, ran into a thicket for refuge. One of the hunters fired an arrow at random where the hind had disappeared. When the hunters burst through the undergrowth, they found St Giles nursing the frightened animal in his arms, with the arrow intended for the deer protruding from the saint's own back. Centuries of orthodoxy have taught us about substitutionary death, but should we not, like Giles, make our own sacrifices to bring wholeness — salvation, indeed — to the living creatures which share the same physical space that we do?

It is surely disingenuous to ask God to save us or our community from catastrophe when through our own consistently wilful actions we create the very conditions where destruction becomes inevitable.

5. Openly acknowledge the power of education
That education itself is genuinely powerful should give educators confidence. There is growing evidence that many members of Generation Y – those in secondary school and those in their twenties – are already making interventions, altruistically, selflessly and courageously, in ways never characteristic of the baby boomer generation. They have vigorously engaged with the Third World, with new frames of reference, and with the post-Einstein worldview. They are already showing a propensity to get up and do something creative and constructive about the state of the world.

Education opens the door for life chances. In launching the UN's 1998 *World Employment Report*, the ILO Director-General (*The Age*, 25/9/98: C3) emphasised that the Asian economic miracles of the 1990s were set alight through education. Put simply, in this century we may at last comprehend how deep and wide are the returns from investment in education, worldwide.

Our last point may therefore be the most startling. The single most

effective device for controlling the world's runaway birth rate – and averting population and other disasters – is to educate the world's women beyond age 14. James Martin (2006, pp.62-63) designates four stages relating to women's fertility rates:
1. When women learn to read, they have access to birthing information and their fertility declines.
2. A girl who is at school is less likely to be a chattel at home and available to conceive.
3. When women and girls are educated well enough to have a job, fertility drops further, for they gain independence and some power over their own destiny.
4. When women become ambitious and aspire to the more impressive jobs in society, the fertility rate falls to well below the replacement level.

An educated woman is able to take control of her own life, join the workforce on equal terms with the men, and remove herself from child-bearing if and when she wishes.

Conclusion

There is a strange but accurate natural conclusion to these facts. One of the most potent means of confronting the world's population explosion, of combating the life styles which feed environmental degradation, of building a powerful economy, and of bringing wholeness to the earth before it is too late is *universal education*. So we should be asking questions about the worldwide distribution of *educational* resources. Would that the trillions of dollars now being poured into warfare around the globe were diverted instead into the constructive provision of universal education!

References

Abramovitz, J.N. and Mattoon, A.T. (2000) Recovering the Paper Landscape. In Brown, Flavin and French (2000). pp.101-120.

Backman, M. (2000) Will Asia keep up with the 21st century pace? *Age* 22/1/2000: Business section. p.1.

Bita, N. (1991) Making woopie: the trend for business in the '90s. *Weekend Australian*. 23/3/91 p.3.

Bone, P. (1999) Hitting 6 000 000 000. *The Age* 12/10/99. Features, p.13.
Bright, C. (2000) Anticipating Environmental 'Surprise'. In Brown, Flavin and French (2000). pp.22-38.
Brittain, V., and Elliott, L. 1996) Gulf grows between rich and poor. *The Guardian Weekly* 155(3) 21/7/96.
Brown, L.R., Flavin, C. and French, H. (eds) (2000) *The State of the World 2000: A Worldwatch Institute Report on Progress Toward a Sustainable Society.* New York: W.W. Norton & Co.
(Brundtland Report) United Nations World Commission on Environment and Development: Chair, G.H. Brundtland. (1987) *Our Common Future.* Oxford: Oxford University Press.
Cairncross, F. (1998) *The Death of Distance: How the communications revolution will change our lives.* Cambridge, Mass.: Harvard Business School Press.
Chandler, J. (2007) Scientists in unison: we're ruining earth. *The Age* (Melbourne), 27/1/07, p.1.
Davis, M. (2006) *Planet of Slums.* London: Vers.
Dunn, S. and Flavin, C. (2000) 'Sizing up Micropower'. In Brown, Flavin and French (2000). pp.142-161.
Fannin, P. (2001) Why we will stop at 25 million people. *The Age* 2/8/01 p.1.
Huntington, S. (1997) *The Clash of Civilisations.* New York: Simon & Schuster.
Kluger, J. (2000) The big crunch. *Time*, Special edition for Earth Day 2000. April-May 2000. pp.44-49.
Laszlo, E. (2006) *The Chaos Point: The World at the Crossroads.* London: Piatkus Books.
Lovelock, J. (2006) *The Revenge of Gaia: Why the Earth is fighting back – and how we can still save humanity.* London: Allen Lane (Penguin Group).
Lovelock, J. (1988) *The Ages of Gaia: A biography of our living Earth.* Oxford: Oxford University Press.
Martin, J. (1981) *The Telematic Society: A Challenge for Tomorrow.* Upper Saddle River, NJ,: Prentice Hall.
Martin, J. (1995) *The Great Transition.* New York: AMACOM (American Management Association).
Martin, J. (2006) *The Meaning of the 21st Century.* New York: Riverhead (Penguin Group).
Meadows, D.H., Meadows, D.L., Randers, J., and Behrens, W.B III. (1972) *The Limits to Growth.* London: Pan Books.
Meadows, D., Randers, J., and Meadows, D.L. (2005) *Limits to Growth: The 30-year Update.* London: Earthscan.
Minchin, L (2007) 'Reef facing extinction'. *The Age* (Melbourne), 30/1/07, pp.1, 11.
Monbiot, G. (2006) *Heat: How to stop the planet burning.* London: Allen Lane.

Neilsen, R. (2005) *The Little Green Handbook: A guide to critical global trends.* Melbourne: Scribe Publications.

Ohmae, K. (2001) *The Invisible Continent.* London: HarperCollins.

Ohmae, K. (1990) *The Borderless World. Power and Strategy in the Interlinked Economy.* London: Collins.

Rees, M. (2003) *Our Final Century.* London: William Heinemann.

Rosenblatt, R. (2000) A letter to the Year 2100. *Time* 1/1/2000. pp.42-47.

Saltau, C. (1999) Six billion in a stifled world. *The Age.* 12/10/99. p.3.

Sayles, M. (1998) One nation, no future. *Age* 30/4/98. p.13.

Six billion and more. *Sunday Herald Sun* (Melbourne). 24/10/99. pp.48-49.

Swimme, B. (1996) *The Hidden Heart of the Cosmos.* Maryknoll, N.Y.: Orbis Books.

Worldwatch Institute (Director, Lester R. Brown) (2000) *The State of the World.* New York: W.W. Norton & Company.

Zachary, G.P. (2000) *The Global Me: Why nations will succeed or fail in the next generation.* St Leonards, NSW: Allen & Unwin.

PART THREE
Leading Catholic Schools into the Future

13
Restoring Venice:
A call to New Evangelisation

Dan White

In 2006 the Archdiocese of Hobart initiated an ongoing process of dialogue and critical reflection surrounding the evangelising mission of Catholic Schools in Tasmania. A Day of Discernment was conducted involving pastors, principals, representatives of various Governing Bodies and senior personnel from the Catholic Education Office. Flowing from the gathering, the Tasmanian Catholic Education Commission (TCEC) established a 'Call to New Evangelisation' working party to follow up on the many challenges that were raised. The brief of the working party was to recommend to the TCEC a range of policy options and strategies that could address, in a practical manner, the issues that had been identified.

The purpose of this chapter is to initially articulate a range of challenges discerned by the Day of Discernment associated with the evangelising mission of the Church within the context of the Archdiocese of Hobart. Secondly, it will reflect upon the necessity and capacity of Catholic schools to respond to a growing awareness that we have moved into a phase of 'new evangelisation' within many Catholic communities across Australia. Finally, the chapter will explore, in a practical manner, some of the emerging policy initiatives and strategies being formulated in response to the challenges associated with the identity and mission of Catholic schools.

A modern parable

Visitors to the medieval city of Venice would be aware of the continuous struggle of Venetians to save and restore their culturally rich and beautiful city. The city has continually sought to maintain a delicate ecological balance between the needs and aspirations of its inhabitants and the natural environment that surrounds it. The gracious waterways and canals are both aesthetically pleasing and the potential source of its destruction. The removal of artesian water and the decaying foundations have made the city increasingly vulnerable to high tides and rising sea levels. In essence, Venice is slowly but surely sinking into the mud.

During the original construction of Venice the wooden foundations for the buildings were driven through many layers of silt and set firmly on the underlying bedrock. The portions of timber that were inserted into the soft mud have, over time, become petrified and are now inextricably linked to the bedrock upon which they rest. However the sections of the timber underpinnings directly connected to the houses that sit in and above the waterline are progressively deteriorating and rotting from within. Gradually, but unmistakeably, the upper strata of the foundations are sagging under the weight of the impressive structures they support.

The civic leaders of Venice are fighting a constant battle to maintain its viability and beauty for future generations. The solution lies not in attempting to demolish every unstable edifice or by replacing the entire foundations for every building that is slipping below the waterline. Rather, the leaders have focused primarily upon restoring the substrata scaffolding that lies in the 'gap' between the mud of the channel floor and surface level of the buildings. The restoration is a complex and delicate process whereby the original building is 'jacked up' and the foundations critically examined. As necessary a new network of supporting crossbeams and secondary posts are installed through the subterranean level of the building and only on the rare occasion is it a necessity to 'drive' a totally new foundational pillar through the silt to the bedrock. Lowering and reattaching the restored infrastructure to the original 'petrified' pillars ensures that a 'solid connection' is once again restored to the underlying bedrock.

In many respects the 'Venetian parable' is a metaphor for what is occurring in Catholic Education in Tasmania. Like the entire system of Catholic Education in Australia, the 37 Tasmanian Catholic schools have been seen as 'one of the jewels in the crown' of parish pastoral ministry for over 160 years. In 2008, the school system is a vibrant, growing reality serving the needs of over 15 000 students which has grown by over 10% over the past five years. On the surface, Catholic schools are highly valued learning communities with rich charisms and a deep commitment to nurturing the Catholic ethos.

The Day of Discernment process provided an opportunity for the institution of Catholic education to be gently lifted from its foundations and a critical examination undertaken of the underlying pillars and beams. As with Venice, the exercise was not a response to a 'deficit model', whereby Catholic schools were being perceived as failing institutions that should be dismantled and consigned to history. Equally, there was great confidence in the depth of their 'petrified' foundations and the ensuing connection with the 'bedrock' of faith in Christ within the Catholic tradition.

A central premise of the Call to New Evangelisation process is for schools in Tasmania to continue to be vibrant Catholic learning communities aware of and connected to their spiritual bedrock. The process of restoration will focus on identifying and preserving what is really worth keeping, reinforcing existing structures and, in some places, building new supporting crossbeams in response to a changed secular and pastoral environment. As noted by the Secretary for the Congregation of Catholic Education, Archbishop Miller,

> The Holy See… recognises the priceless treasure of Catholic schools as an indispensable instrument of evangelisation. Ensuring their genuinely Catholic identity is the Church's greatest educational challenge. (Congregation for Catholic Education, 2007, p.61)

Connecting with the bedrock: What does it mean to be Catholic?

Whilst appreciating that the majority of the restorative work would be focused 'just below the surface', as the Call to New Evangelisation process unfolded in a variety of consultative sessions it became apparent that all stakeholders were vitally interested in touching base with the very essence of their Catholic tradition. At the heart of many discussions (e.g. enrolment policies, spiritual formation programs…) was the fundamental question: *What does it mean to be Catholic?*

In response, a theological reflection paper[1] has been developed by the archdiocese with a view to stimulating prayerful discussion and rearticulating for the next generation of educators and stakeholders what it may mean to be Catholic in an increasingly pluralist, secular and

---

[1] The theological reflections developed by Mrs Helen Healy (Head of Mission & RE) and Dr Drasko Dizdar ('Theologian in Residence') are particularly acknowledged and have been incorporated within this chapter.

consumerist society. In particular, it is envisaged the theological reflection will become a seminal document that will inform a range of formation programs for staff employed in Catholic schools.

The reflection paper resonates with two main beliefs. Firstly, an emphasis on the nature of Catholicity being grounded in a broad theological context which incorporates and synthesises a diversity of sources and does not simplistically rely on a uni-dimensional theological perspective. In particular recognition is given to Revelation and the lived experience of faith, hope and love; scripture; tradition; the magisterium; scholarship and reason; and prayer and spirituality. Secondly, the nature of Catholicity is held together by the essential 'marks of the Church', especially as articulated in the Nicene Creed: one, holy, catholic and apostolic. The reflection highlights connectedness with the 'Body of Christ' and the organic interaction of being 'called' and 'sent' particularly within the uniquely sacramental dimension of the Catholic experience. As noted in *The Catechism of the Catholic Church*,

> The word 'catholic' means universal, in the sense of 'according to the totality' or 'in keeping with the whole'. The Church is catholic in a double sense: First, the Church is catholic because Christ is present in her. 'Where there is Christ Jesus, there is the Catholic Church.' (St. Ignatius of Antioch, Ad Smyrn. 8,2). Secondly, the Church is catholic because she has been sent out by Christ on a mission to the whole of the human race. (Libreria Editrice Vaticana1997, #830 & #831)

Testing the 'petrified pillars': A shift in focus — evangelisation, catechesis or New Evangelisation?

Over recent years there has been a growing awareness in the Australian Church of a need to reconnect with a growing number of Catholic families who, for a variety of reasons, have become disconnected from the active life of their parish community. Pope John Paul II in his encyclical *Redemptoris Missio* (#33) recognised that people need to be invited and socialised into situations of vibrant faith. Three challenges for the Church of today were identified: firstly, the importance of the primary proclamation of the Gospel and the establishment of new communities of faith; secondly, the pastoral care of those communities where faith is healthy, mature and fervent; and thirdly, to attend to those Christians who have lost a sense of faith or whose faith has never had the opportunity for faith formation. John Paul II therefore identified a new challenge for the Church particularly in western, secular society: the call for a *Re-evangelisation* or a *New Evangelisation*.

The Day of Discernment process was unambiguous in recognising that many of the philosophical pillars upon which the system of Catholic schools has been built have served the test of time. The deeply grounded principles of faith transmission, equity and social justice, Catholic spirituality, worship and ritual, inclusiveness and welcome, pastoral care and stewardship are as relevant and significant for today's generation of schools as they have been for the past 160 years. Notwithstanding the confidence in these enduring structures and foundations, a critical issue being faced by Tasmanian Catholic schools is a growing awareness that one of the corner stones of their mission has shifted markedly in recent years.

When the Sisters of Charity first accepted an invitation from Bishop Willson to serve the Tasmanian community their ministry with the women of the 'Female Factory' was one of evangelisation through service and love. Their work gave flesh to the mission of the Church, 'to enable all people to experience the abundant goodness, justice and peace of an infinitely loving God by knowing the person of Christ' (John Paul II, 2001a,#1). Inspired by the charisms of many religious communities Tasmanian Catholic schools have continued to embrace the inherent nature of the evangelising mission of the Church. In the words of Pope Paul VI,

> For the Church, evangelisation means bringing the Good News into all strata of humanity, and, through its influence, transforming humanity from within and making it new… The purpose of evangelisation is therefore precisely this interior change… the Church evangelises when she seeks to convert, solely through the divine power of the Message she proclaims, both the personal and the collective consciences of people, the activities in which they engage, and the lives and concrete milieux which are theirs (Pope Paul VI, 1976, #).

As the system of Catholic schools flourished across the state in the service of a clearly identified community of Catholic families, the evangelising mission shifted in focus from the early stages of 'primary proclamation' to 'initiatory' and 'ongoing' catechesis to a relatively homogeneous Catholic community whereby the truth of Christian faith was proclaimed in a context 'that called forth a faith response upon the part of the hearer' (Holohan, 1999).

The pastoral climate within which Catholic schools operate has shifted significantly over the last generation. The assumption of a comparatively homogeneous Catholic student population, which allowed for a catechetical focus both in terms of religious education and pastoral formation, can no longer be sustained. Consequently, Catholic schools in Tasmania at this time are being called to operate as agents of evangelisation at four distinct levels:

- Primary proclamation (especially to the 44% of non-Catholic enrolments)
- Initiatory catechesis (particularly in response to the lack of home-based formation prior to children entering school)
- On-going catechesis (to the much smaller group of approximately 10% of students, directly involved within their parish community, who need explicit support in their growing faith awareness); and
- New Evangelisation (reaching out to the 90% of Catholic families who are not directly connected to their parish Eucharistic community).

This shift in the nature and spiritual needs of the families enrolled in Catholic education evokes a challenge to reconceptualise one of the central paradigms of ministry upon which Catholic schools have been premised. Whilst affirming the integral nature of evangelisation and catechesis, it is appropriate for schools to begin exploring and constructing a third philosophical 'pillar' in the form of a commitment to the process of New Evangelisation.

Distinct from primary evangelisation and catechesis is the call for a renewal and enlivening of faith. New Evangelisation is for all who have lost or those who have never developed a living sense of faith. New Evangelisation is a response to those who are hungering for Christ within a context and a time when the message of the Gospel is only one voice within our modern culture of secularisation and materialism. From the perspective of a Catholic school, New Evangelisation recognises that many baptised children, in fact the majority of students, are drawn from families who have become disconnected from the practice of their faith.

Examining the subterranean scaffolding: key issues of concern

The Day of Discernment and subsequent deliberations have shed critical light on a number of the crossbeams that underpin the nature and culture of Catholic schools in Tasmania. Some issues, such as enrolment trends, were readily visible and objectively measurable, whilst others were far more subtle and difficult to define. Initially, there was a tendency to focus on what was easily observable (above the waterline), such as the proportion of non-Catholic students within each school or the religious education qualifications of staff. However, as the process has unfolded all stakeholders have begun to probe deeper and test the strength and resilience of the structures that lie further below the surface. Amongst a myriad of issues the following four questions were specifically identified:

- What are some of the specific hallmarks of a Catholic school that should always be proclaimed and celebrated?
- What is the nature and balance of the enrolment profile of Catholic schools?
- How can Catholic schools more proactively reach out to all Catholic families who have lost contact with their faith community, with a particular emphasis on those who are marginalised and disadvantaged? (The challenge of New Evangelisation.)
- What formation strategies will help ensure staff employed in Catholic schools continue to have a deep understanding and commitment to their changing ministry?

Restoring the scaffolding and crossbeams: a practical response to the call to New Evangelisation

Developing a Charter and mandate for Catholic education

All Catholic schools have developed appropriate vision and mission statements that unambiguously place the evangelising mission of the Church at their central core. It was felt that now it was timely for the archbishop to develop a Charter for Catholic education that clearly articulated his vision for, and expectations of, Catholic schools. The Charter articulates eleven key 'foundational' principles that, amongst a range of issues highlight: the relationship with the parish community; the centrality of teaching a 'Catholic' curriculum; the recruitment and formation of staff; the review of enrolment policies; and the role of schools in responding to Catholic social teaching.

What is significant about the Charter is that it moves beyond broad philosophical statements and, for the first time in the Tasmanian context, spells out the specific expectations of the Archbishop with regard to the conduct of a Catholic school. For example, the expectations associated with the Charter place much greater emphasis on selecting teachers on the basis of commitment to the Catholic tradition and involvement in ongoing formation linked to a revised accreditation policy. Similarly the imperative of working towards a system-wide target of enrolling at least 75% of the student cohort from Catholic families is especially highlighted.

In terms of Religious Education, schools will be challenged to introduce a triangulated model of assessment that replicates assessment processes being proposed in other Key Learning Areas. In essence, the archdiocese is planning to adopt a model of moderated assessment against explicit standards that involves internal and external moderation in association with standardised Religious Literacy tests at Grades 4 and 8.

Schools will also be 'challenged' to reflect upon the signs and symbols that will distinguish them as uniquely Catholic. For example with the growth in Tasmania of a number of independent and Christian schools, local school communities will be asked as to whether the inclusion of the term Catholic (eg. St Aloysius *Catholic* College) should be explicitly included in their nomenclature and promotional material.

Following the promulgation of the Archbishop's Charter, as part of the newly introduced School Improvement process, each Catholic school in Tasmania will be requested to develop a detailed response to the Charter. Over the next two years leadership teams will be afforded a two-day formation opportunity to 'unpack' the Charter and explore strategies for formulating a response to the Archbishop's 'expectations' in association with their local communities. It is anticipated the Archbishop will contribute in a major way to the input during the formation program.

Of special significance, each Catholic school in Tasmania will be expected to submit a detailed response to the Charter in order to obtain, from the Archbishop, a mandate under Canon Law[2] to function as a Catholic institute. The external validating component of the cyclic School

---

[2] Canon 806 : 'The diocesan Bishop has the right to watch over and inspect Catholic schools in his territory, even those established or directed by members of religious institutes. He also has the right to issue directives concerning the general regulation of Catholic schools; those directives apply also to schools conducted by members of a religious institute, although they retain their autonomy in the internal management of their schools.'

Improvement process, once every six years, will be utilised to ensure that, over time, the Archbishop's mandate is progressively affirmed and refined in each school community.

Discerning an appropriate enrolment profile

In 2007, 56% of enrolments in Tasmanian Catholic schools came from Catholic families, the lowest proportion of any state or territory in Australia. Concurrently census data indicated that approximately 50% of Catholic children are being educated in State (lower income families) or independent (higher income families) schools.

Reflecting upon this data at the Day of Discernment brought forth a number of key issues. First and foremost debate centred on the intrinsic purpose of Catholic schools. From one perspective the evangelising mission of the Church reaching out into the wider Tasmanian community was counter-balanced by the theological imperative of supporting the catechetical formation of baptised Catholic children. At a more subtle level concern was expressed as to whether the absence of a 'critical mass' of Catholic children could potentially undermine the mission and potency of a Catholic school, especially in a secondary college context. Furthermore it was suggested that some families, whilst accepting enrolment in a Catholic school, might not fully appreciate its core purpose and potentially not encourage their children to participate fully in the spiritual life of the school community. Finally, anecdotal evidence was presented that, within the context of some Catholic schools, committed Catholic students felt the burden of peer pressure and were disinclined to admit to the witness and practice of their faith.

Addressing the issue of finding the appropriate enrolment mix between Catholic and non-Catholic students has sparked a rich and vibrant debate both within the Catholic education sector and the wider secular community. In terms of a policy response, the TCEC has adopted a measured and realistic approach. The major philosophical foundation of a revised enrolment policy is premised on the notion of actively encouraging and inviting a greater number of baptised Catholic families to consider enrolling in Catholic education.

Overall the Catholic sector in Tasmania has committed itself to working towards a target of 75% Catholic student enrolment across the entire system of schools. Firstly, local communities are to discern an appropriate *Catholic enrolment target* for each individual school taking into account current demographics, economic viability and enrolment demands. Secondly, in high demand enrolment areas, schools will be encouraged to reserve enrolment places for Catholic families who transfer into the area after the traditional enrolment periods. Finally in 2008, the TCEC will introduce a pilot program specifically aimed at reaching out to Catholic families who may not be regularly attending Mass in the parish. Simply stated, the initiative involves the parish priest sending a *baptismal anniversary* card to each child who has been baptised in the parish over the past five years and including in the card a small symbolic gift, information about the parish and invitations to key liturgical and sacramental events.

Reaching out to marginalised and disadvantaged families

In economic terms Tasmania is the most socially disadvantaged state or territory in Australia. Over two thirds of Catholic primary schools fall into the bottom quintile (20%) of the national socio-economic index. Whilst not subject to extreme poverty, average family incomes are relatively low and unemployment levels are significantly higher than the national average. The *Day of Discernment* questioned whether Catholic schools in the 21st Century are now more actively catering for 'aspirational' middle class families in contrast to authentically reaching out to marginalised or financially disadvantaged family units?

The assembly concluded that the Catholic system in Tasmania needed to revisit its founding purpose and renew its efforts to reach out more tangibly to families who live on the margins of society. Grappling with this complex question is one of the most vexed and difficult areas currently confronting the TCEC. At the time of writing, a response to this issue is very much work in progress. To date, two key strategic ideas have been piloted.

In partnership with the archdiocese, an Archdiocesan Catholic Education Foundation has been established. Supported by bequests and some systemic funding, the Foundation will financially support low-income Catholic families in accessing Catholic schools, especially at the Kindergarten entry level. Managed by archdiocesan trustees the Foundation proposes to provide establishment grants of approximately $400 to disadvantaged families to assist with the costs of starting school. Tasmanian research conducted by Anglicare identified the burden of the on-costs (uniforms, bags, books, excursion levies...) was a major concern for low-income parents. It is also proposed that the Foundation will pay a grant of up to 80% of the annual school fees for the first three years of a child's enrolment; after that point it is hoped the normal, pastorally-oriented school based fee relief protocols would be activated.

Following a detailed study into the needs of refugee families in Tasmania a range of educational and pastoral initiatives to help further support humanitarian entrants have been developed. Apart from financial assistance (via the Archdiocesan Foundation), recommendations have been acted upon that will see the establishment of an intensive language centre potentially operating on a summer and winter school model, improved trauma counselling services, cultural awareness professional development and the employment of a community liaison officer.

Enhancing the spiritual formation and commitment of staff

Of paramount concern to the assembled community at the Day of Discernment was an appreciation that the strength and maintenance of a vibrant Catholic culture and ethos in school communities were directly proportional to the quality of formation and commitment of the staff. A constant theme that emerged from the discernment process was a call to develop strategies that promoted a deep understanding of and an enduring commitment to the ongoing ministry of the Church in Tasmania. At every level from staff recruitment, to induction, to ongoing professional learning and spiritual formation and ultimately staff appraisal, questions were posed as to whether more could be done to ensure every staff member was adequately equipped to fulfil the mandate conferred on them by the Archbishop.

For a variety of reasons which include the historical (the lack of access to a campus of a Catholic university), cultural (the primacy of the Department of Education as an 'employer of choice') and matters of resource (declining enrolments in the 1990's severely limited the capacity to initiate formational programs), Catholic schools in Tasmania have not been able to offer a coherent, integrated program of staff induction and ongoing spiritual formation. It was noted that a significant percentage (37%) of teachers were teaching Religious Education (RE) without the appropriate levels of archdiocesan accreditation. Additionally, the staff employment profile indicated 40% of teachers were affiliated with other Christian faith traditions and, in a number of cases, were being called upon to teach Religious Education. Whilst acknowledging the absolute sincerity and dedication of these teachers in supporting the Catholic ethos, uncertainty was expressed as to whether teachers from another faith tradition could effectively move beyond the instructional mode in Religious Education and, with authenticity, engage students in catechetically-oriented formational and transformational experiences within the Catholic tradition.

In response, the Catholic Education Office has named spiritual formation as one of its major strategic and budgetary priorities for the next quadrennium and beyond. In this respect a detailed, integrated plan has been developed that will see funding for formation initiatives increase five fold over the next four years. Key aspects to the plan will see an expansion of personnel in the Mission and Religious Education team so as to place even greater emphasis on adult spirituality. Key aspects of the emerging archdiocesan plan include:

- The appointment of a *theologian in residence*
- The introduction of two day *retreats* based on Parker Palmer's Courage to Teach program
- The introduction of a four-day *spirituality of teaching* retreat program, broken into two, 2-day experiences for prospective beginning teachers
- The provision of *spirituality grants* of approximately $2 000 annually to each systemic school
- Creating the opportunity for teachers to become involved in an *immersion program* and attend the Tantur spirituality program in Jerusalem each year
- Revising the current Accreditation program to introduce provisional accreditation for newly appointed RE teachers and leaders.
- The appointment of jointly funded and shared *School/Parish Pastoral Associates*.

Beyond 2008: Other Strategic Priorities

The Catholic Education system in Tasmania recognises that the Call to New Evangelisation project is simply work 'in-progress'. Many other supporting beams need to be developed in order to strengthen and reaffirm the Catholic identity of the school communities. At the time of writing a variety of further issues are under consideration. Major initiatives include: investigating parish based child-care provision in disadvantaged areas; strengthening formation programs for school boards particularly with respect to Catholic ethos; developing a Charter for Parents which focuses on the tripartite relationship between parish, school and families;

and supporting action research projects in direct response to the New Evangelisation agenda.

Conclusion

Restoring the city of Venice is a never-ending story; the advances in technology and human ingenuity are being constantly pitted against the eroding influence of climate change and human indifference. Similarly Catholic schools in Tasmania need to be totally committed to an ongoing process of *School Improvement* that has at its centre the constant strengthening and revitalisation of the pillars and structures that underpin a vibrant Catholic ethos. The challenge of New Evangelisation requires a heightened awareness on the part of Catholic schools that they now minister within a very different and rapidly changing social milieu. If the beauty and richness of Catholic Education is to be sustained it is simply not sufficient to 'paint over the cracks'. Rather schools and system authorities need to periodically 'lift up the building', strengthen the enduring foundations and insert innovative scaffolding that is responsive to the mission of evangelisation in a contemporary world.

References

Canon Law Society of Great Britain and Ireland. (1983) *The Code of Canon Law in English Translation.* Sydney, NSW: Collins Liturgical Publications.
Libreria Editrice Vaticana. (1997) *Catechism of the Catholic Church* (2nded.). Homebush, NSW: St Paul's Publications.
Congregation for Catholic Education (2007) *The Holy See's Teaching on Catholic Schools*. (Australian Edition). Strathfield, NSW: St Paul's Publications.
Holohan, G.J. (1999) *Australian Religious Education – Facing the Challenges*, Canberra, ACT: National Catholic Education Commission.
John Paul II (2001a) *Novo millennio ineunte.* Strathfield, NSW: St Paul's Publications.
John Paul II (1991) *Redemptor missio.* Homebush, NSW: St Paul's Publications.
Paul VI (1976) *Evangelii Nuntiandi.* Homebush, NSW: St Paul's Publications.

14
Taking the Next Step:
Catholic schools and the cry of the poor

Anne Benjamin

Hope strives to create conditions [which are] favourable to [those] who are most loved by God, - the poorest and the weakest (Kerstiens, 1975, p 655).

Catholic schools have always been charged with a special mandate to offer hope to those who are disadvantaged, and this 'special attention for those who are weakest' (Congregation for Catholic Education, 1997, #15) is a cherished part of the Australian Catholic school story. Of the various significant issues which it is timely for Catholic school leaders to explore at this time in history, this chapter focuses on the mission of Catholic schools to those who are neediest.

This issue has long continued to be the subject of serious concern within the Australian Church (see, for example, Johnston & Chesterton, 1994; Chesterton and Johnston, 1998; Catholic Education Commission Victoria, (2004a & 2004b). In 1972, Monsignor James Bourke, as Director of the Federal Catholic Education Office, spoke of the 'troubling question' of the degree to which, in a time of rising costs, 'the choice of a Catholic school can be kept open for the less well off' (Gill, 1972, p 6). In 2007, the NSW Catholic Bishops noted as one of their concerns relating to enrolments in Catholic schools that '...poorer Catholic children are increasingly attending State schools, while wealthier Catholic children go to non-Catholic non-government schools' (Bishops of NSW and ACT, 2007, p 8).

This chapter responds to this continuing concern and proposes that the high level of public credibility presently enjoyed by Catholic schools in Australia offers an ideal opportunity for school leaders to revisit the issues of access and take Catholic schools into a new chapter of their history in which they more comprehensively serve children, especially those who are poor and disadvantaged. The chapter commences with an overview of the contemporary status of Catholic schools in Australia and then explores the challenge of the Church's mission to the neediest as well as some of the conditions which might facilitate access to Catholic schools by those who are needy.[1]

Contemporary Catholic schools in Australia

A few indicators of the strength and influence of Catholic schools in contemporary Australia are noted below.

Enrolments

In the first place, Catholic schools are well supported by enrolments. There is a complex set of issues associated with enrolment trends in Catholic schools.

In 2007, there were 690 621 students in Australian Catholic schools, an increase of 5351 from 2006, and an increase of more than 115 000, students since 1985 (National Catholic Education Commission (NCEC), 2008). Yet, as Monsignor Bourke in 1972 noted, increased enrolments still met a decline in the *proportion* of Australian children attending Catholic schools. Bourke indicated that in 1965, there were 477 000 children enrolled in Australian Catholic schools, representing a little under 20% of the Aussie school-going population. In 1970, there were nearly 494 000 children enrolled in Catholic schools, representing only less than 18% of the Australian school-going population. So numbers had increased, but the Catholic 'share' (as they say) of the total school enrolments in Australia had declined. Similarly contemporary Catholic school leaders are questioning changing patterns in Catholic school enrolments. (Bourke, in Gill, 1972). Of the total student population in 2006, 25% (170 551) were students who were non-Catholic and some of the increase in enrolments since 1985 comes from this group of students. A retention rate of 117.7% for students from Catholic primary to Catholic secondary schools nationally indicates that students from other schools are enrolling in Catholic secondary schools.

---

[1] In preparing this paper, I have been assisted with advice from Crichton Smith, NSW Catholic Education Commission, and colleagues at ACU National.

Staff

The total number of staff serving Australian Catholic schools in 2007 was 76 194, with 52 925 being teachers. The professional calibre of the teaching staff is an inestimable resource. Although Catholic schools in the past have experienced challenges in attracting qualified staff, current teachers are universally tertiary-qualified. Present regulations for teacher registration implemented across Australian states in the past five or six years prescribe a certain level of qualification. However, prior to this there had already been a well-established commitment to ongoing professional development amongst Catholic school teachers, generously supported by diocesan education offices and congregations. The partnership between Catholic school systems and higher education providers, especially Australian Catholic University, has been a most productive one in terms of creating highly-professional teachers and educational leaders. A positive outcome of this commitment to ongoing learning has been the emergence in recent years of a sharper focus by Catholic schools upon the quality of their learning and teaching outcomes for students.

Pastoral care

Another character of contemporary Catholic schools is the quality of their community life and the culture of pastoral care for students, staff and families. This commitment to pastoral care has sometimes been criticised for being valued by staff more highly than their teaching outcomes. Some observers would see the quality of school community life being more easily observable in primary schools than in their secondary counterparts. Despite these reservations, it is undeniable that Catholic schools offer great hospitality and care to their members.

Because of their size and the culture in which they are immersed, by and large, Catholic school systems (both diocesan and congregational) have a capacity for devolvement, creativity and flexibility. This, together with a healthy sense of community, facilitates the maintenance of positive morale amongst staff and a willingness to take initiatives.

Systems

A fourth strength of Australian Catholic schools is the quality and competence of the systems and organisational structures supporting them. Sophisticated systems effectively support the work of teachers in governance, planning, human resources, finance, and especially, curriculum, special education and professional development (cf Benjamin 2007). In the larger domain, Catholic educators contribute to policy development at both state and federal levels and their advice is well-regarded.

A Catholic spirit

Finally, it is my experience that Australian Catholic school leaders and staff are seriously committed to honouring their mission as *Catholic* schools, and do so diligently. This is evidenced in the practices, communications, prayer, curriculum and culture of schools. In 2003, I had the opportunity to meet with Archbishop Guiseppe Pittau, SJ – then Secretary for the Congregation for Catholic Education in the Vatican. He applauded the work of Australian Catholic schools along these lines:

> I am very, very impressed with the way which in a very short period of time the transition from religious to lay leadership and staffing has occurred in Australia. There has been a strong commitment to professional development which has made this possible. It is amazing! The Catholic spirit in your schools is very strong. Take care of it. Catholic schools must be excellent schools. I have great admiration for Australian Catholic education. It is a jewel. I congratulate you most warmly and thank you so much for all you are doing for Catholic education in Australia (Personal notes, 2003).

The present systems of Catholic schools in Australia owe much to the determined commitment of the bishops of the late 19th century to provide a religious education for Catholic families in the colony. They persisted with their hope in a climate which was hostile to Catholicism, resisting the bitterness which sought to separate education and religion. The bishops' vision was brought to life by the women and men of religious congregations who responded courageously to the invitation to teach the faith in this rough land and to give opportunity to young Catholics to rise beyond the poverty in which many of them lived. By the 1950s and 1960s, inadequate Catholic classrooms were bulging with locally-born and new post-war immigrant children. This growth necessitated strategies to provide sufficient teachers and for funding to provide more appropriate facilities. In 2008, teachers in Catholic schools enjoy working conditions which are comparable to their colleagues in government schools.

This overview is deliberately global, and at the local level, there are, of course, many nuances. Catholic schools and their people have the same shortcomings as others: for example, a principal who avoids parents, is rude or even harsh, who is ensconced in a corporate-style office, who does not visit parishes; or a teacher who neglects professional development, who fails to challenge students, who undermines Catholic ethos; or a parish priest who avoids the school, or neglects his own learning; or the governing bodies which fail to recognise the faith journey of young teachers or which allow some children to go unnoticed through school towards mediocre under-achievement. These are there, of course, but in my experience of over 40 years with Catholic schools, they are the exception. My over-riding knowledge is of generous, committed professionals, many with a strong sense of religious vocation in their teaching, who work hard to bring the hope promised by Catholic schooling to reality in the lives of young people.

Contemporary Catholic schools and the poor

Previous studies relating to access to Catholic schools have drawn their data from the *perceptions* of school and community personnel about the groups of children who were excluded or under-represented in Catholic schools (eg, Chesterton & Johnston, 1998; Johnston & Chesterton, 1994). The 1994 report commented on the lack of a 'generally acceptable measure or set of procedures' by which the poor could be identified (ibid, p 68). Subsequently, the NCEC established a mechanism to obtain and analyse national census data using descriptors of income level from the census. Statistics relating to the SES status of students' families are now available and the ongoing analysis of trends relating to enrolments is timely and valuable. It is also challenging.

Trends

Some selected emergent trends (based on the 2006 Australian Government census figures and reported by the NCEC) follow:[2]
- More than half of students from Catholic families do not attend a Catholic school. 49% of Catholic families attend a government school and 8% attend a non-Catholic non-government school.

[2] These figures have been drawn from a series of Reports prepared by the Australian Catholic Education Statistics Working Group of the National Catholic Education Commission and available on the NCEC website, http://www.ncec.catholic.edu.au.

- Low income Catholic families are twice as likely to be enrolled at a government school rather than a Catholic school (63%:32%).
- Increasingly, Catholic families are choosing to send their children to non-government schools which are not Catholic, rather than to a Catholic or government school. This is especially so for higher income Catholic families, as 17% of high income Catholic families have students in these Other non-government schools.
- This trend is even more apparent for secondary students, with more than one in every five students (21%) from higher income Catholic families (up from 13% at the 1996 Census and 17% at the 2001 Census).
- Recent growth in Catholic school enrolments have come from students whose families do not identify as Catholic.
- The majority of students from low income families in Catholic schools are Catholic, but when the incomes of Catholic and non-Catholics families in Catholic schools are compared, the proportion of low income non-Catholic students is larger (20% of non-Catholic students) than the proportion of low income Catholic students (11%). For students from high income families, the trend is the opposite, as only 14% of the non-Catholic students are from higher income families, while 21% of the Catholic students in Catholic schools are from higher income families.
- The number of Aboriginal and Torres Strait Islander students in Catholic schools has grown from 5423 in 1985 (0.9% of total Catholic school enrolments) to 12 945 in 2007 (or 1.9% of Catholic school enrolments). However, Catholic schools still enrol less than half of the expected Catholic sector student share of Indigenous students. In other words, Catholic schools enrol 20% of Australia's students, but only 10% of Australia's Indigenous students. Furthermore, only one quarter (25%) of Indigenous students who are Catholic attend a Catholic school.
- Catholic schools have significantly increased their enrolment of Students with a Disability (SWD) (From 1392 in 1985 to 21 599 in 2007). They presently enrol 14% of the total *funded* students with disabilities in Australian schools. In 2006, 2.9% of students in Catholic schools were funded SWD students – lower than the 5.2% of students in Government schools, but higher than the

1.8% of students in other non-government schools.[3] (Productivity Commission, 2008, Table 4A.21)
- At the same time, the number and proportion of Indigenous and SWD students in Catholic schools have been increasing in recent decades, and the increase of 733 Indigenous students in Australian Catholic schools from 2006 to 2007 was the largest increase since 1985, while the increase of 1756 SWD students was the largest increase since 1991. These two groups combined represent almost half of the growth (47%) in enrolments in Catholic schools in the past year.

The challenge to mission

Many questions are suggested by these figures. Are Catholic schools being challenged in their mission by their own success? Diocesan Catholic schools maintain the principle of 'being comprehensive', yet, the figures given above threaten that comprehensiveness, with both 'ends' – high income and low income families – moving away. The early Australian Catholic schools which set out to give opportunity to the children of poor Catholics in the colony appear to have succeeded: higher-income Catholic families aspire for more expensive schooling, while significant numbers of those for whom Catholic schools have a special mandate – students from low income families, students with disabilities, Indigenous students – are not attending Catholic schools.

Do the families of these children freely *choose* not to attend a Catholic school? Or are there factors which create barriers so that Catholic schools cease to be a feasible option for them? To the extent that families of needier students do feel excluded, then Catholic schools are failing in their mission. Secondly, to the extent that the poorest and wealthiest families are sending their children elsewhere, Catholic school education becomes impoverished and risks providing neither a truly 'comprehensive' education nor a truly 'ecclesial' experience.

Poverty and educational disadvantage

Poverty rarely appears as a single disadvantage. Low income has been associated with:

[3] This paper uses the Productivity Commission figures as one way to address definitional issues associated with identifying the SWD population.

higher impacts in the areas of family break up, violence, crime, incarceration of family member, presence of troublesome outsiders and higher parental involvement in student disputes...offending, truancy, racism, bullying of others, violence, defiant or negative classroom behaviour, running away, lack of pathways for less academic students and rudeness to staff (Catholic Education Commission of Victoria, 2004a & 2004b).

Furthermore, 'in most OECD countries, children from poorer homes are between three and four times more likely to be in the lowest scoring group in mathematics at age 15' (OECD, 2007, p 13). The odds for 15-year-old Australian students from poorer backgrounds to be in the lowest scoring mathematics groups are 3:1. (OECD) Aboriginal students as a group achieve lower scores than non-Aboriginal children on public tests. Poverty carries not just the disadvantage of uncertain income, but complex multi-headed impacts on educational outcomes, and hence on subsequent employment and earning opportunity, so that the cycle reproduces itself into the next generations.

Reconsidering the Church's mandate to schools

Catholic schools are premised on the fundamental dignity of each individual person. Part of the challenge posed by Jesus to the Jewish establishment was that he associated with the marginalised. Traditional enrolment policies governing Catholic schools give priority of enrolment to children of families who are active in a parish. However, given the Church's mandate to Catholic schools to have a special place for those who are most vulnerable, surely it is timely to reconsider how students are accepted into Catholic schools and which students are excluded.

Removing any barriers which exclude those who are poor is one step. Reaching out to invite those who are poor requires that we go further. The Congregation for Catholic Education (1997) refers to 'new forms of poverty' which leaves families with no sense of meaning in life; without values and without faith; broken and dysfunctional; slaves to a poverty which promises a future only of unemployment and marginalisation (ibid, #15). It is for the children of these new poor, 'especially the poor and marginalised', that Catholic schools are mandated by the Church to offer 'in a spirit of love', the *opportunity of an education, of training for a job, of human and Christian formation* (ibid).

For the marginalised of a society to feel valued – that is, to experience something of the love of God – demands a deliberate sustained hospitality. Statistics indicate that, at present, it is government schools more than Catholic schools who are offering that hospitality. Furthermore, if low-income Catholic families continue to enrol in government schools, there will be a concentration of poverty and its concomitants in the public system, with potential impact upon the quality of government schools (cf Catholic Education Commission of Victoria, 2004a, p 3). This damaging impact should concern all educators.

At this time when Australian Catholic schools are both successful and popular, there is an ideal opportunity for Catholic school leaders to open up discussion about taking the extra step to open Catholic schools to all those who are needy, whatever their faith, or lack of faith. There are obvious challenges for classroom practice and school leadership in opening schools to a more comprehensive student body which includes a greater number of those 'new poor' as characterised by the Congregation for Catholic Education. The greater social and personal uncertainties which children bring to school certainly impact seriously upon classroom and school yards. Yet, Catholic schools are resourced as never before in their history to face these challenges, for example, through:

- Resources and school facilities (eg, counsellors, special education funding)
- Qualifications of staff and school leaders
- Ready access to ongoing professional development
- Developments in the discipline of learning and teaching
- The capacity of church/system leaders to influence government funding policy, not only for students in Catholic schools, but for all students who are needy and vulnerable.

Space has not permitted focus on those children who bring specific learning disabilities (SWD) to their education. Traditionally, very few Catholic schools have enrolled children with more substantial learning needs. However, pleasingly, there have been significant increases in the last twenty years both in the number of SWD students enrolled in Catholic schools and in the level of disability. Some Catholic school systems have begun to establish classes for children with higher levels of learning disability and also to cooperate with agencies such as the Autistic Association to establish classrooms within Catholic schools.

The missionary nature of the Catholic school

Any frank discussion which reassesses enrolment priorities for Catholic schools is assured of being demanding and thorny. So it should be. The issue of enrolling more of the neediest in Catholic schools relates directly to the missionary nature of Catholic schools.

Discussions about Catholic school enrolment have sometimes argued that only practising Catholics should be enrolled because it was money from the local parish that had built and developed the school. Similarly, sometimes children of families who did not contribute to the parish's planned giving were excluded. Another confusing argument excluded children who, because of their circumstances and family, had been deprived of a religious background. The generosity of faithful parishioners over many years is a treasured legacy. But are any of these arguments consistent with the *missionary* nature of the Church? Where is the sense of *mission* in excluding these children? There are even more extreme positions than this, but they are genuinely exceptional, and so do not merit attention here.

The particular focus of this chapter is upon that sense of mission in reaching out and inviting into Catholic schools those who are poor and marginalised. That specifically includes children of low-income families as well as the 'new poor'. Many of these children are, of course, Catholic, and the impediment to their enrolment is more likely to be financial and cultural rather than religious. But others will be children from other faiths and other Christian traditions, as well as those without a faith experience.

If Catholic school leaders are to take seriously the missionary and ecclesial nature of Catholic schools, then they need to look beyond those who meet the technical 'religious affiliation and practice' requirement. The line between many of the children from families who identify themselves as 'Catholic' and children from families of no religious affiliation has become quite blurred. In one of the most persuasive discussions I have read on this matter, Therese D'Orsa, proposes that

> *recognition of the missionary character of Catholic schooling is also recognition that **every** child is called into relationship with God, that **every** child has a right to know God's invitation to relationship, and that **every** child should have the opportunity to access the way of life exemplified by Jesus* (D'Orsa, 2001, p 8).

In particular, I wish to highlight two of the propositions which D'Orsa had put forward for discussion in her role as Director of Schools in the Diocese of Sale, namely:

1. The Catholic school is of its very nature ecclesial. The Church is of its very nature missionary. Therefore, the Catholic school must give genuine expression to the missionary nature of the Church, and
2. Catholic schools can and must today play two roles. They must be places both of pastoral care of the faithful and centres of missionary outreach extended to Catholics and other Christians with limited faith background. This background may also extend to those of no faith background and, at times, to those adhering to world religions other than Christian (D'Orsa, 2001, pp 8-9).

In my experience with Catholic schools in western Sydney, principals commonly reported that the enrolment of a child into a Catholic school can lead to a conversation with parents about faith and some kind of reaching out towards church. Families of the 21st century in our countries seem to seek spirituality and meaning, but not formal religion; they are said to want the Kingdom, but not the Church. However, — and this is a key challenge for Catholic schools — these young families need their tentative inclinations towards (or back towards) religious practice to be recognised and sensitively supported. Interestingly, the overwhelming majority of growth from 1962 to 2006 in the number of schools in the 'Other non-government sector' has been in religious schools – especially 'Christian Schools' – rather than, for example, non-religious schools founded on particular educational orientations.[4]

The invitation to faith
Part of faithfully living out a school's Catholic identity involves a missionary outreach which invites others – through the way a school's staff lives and works – to be part of this community of faith. Some students and teachers are received into the Church each year. 'Many parents who send their children to Catholic schools are begging to be more invited to the Catholic Church,' a parish priest once wrote to me.

---

[4] Like many of the other statistics quoted in this paper, this one raises a number of interesting possibilities and issues.

'Our policy is to open doors, the best we can…Unfortunately we are not very good at inviting' (Personal correspondence, 2006).

I have always chosen to assume that, whatever appearances to the contrary, the fact that families seek a Catholic education for their children means that, in some way, even unconsciously, they are open to their children discovering a religious way of life, even when it is within another faith tradition . It is for us to invite them, or in other words, '*it is impossible to justify walking away from the genuine desire of many good people for a gospel-based education'* (D'Orsa, 2001, p 8).

The appropriate locus for this invitation is in the interaction of the local Catholic school within its local parish community, or communities. By and large, there is a healthy cooperation and mutual respect between schools and the parish in which they work. Perhaps, it is time to take this relationship further so that local church and school exploit their mutual resources to plan together for a more mission-oriented approach (Cf Benedict on *Hope*, #25). Those parish and school leaders who work together to seek out those families who are in greatest need and invite them into the community of Catholic schools show us the way.

Taking the next step: A national Church focus on offering hope to the neediest

In 1994, Johnston and Chesterton concluded their report on the poor and Catholic schools with a warning that the 'gravity of the situation cannot be ignored or delayed' (p 71). In 2008, are there any reasons why there should be further delay? The way forward is already in place, *in seed,* in many places, and the concern for greater inclusion in Catholic schools is shared by many. But, what does it mean for Catholic schools to take the next step to create conditions which will be favourable for greater inclusion of those 'who are most loved by God – the poor and weakest'?

Commitment

One thing which is required is a more deliberate, explicit and systemic commitment to bring this mission to the poor to life and to make the Catholic school system *as a whole* more truly comprehensive – catholic – by opening schools to a far greater number of those who are most vulnerable. This issue belongs to the whole Australian Church; it cannot remain the option of individual schools, dioceses or congregations. The

NCEC data now being made available and analysed offers both challenge and resource. It is timely for Australian Catholic education leaders to work together in a direct national focus on this wound which is at the heart of the mission of an authentically Catholic school system. It is time to take some risks in honouring our mission, *especially* for those who are poor and in any way afflicted – to make God and his incarnate Son present and, in a sense, visible (Vatican Council II, *Gaudium & Spes*, #1, #21).

Starting points

The Australian Catholic education systems have a wealth of people of commitment and imagination to address this creatively and prudently. A starting point is to build on the quality of care which Catholic schools presently extend to those who are already part of their communities. Catholic school leaders need to discern the critical questions together, as Church, and then try to answer them. Some starting points, for example, might be:

- Are we willing to take the risks needed so that Catholic schools more comprehensively reach out to *any* child who is 'socially and economically disadvantaged' (Congregation for Catholic Education, 1997, #15) – no matter their faith and religious practice?
- What mechanisms of welcome can Catholic schools develop to replace asking low-income families to declare themselves 'unable to pay'? (eg, use of health cards, or for Catholic schools simply to promote themselves as 'fee-free' for all children from families up to a certain income level, with an invitation to families at the highest-income levels to sponsor other students)?
- How would enrolment profiles in schools change if school and system enrolment policies were reviewed to give a higher priority to mission and evangelisation?
- How would enrolment profiles in schools change if school and system enrolment policies were reviewed to give a higher priority to those who are most vulnerable?
- What resources of experience, pastoral care, faith and piety are we excluding from the lives of students in Catholic schools when parishioners – especially older parishioners – are not invited to contribute to the mission of the local Catholic school?

- How should the Church resource its school leaders, teachers and staff to honour this mission to the poor?

Ultimately, the test of an authentic Catholic school is as it always has been: do the students graduate competent and confident in their own gifts, skills and capacity to keep on learning? Do they go with a commitment to live good, virtuous and productive lives which leave their world a better place? Do they go heartened and enlivened because they have encountered something of the saving love of God in the substance and process of their schooling? Do they leave more deeply religious because they have been educated in spirit in the totality of their person? Do they go with a sense of their dignity as children of God, whatever their background, religion and circumstances?

References

Benedict XVI, (2007) Encyclical Letter *Spe Salvi*, http://www.catholicnewsagency.com, accessed, December 2007.

Benjamin, A. (2007) Directions for Catholic Educational Leadership: A Personal Retrospective, paper presented to the Catholic Educational Leadership Conference, Flagship for Creative and Authentic Leadership, Australian Catholic University National, Sydney, 31st July-2nd August.

Bishops of NSW and ACT, (2007) *Catholic Schools at a Crossroads*, Pastoral Letter, Sydney, Bishops of NSW & ACT/CEO Sydney

Catholic Education Commission of Victoria, (2004b) *The Welfare Needs of Victorian Catholic Schools*, Seminar 3: May.

Catholic Education Commission of Victoria, (2004a) *The Affordability of Catholic Schools in Victoria*, Seminar 2: March.

Chesterton, P. & Johnston, K. (1998) *Access to Catholic Schooling*, National Catholic Education Commission and Australian Catholic University.

Congregation for Catholic Education, ((1977) *The Catholic School*, Sydney, St Pauls.

Congregation for Catholic Education, (1998) *The Catholic School on the Threshold of the Third Millenium*, Strathfield, St Pauls.

D'Orsa, T. (2001) *Catholic Schools and the Mission of the Church*, Discussion Paper, Sale, Catholic Education Office.

Gill, P. (1972) *Catholic Education. Where is it going?* Melbourne, Cassell Australia.

Johnston. K. & Chesterton, P. (1994) *The Poor and Catholic Schools*, Annandale,

Conference of Leaders of Religious Institutes (NSW).

Kerstiens, F. (1975) 'Hope', *Encyclopedia of Theology,* Ed. Karl Rahner, London, Burns & Oates.

National Catholic Education Commission, (1991) *Statement on National Curriculum,* http://www.ncec.catholic.edu.au, accessed 5th December 2007.

National Catholic Education Commission, (2007) *Catholic School Enrolment Trends 2006,* Report from the Australian Catholic Education Statistics (ACES) Working Group, February. Accessed from NCEC website, January 2008.

National Catholic Education Commission, (2008), *Catholic School Enrolment Trends 2007,* Report from Australian Catholic Education Statistics (ACES) Working Group, February. Accessed from NCEC website, February 2008.

Nouwen, H. (1978) *Creative Ministry,* New York, Doubleday.

OECD, (2007) *No more failures: ten steps to equity in education,* Executive Summary, accessed December 2007.

Prendergast, N. & Monahan, L. (2003) *Re-imagining the Catholic School,* Dubln, Veritas.

Robinson, Bishop G. (2007) *Confronting Power and Sex in the Catholic Church. Reclaiming the Spirit of Jesus.* Melbourne, John Garratt Publishing.

Vatican Council II, (1966) *Gaudium et Spes,* in *The Documents of Vatican II,* London, Geoffrey Chapman.

15
A Journey of Healing:
One in spirit embracing difference

Joan Hendriks

The ongoing journey of Reconciliation in Australia has been enhanced and moved forward with the apology that was read by the Prime Minister Kevin Rudd and tabled in Parliament on the 13 February 2008. This historical moment was witnessed throughout Australia and around the world. The overwhelming relief was evident. It was a time to be still and sense the movement of the Spirit of Reconciliation. With this action, the pathways to reconciliation have widened and there is evidence that more Australians are seeking involvement in 'walking the talk' to find their own niche to move forward and be a part of dealing with the unfinished business of Reconciliation.

As we build on these positives, the negatives will be eliminated if we have faith and trust in the Spirit of living faith in public place. However, in making this hopeful comment, it doesn't mean that we can just sweep those attributes which are continuing to erode some aspects of Reconciliation under the carpet, as the saying goes. We cannot ignore the obstacles to Reconciliation. We need to address those issues that can be discussed as a means of educating to make a difference.

It is time to draw strength in realising that from 'little things we can grow bigger and better things'. We are steadily growing in numbers and we will continue to do so. Our faith in one another must remain strong as we place our trust in the one God of whole creation.

Attitude is a priceless possession and it is unfortunate that for many years this powerful individual attribute has been misused; and has been a stumbling block in acknowledging, accepting and being responsible for seeking justice and equity for all peoples of Australia. In forwarding Reconciliation there needs to be a change in attitudes so that we can 'Close the Gap', in particular, in the education and health sectors.

Educating to make a difference

In 2003, I was invited to present the 2003 Jack Woodward memorial lecture (Hendriks, 2003). In that lecture, 'Catholic Education's Response to the Challenges of Reconciliation', I reminded the audience that 'reconciliation presents a number of challenges to this country and the Catholic community has a special responsibility to promote the dignity and respect of all humanity.' These words of compassion certainly flame the passion I have to continue to nurture and strengthen the spirit for true Reconciliation. Five years later and further down the road to Reconciliation, the same will to win remains. There is still a long way to go and our Catholic community must continue to promote the dignity and respect of all humanity if we truly believe that we must 'Act justly, love tenderly and walk humbly with our God of whole creation' (Micah 6:8).

Dealing with discriminative attitudes

Reflecting my conviction about the value of education in the Reconciliation process, over a number of years I have been involved in an ecumenical reconciliation workshop program, called 'Education: a Key to Reconciliation Workshop Program.' A section of the program focuses on 'Dealing with Racism'. The particular exercises involved reveal that discriminative attitudes still exist – even in the 21st century – within the various groups, and this has been the case without exception in any one group to date. For example, the word 'Aboriginal' is used in the discussion seeking off the cuff comments. Positive comments include, for example, *spiritual people, value of land, relationships to land, importance of family*, and so on. However, negativity invariably will emerge in the discussion, with examples such as, to name but a few, *alcoholics, lazy, dirty, uneducated*, and so on.

The group taking part in the program is responsible for the outcome of the exercise and the next step is to debate and discuss further the reasoning behind the values portrayed. The objective is to elicit – entice – a change in attitude if possible. There are certainly many positive outcomes but also, surprising to some people, there are group members who stand firm and hold on to their views, so that their 'I believe what I believe and so be it' attitude remains. It is difficult to offer the olive branch and be turned away like this, but this kind of discussion is an opportunity to make a difference and work on changing attitudes. Without a change in attitudes there is no real possibility for change in those who reject embracing difference. However, there is always the hope that even if this situation remains, perhaps the thought that has been offered in discussion may dwell on within deaf ears and the blind will learn to see through the lens of the spirit and the example of others. Every single person can make a difference in exercising their faith to promote Reconciliation.

Sorry Time
Another example is the 'Sorry Day Journey of Healing' commemorative ceremonies that have become an annual event. It is not unusual to have someone pass the remark '*We've said sorry – how many more times are we expected to say sorry?*' Defining the word *Sorry* from an Indigenous perspective relates to compassion for the pain and suffering the person and family are enduring at the time.

Sorry in the Indigenous way has a different meaning to western interpretation. *Sorry Time* is about losing a family member or a tragic event happening and is a time of deep mourning and a spiritual journey of the fare-welling of a loved one. It becomes Sorry time for the whole community which shuts down for days. In particular this is distinctly noticeable in remote communities where traditional burials are still practised. In visiting a community during a time of Sorry Business one's spirit is stirred by the intensity of the respect that is witnessed and felt.

I recall a non-Indigenous colleague writing in a report that argued the importance of understanding cultural difference that 'every non Indigenous person should attend an Aboriginal funeral – it's good for the spirit within oneself'. The whole community joins the family in the funeral ceremony and rituals. Funerals are held over until community members can travel back to their homeland to attend regardless of the distance of the journey. This is the true meaning of Sorry Time.

Determining direction in schools
2008 has brought us to the interface of the events of the past year and the need to follow the signposts of what is best practice and how to determine direction as we face the road ahead. The Government has prioritised Health and Education as key areas for funding and with this

initiative has forged guidelines of policies, procedures and outcomes to legitimise the expenditure. The current Government Intervention programs that are being enforced will also influence the attendance of children in schools. These children will need qualified staff who have an understanding of the history and background of their students. Equally important is the empathy and rapport to accept the situations that will need to be endured. The desire to meet the challenge to develop a genuine relationship with the students has to be the real commitment to those who have not had the same happy family environment that has been a natural for other students. It stands to reason that the parents of these children have themselves, in many instances, been the victims of the cycle of life that continues to plague the lives of the children today.

Targetting the holistic health of students
The current focus on 'Closing the Gap' will require also a commitment to understand the reasoning behind years of layers of injustice, dispossession of family, and dispersal from country of spiritual and cultural identity. There will be students who will have extra special needs and not simply special treatment as is a common misconception. The message here is that it is the holistic health of the student which will need to be the main focus. Loss of identity is a complicated issue that is often not understood and as a result is not properly addressed. Reparation of the broken spirit within must be of primary importance and requires love that is patient and gentle and steeped in understanding, compassion and respect for the downtrodden soul of the person. The importance of having qualified Indigenous role models working in partnership with staff and students cannot be over emphasised. The expertise they bring through personal experiences and cultural understanding is a learning tool for all staff and students alike. In forging this partnership there is the opportunity to learn and journey together, dealing with the unfinished business of a search for a new core of creativity in the lives of those who have endured the flames of a conditioned way of life.

The ongoing saga of the portrayal of negativity continues to plague the image of Indigenous peoples and becomes the cornerstone in the projection of attitudes that resist, rather than accept the opportunity to further Reconciliation. Changing attitudes will depend entirely on the spirit in which the message of Reconciliation is delivered. And it requires the co-operation of all parties concerned.

The Churches and social justice

> In addressing this issue we have to continue to challenge to eliminate the forms of discrimination and blatant racism that exist within our Australian society and which have become more public and prevalent with the changing nature of our Australian society. The search for meaning and new life is dampened and damaged by the many facets of discrimination and racism.

The World Council of Churches (WCC) resource guide, *Transformative Justice: Being Church and Overcoming Racism* (WCC, 2004) has been a worthwhile document. The words of Introduction include the following message:

> The paths for the journey towards racial justice are many and varied. The issue is complex. The more ground that is covered, the more there is to be done. The journey towards racial justice is collective, community-based and inclusive. It has to be a journey that is rooted and centred on people their participation and their relationships. To be effective, the journey should touch our souls and spirits, our hearts and our minds. (WCC, 2004, p 2)

Racial justice

Section 1 of the resource relates to 'The Sin of Racism' and states that

> Racism has some of its origins in the history of European expansion and colonialism and, subsequently, in the history of colonised continents. People continue to be subjected to the consequences of both colonialism and racism. (WCC, 2004, p11)

There are many ways of defining 'racism'; the historical roots have been seeded in the development of capitalism and thrived particularly in countries where colonisation has taken place.

The most common definition is 'that members of one racial group consider themselves intrinsically superior to members of other racial groups' (WCC, 2004, p16). This is the foundational factor that causes discrimination, whether it is discrimination against color, race or creed. It grows from the discomfort of one person by another; and can be responsible for permeated racism that breeds contempt. This in turns compounds a racist attitude which can be handed down from generation to generation. With the growth of multi-culturalism in Australia, the need to consider the issue of racism has become in itself a problem and is under consider discussion in the campaign for 'A Fair Go' and 'Justice for All Australians'. United we stand and divided we fall in a society built on dominant views and attitudes.

The Royal Commission into Aboriginal Deaths in Custody (RCIADIC) National Report reminded us all that 'Non-Aboriginal Australia has developed on the racist assumption of an ingrained sense of superiority that it knows best what is good for Aboriginal people'. (RCIADIC, 1991)

If we truly believe in the Spirit of Reconciliation, the continuing journey of moving with the spirit of reconciliation towards a more just and equitable society of Australia relies on the elimination of discrimination and racism and is the responsibility of all Australians. The truth sets us free and together we can make a difference.

Education and social justice

The Human Rights and Equal Opportunity Commission (cf. HREOC website) relates that education is one of their main roles and impresses that human rights are everyone's responsibility and must be applied to everyday lives.

> Within Catholic Education we are called to 'Act justly, love tenderly and walk humbly with the one God of all creation'. (Micah, 6:8)

The Role of History
The influence of history and politics has determined the aftermath of the living conditions and poor health that perpetuates today's way of life for Indigenous peoples. It is a way of life that has been seeded in a clash of cultures that has thrived on loss of identity and devaluation of self; a way of life that is entrapped in the cycle of an inherited way of life accorded to the authorities of the time. It is important to take into consideration that many of the communities that are currently undergoing Government Intervention were founded as Government Reserves and Missions.

The state of poor health of the community is the result of whether the community has survived the depression of the historical association by removal to a reserve or mission or is a community that has remained affiliated to their land of heritage. The layers of removal from place of belonging, separation of families and institutionalisation over several generations is the core issue that needs to be taken into consideration when addressing process, practices and partnership in realising positive outcomes in health and education. This inherited way of life is symptomatic of the problems that are currently being addressed in the critical situation that is being faced today. It is especially pertinent in the instance of those communities who are currently undergoing Intervention

Catholic education and Reconciliation

On a more positive note, in the midst of dealing with the challenges to many contemporary Indigenous communities, there is much to be celebrated. In seeking a means of forwarding Reconciliation through education there is much to be celebrated. Catholic Education across the States and Territories has endeavored to be a part of the Reconciliation movement since the formation of the Council for Aboriginal Reconciliation. Quality input, as always, relies on the goodwill of those involved across the education system. Some of these projects and programs, especially from a Queenland perspective, include, for example:

- In the mid 1980s Brisbane Catholic Education Office (BCEO) began a conversation with invited Indigenous Elders and Community members to establish a Cultural Centre in Brisbane. Ngutani Lui was officially opened in 1988 and provides Cultural Awareness workshops to Catholic Schools and Staff, Queensland State Schools, and other sectors of the Community on request.
- Education Diocesan Co-ordinators and Participation Officers have also been part of the Catholic systems since the late 1980s.
- In 1989 Australian Catholic University (ACU) National opened the Weemala Indigenous Support Unit. Other ACU campuses have also been part of this partnership in supporting Indigenous education.
- (ACU McAuley has been showcased for the Reflection Space that is an outside area at the Weemala Indigenous Unit. This space is a place for regular prayerful reflections, memorial services and liturgies.)
- In 1993 a position was put in place for an Indigenous person to be a member of the National Catholic Education Commission

(NCEC) and over the time span since three Indigenous people have held this position.
- 1996 was the year that the Queensland Catholic Education Commission (QCEC) appointed the first QCEC Indigenous Education Officer and likewise other States and Territories now have a State Indigenous Co-Ordinator.
- Some of the Catholic Schools also have Participation Officers within in school. Others may cluster and share the role of one paid person.

Taking into consideration the diversity of communities and the varying numbers in schools it stands to reason that some dioceses have a larger workload and therefore require more Indigenous Support Persons. In Queensland, this is the case of dioceses like Townsville, Rockhampton and Cairns, while other states have their own particular variations in population. There is room for improvement in all areas but we have started to move with closing the gap in working in partnership within the Catholic education system. Another positive example is the regular QCEC Indigenous Education Committee meetings which are of good value and allow the teams from the five Queensland dioceses to meet and share the needs and aspiration and successes as a co-ordinated team.

Within Catholic education there are individual schools that have embraced difference and accepted the challenges of education in the 21st century. Personal experiences allows for a focus on one particular school, again in Queensland, that has taken up this challenge.

Lourdes Hill College, Brisbane
Lourdes Hill College in Brisbane has taken the challenge to 'Dare to Lead' and is one of the first Colleges to have endorsed a Reconciliation Action Plan (RAP). The recent accreditation is grounded in the excellence of the overall presentation of education and outlook on Christian ethos and social justice practices.

This school has become a 'home away from home' for many Indigenous students, overseas visiting students and all who call Australia 'home'. The charism of the Good Samaritan Sisters' Benedictine ethos is vibrantly alive in the attitudes of students, staff, parents and associates alike. The students are nurtured into caring and sharing the good and not so good sides of living with the Spirit and exemplifying goodwill to all.

Included in the Lourdes Hill College 2007-2008 Annual Report was the message that 'while strength is drawn from the past, our vision for the future addresses the changing needs of all students in today's contemporary society.' Further, it added, 'As knowledge informs the lives our students will lead, all learning at Lourdes Hill College is grounded in a Catholic, holistic vision of life.' (Annual Report, 2008) The foundations of the Charism of the Good Samaritan Sisters remains grounded in the inherited values of the Benedictine ethos of being proud to be a Lourdanian.

The importance of heritage and environment

There are many words that assist in describing culture and some that come to mind are family, country, customs, traditions, ethos, nation, and civilisation.

Culture is here, there and everywhere and the highly regarded text on Aboriginal health, *Binan Goonj,* relates that culture is:

> A view of the world that has meaning … A blue print for all human behaviour. Culture is the sum or totality of man's learned or behavioural traits in an identifiable society. Culture is more than 'a people's way of life'. Culture tells us what is pretty and what is ugly; what is right and what is wrong; culture influences our preferred way of thinking, of behaving, of making decisions. (Eckermann et al, 2005, p 6)

Peoples and places are of great importance in the moulding of our spiritual connectedness with the Creator God. 'Who's your family' and 'Where you come from' is at the essence of Aboriginality, and central to the holistic approach that determines self-worth and well-being of body, mind and spirit.

The Dreaming

Indigenous peoples have lived with the myths of creation as handed down from generation to generation for thousands and thousands of years. There is depth in the paralleling of the Dreaming and the Genesis stories of creation. The Earth our Mother and the Spirit of our Dreaming provide a holistic, healthy, physical and spiritual lifestyle: it is essentially a non-materialistic way of life that existed thousands upon thousand of years since the very beginning of God's creation.

Patrick Dodson (1988) relates the essence of our Dreaming in his talk 'The Land our Mother, The Church our Mother'. He writes:

> Sacred sites help to make present the powers of 'The Dreaming' and so help to sustain people in the present. They are vital for the continuance of religion and culture, for the maintenance of kinship ties and environmental balance, and to be a source of continuing pride and self respect… Clearly Aboriginal religions have a beautifully worked spirituality complete with a full and coherent sacramental theology…

> You would husband the land. You would burn the grasses to promote new growth and to make sure that the delicate balance of nature that has been created is preserved. There is a rich and complicated legal system which is administered by elders and to which all are bound. The blind, the lame, the mentally defective are all to be looked after. Your spiritual and religious life is as rich as your material life is simple. The children are more deeply loved than perhaps any children on earth. Until puberty and initiation they can do no wrong. They are cuddled not chastised. They learn from love and from example. The children grow in security and confidence. They are tutored in the life of the spirit, in respect of the elders and kinship and the ways of the country.

Six remote Indigenous communities that were founded by Christian missionaries from the various denominations were visited in 1994 for the purpose of recording what was happening in these communities in terms of the Christian Movement.

One of those interviewed was Fr. John Leary who went to the Northern Territory from the seminary and spent 50 years of his priesthood working with the communities of Daly River and Wadeye. While the following excerpt is very long, there is much to be considered in the words he shared on the video.

> You don't have to be here long before you realise that these people they are still very traditional people. They have their own ceremonies. The men's business and the women's business; and actually the church too is a ceremony thing.

> I remember a non-Catholic minister years ago telling me. He said 'You Catholics should have it made with your Sacraments and your Mass

and your ceremonies; and I remember thinking about this and I said 'We should have it made but we haven't made it'; because the two are quite distinct. And it's always been my ambition to wed the two. And that's why when we started to talk about baptism and how it related to basic things in religion culture; that I started to realise that the ceremony of the sacrament of Baptism especially; the sacraments could be indigenised if we used that word. But it must not be done by Leary or anyone else.

Someone had read about St Paul as going down into the grave to die with Christ in order to rise with him; and one of them said 'We have in our ceremony something like that. A high thing; a dying in order to live a higher kind of life. And we have a myth: where the old lady, the earth mother, represented by the serpent, the sun snake, swallows the men after they die … and after sometime she regurgitates them out and they later reappear as mystical men with responsibilities and with knowledge. That business about St Paul dying and coming out again is very much on our level.

So we spent three or four days talking about that; how to express this in religious ceremony. And that is this how this ceremony originated. And really it did ring bells deep down and there's a resonance there. And I think that's what we're on about: unless this happens, this connection between the way they think their spirituality and the Christian thing; there's no honesty of expression. I think there's no real Aboriginal Christian spirituality arising.'

Meeting the challenges of a way forward

There needs to be an awareness of the characteristics of living in community and dealing with different levels of attitudes towards what is best practice.

Values of what is best practice differ within communities and this relates directly back to the passage through life that has been the lot of particular families. People are returning to communities in an effort to rebuild their links with the land and life in community with family. As a result of the lifestyle that has engaged them for many years, some of these people return with a different outlook on what are appropriate ways to live specifically in Indigenous community. And so there needs to be a working through of the problematic issues.

Today there are people who want to move on and forget about past experiences and start a new beginning. Others have endured the past and continue to immerse their innermost depression in whatever comes to hand, in an attempt to alleviate the despair. This has resulted in many instances of self-harm and death because of psychological breakdown or poor health.

All in all, there is much work to be done and time is needed to open the doors to work on relationships within the boundaries and the interfacing of a changing culture.

What has happened in the past cannot be mended overnight and requires justice in our dealing with one another. There is a need to work in solidarity in an effort to build relationships; and throughout the journey of working and living in community be ever ready to follow the protocols as outlined by the community.

Community empowerment must be the vision to determine each community's own destiny of a healthy, stable and viable community leadership. Self-empowerment is of little value if this is not channelled to community empowerment by those in a leadership role. Shared leadership is culturally appropriate for Indigenous communities. Shared leadership calls for individual leadership to work collectively to build partnerships that will determine more positive outcomes in a way which reflects and respects the complex and less structured mode of Indigenous leadership.

References

Annual Report, (2008) Lourdes Hill College, Brisbane, available at http://www.lhc.qld.edu.au/ANNUAL_REPORT_2007-2008.pdf.

Eckermann A, Dowd T, Chong E, Nixon L, Gray R, et al. (2005) *Binan Goonj: bridging cultures in Aboriginal health*. 2nd ed. Edinburgh: Churchill Livingstone.

Council for Aboriginal Reconciliation, (2000) Corroboree 2000, Australian Declaration for Reconciliation, Council for Aboriginal Reconciliation ACT.

Dodson, P (1988) 'The Land our Mother, The Church our Mother', *Compass*,1 no 2 -1988

Hendriks, J. (2004) *Catholic Education's Response to the Challenges of Reconciliation*, Federation of Parents and Friends Association of Catholic Schools in Queensland Inc.

Hendriks, Murphy J., (1996-2004) *Education: a Key to Reconciliation Workshop Program*. Churches Together Aboriginal Partnership, (CTIPP). Queensland Churches Together.

HREOC website, Australian Human Rights and Equal Opportunity Commission, http://www.hreoc.gov.au/

RCIADC, (1991) Final Report of the Royal Commission into Aboriginal Deaths in Custody, Reconciliation and Social Justice Library, http://www.austlii.edu.au/au/special/rsjproject/rsjlibrary/rciadic/rciadic_summary/rcsumk01.html, accessed 30th March 2007.

Stanner W.E.H. (1989). *On Aboriginal Religion*. University of Sydney, NSW

World Council of Churches (2004) *Transformative Justice: Being Church and Overcoming Racism Resource Guide,* Justice, Peace and Creation Team, Geneva.

16
Both 'Catholic' and 'School': Leading learning with moral purpose

MICHAEL BEZZINA

Now, perhaps more than at any other time in the history of Catholic education in Australia, leaders in Catholic schools are being challenged to be explicit about what it is that makes them Catholic. Archbishop Michael Miller, the Secretary for the Vatican's Congregation for Catholic Education went so far as to say that 'ensuring [the schools'] genuinely Catholic identity is the Church's greatest challenge' (2005).

Some see this challenge as growing out of an organic quest for improvement – a natural desire to be the best that Catholic schools can be. Disappointed others look in an overly simplistic fashion at measures such as Mass attendance as evidence that the schools are failing in their purpose and therefore need reform. Their questions focus on the school's perceived impact on the faith life of its students.

Other critics of Catholic schools point to the fact that, over recent years, apparently steady enrolments have actually been built on declining numbers of Catholic students and growing numbers of non-Catholics. There is a temptation for some to reduce the important, yet complex discussion on the identity of Catholic schools to a numbers game. For them, the problem is that there is an average of 23% non-Catholics in our schools (up to 40% in Tasmania, and 36% in South Australia), and the solutions would be to mandate maximum percentages for non-Catholics, or, in a view considered but rejected by the bishops of NSW and the ACT (2007, p.8), 'to downsize our school system to a scale at which we can choose students and staff who readily embrace the mission of the Catholic school'. These simplistic responses are problematic on two counts.

On the one hand, they ignore the Church's own view that the Catholic school has a responsibility to act as an agent of primary evangelisation. Surely this is a key element of the mission to which the bishops refer?

We are reminded in *The Catholic School on the Threshold of the Third Millennium* (1997, n.16) that 'the Catholic school is not reserved to Catholics only, but is open to all those who appreciate and share its qualified educational project'. It names in particular 'those far from the faith' (58). The Catholic school should therefore not be defined by its students, but by its mission to those students.

The second problem with what we might call the 'percentage' approach to Catholic identity is that regardless of who attends our schools, we are still faced with finding ways to address the challenge of 'the synthesis between culture and faith' (*The Catholic School on the Threshold of the Third Millennium,*1997, n.14). The Catholic school is, in the words of the title of this chapter, both 'Catholic' and 'school'. It has both an educational and an ecclesial function, and its deepest moral purpose lies at the intersection of these two. No school that claims the name Catholic can do so unless it seeks to provide the best possible education for its students. How can we ensure that our faith and our educational activities act powerfully upon one another?

The object of all good schools is to promote authentic learning in their students. This calls on schools to connect the learners' search for meaning and purpose in their lives to a variety of personal experiences in the curriculum. They need to enable learners to continuously transform their understanding of themselves, the world in which they live, and their purpose in life. This authentic learning is truly transformative.

Authentic learning at the heart of moral purpose in Catholic schools

What does authentic learning look like? Educators in most schools would agree that it ought to promote the development of personal meaning, respect for the material being learned, the application of learning in life, and the ultimate transformation of the learner.

Starratt's (2004) challenge to educators is to infuse academic learning with a personal dimension, and thereby enrich the whole learning process. He argues, somewhat confrontingly, that learning which is not authentic to the needs of the students' world is not only *inappropriate* but *unethical*. This is a real challenge, particularly for Catholic educators. It is the pursuit of transformational and life-giving learning through this integration which imparts to Catholic schools their unique character, creating a special context for leadership and learning.

All those in school leadership must be centrally concerned with ethics and morality by the very nature of the work they do — with deciding what is significant, what is right and what is worthwhile (Duignan and MacPherson, 1992). This focus is central to Burns' (1978, p20) seminal distinction between leadership that is *transactional* and that which is *transformational*. Transformational leadership 'occurs when one or more persons *engage* with others in such a way that leaders and followers raise one another to higher levels of motivation and morality [and it] ultimately becomes moral in that it raises the level of human conduct and ethical aspiration of both leader and led, and thus it has a transforming effect on both'.

The 'bottom line' for educational leaders is that they help create and support the conditions that promote transformative teaching and learning in their schools (Starratt, 2004). Good educational leaders pay close attention to the quality of teaching and students' learning. Such leaders encourage others to commit themselves to professional practices that are, by their nature, educative. They help create the conditions within which teachers and students take responsibility for the quality of their own teaching and learning. They challenge others to participate in the visionary activity of identifying in curriculum, teaching and learning what is worthwhile, what is worth doing and preferred ways of doing and acting together. The key emphasis is on leading authentic learning and creating processes and conditions that encourage everyone in the school community to be effective learning resources for each other.

Leaders in Catholic schools face unique demands in living out this role. Like all school leaders, they need to have a good understanding of the dynamics of teaching and learning, and how these impact on authentic learning. Like their colleagues in other types of school they need to develop a repertoire of behaviours that they know have the potential to transform teacher actions, and hence student outcomes. But in addition, this whole enterprise needs to be shaped by a uniquely Catholic world view, embodied in a particular set of values and ethics. This world view needs to find expression not only in the traditionally 'Catholic' features of the school (e.g., religious education classes, liturgies, community service, the curriculum of community), but within all the school's curricular and co-curricular programs. In other words, transformative learning approaches have to be embedded in whole-school perspectives within a Catholic ethos. What we teach, how we teach it and how we live it have to be congruent with the values and beliefs of the Catholic school. A Catholic view of the world can only grow out of our personal relationship with Jesus.

Catholic schools are not alone in claiming to have a moral purpose. Whether labelled 'shared whole school vision and goals' (Cuttance et al., 2003) or 'community values' (Andrews and Lewis, 2004) or simply 'moral purpose' (Fullan, 2001; MacBeath, 2005), a shared moral purpose has been consistently identified in the literature as one of the fundamental necessities for bringing about the kind of change and improvement which will deliver desirable student learning in schools. The National College of School Leadership (NCSL) describes shared moral purpose as 'a compelling idea or aspirational purpose, a shared belief (a team) can achieve far more for their end users together than they can alone' (2006, p3). It stresses the importance of student learning as part of this purpose.

The challenge is to find a way to surface this moral purpose and then to make it part of the discourse of the school so that it can be embedded in practice. Somehow we need to avoid falling into the trap of thinking that because it is in our documents it is owned by the school community. There is a need for shared sense of purpose to be grounded in a shared commitment to explicit values (Andrews and Lewis, 2004).

While leaders of Catholic schools are regularly engaged in the ongoing professional as well as religious development of their leadership, with a strong emphasis on both the values base and student outcomes, perhaps these efforts have lacked integration. The remainder of this chapter presents a conceptual model, with which Catholic schools can explore the linkages between leading and learning based on a strong and explicit sense of their unique identity, and the moral purpose which underpins it.

The 'Leaders Transforming Learning and Learners' conceptual model

Leaders Transforming Learning and Learners (LTLL) was a pilot project collaboratively designed by the Flagship for Creative and Authentic Leadership at Australian Catholic University (ACU) and four NSW dioceses (Parramatta, Broken Bay, Wollongong and Maitland-Newcastle). There were nine case study schools, drawn from the four systems. Thirty-three teachers made up the nine project teams who were part of the study. The research team included myself and my colleagues Charles Burford and Patrick Duignan, and the conceptualisation of the model presented in this chapter draws on their insights and those of the practitioners from each of the school systems.

The conceptual framework in Figure 1 was at the heart of the initiative. The researchers made use of the advantage of having a group of schools with a common religious background to work towards an elaboration of moral purpose. The Values elements were developed in conversation with the expert participants from schools, systems and university, drawing on their extensive experience in Catholic education. For the Ethics elements the team owes a debt of gratitude to Professor Jerry Starratt who was engaged in the early stages of the project. His three ethics of presence, responsibility and authenticity had a profound influence on participants (Starratt, 2004). The researchers were then able to align the first two elements in a preliminary way with what they saw as the emerging consensus in the research around leadership and learning behaviours that had been shown to enhance student learning (eg Crowther, Hann and Andrews 2002; Crowther, Kaagan, Ferguson and Hahn, 2002; Cuttance, et al., 2003; Marzano, Waters and McNulty, 2005).

Figure 1: The LTLL Conceptual Framework

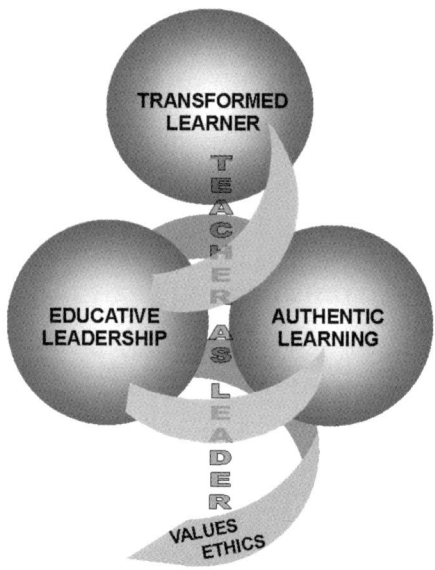

In this framework, the moral purpose is oriented towards a vision of transformed learners that can be attained by means of a series of behaviours in the educative leadership and authentic learning domains (which are themselves value based and ethical).

Figure 1 can be considered in two broad sections: the first might be described as encapsulating moral purpose, and is made up of the Values, Ethics and Transformed Learners elements, which were brought together for the first time in this project, responding to the perceived need for greater explicitness in these areas; the second comprises the Educative Leadership and Authentic Learning elements, which began as a broad adaptation of the National Quality Schooling Framework (Cuttance et al, 2003) but have been considerably refined through the experience of the pilot. The resultant conceptual framework provides what the project team believes is the first serious attempt to devote the same attention to the moral dimension of schooling as to the leadership and learning behaviours which they underpin. If the model is to be useful, though, as a basis for reflective practice, it will be necessary to tease out each of the domains in more detail, and to understand how they are inter-related.

Elaborating the LTLL framework

Each of the domains in the model can be elaborated at two levels: the separate elements which make it up, and sample indicators. In fact, in the LTLL project itself, both levels were provided in a reflective tool used in a range of ways by the different schools. The material which follows is a refinement and simplification of the original material which grew out of the pilot. Leaders in Catholic schools might choose to use it (whole or in part) as a stimulus to reflection with their colleagues.

The transformed learner
In our commitment to authentic learning, based on our values and ethics in action, we promote learning that is transformative for our students and their society. Transformed learners will take delight in both the subject and the process of learning, for which they take responsibility as part of a life-long journey. Their growing understanding reflects a rigorous, critical and respectful approach to the subject matter and to their fellow learners. They will be committed to their own growth – physical, intellectual, social and spiritual and filled with the hope of

a Catholic world view. Transformed learners will engage actively with society as engaged citizens seeking to make a difference.

Values

Our values shape our behaviours. If we genuinely hold particular values, they should be visible in what we do in schools and how we do it. Different schools may choose to name different values as central to their activities. The LTLL model proposes five – Catholicity, justice, excellence, the common good and transformation as a starting point. Different school communities and different systems may choose different names or sets of values.

Catholicity is the defining characteristic of our schools. They are a work of love for the full human development of our students, grounded in the teachings of Christ and at the service of society. They work closely with the parish as a key element of the evangelising mission of the Church in their work of bringing culture and faith into harmony in the school community. This 'value' is an attempt to capture the unique dimensions of our religious tradition, such as eucharist, sacrament, scripture, spirituality, morality and a hope filled world view. This tradition is made explicit in liturgy and prayer, the religious education program and the lived daily life and culture of the school.

There is no contradiction between good pastoral care and the pursuit of *excellence*. Catholic schools must be good schools. In fact, to seek the very best outcomes for students is to undertake the fundamental pastoral responsibility. This comes down to ensuring the highest quality of learning both for staff and students, in a culture of high expectation and strong support which recognises and responds to individual differences.

The good Catholic school must pursue *justice* unhesitatingly. The document *The Catholic School on the Threshold of the Third Millennium* makes it clear that Catholic schools should have 'a special attention to those who are weakest' (n15), and are 'at the service of society' (n16). Catholic schools are challenged to be inviting, inclusive and just as they embrace the diversity of peoples and seek to serve the poor and the marginalised both in their internal workings and their public stances.

Catholic schools must go beyond the informational and even the formational to the *transformational*. As Starratt (2004) says, through transformative learning, the learner becomes a fuller, richer, deeper human being. Transformation is one of the major focuses in Catholic schools for both students and teachers as they strive to make Christ present in the world, to transform not only themselves, but the world they live in. Learning that is meaningful and purposeful promotes self-knowledge and empowerment of students to act in the Church and in society.

In Catholic schools, we see society not just as a collection of individuals but as a community called to share for the *common good*. The common good is best supported within healthy communities which place great value on relationships, promote collaboration and ensure that decision making involves those most affected by outcomes. The values stance outlined here precludes practices which might shape Catholic schools as enclaves of privilege. It requires instead that in living out these values, they place themselves at the service of society.

Ethics

Ethics are the norms and virtues by which members of a community bind themselves to a moral way of living. Starratt (2004) suggests that they are maps that we consult only when the familiar terrain we are traversing becomes a tangle of underbrush. He names three particularly significant ethics: authenticity, presence, and responsibility.

The ethic of *authenticity* challenges us to act in truth and integrity in all our interactions as humans, citizens, teachers and leaders. It is the ethic that demands reciprocity in relationships, learning that has real meaning, and structures that promote and challenge authenticity.

The ethic of *presence* challenges us to relate to others, and to develop self-awareness, in ways are truly open and truly engaging. It requires sensitivity, engagement and affirmation, with attentive communication built on insightful self reflection.

The ethic of *responsibility* challenges us to act in ways that acknowledge our personal accountability for our actions, for shaping learning and for providing growth promoting environments for transforming relationships and learning. It asks us to consider not only those things we are responsible as teachers and leaders but to whom. It calls for the development of school cultures of accountability to not only one-another, but to self for the learning that takes place in the school.

Educative leadership

Educative leadership is understood as the capacity to influence others in order to enhance student learning. Research has identified a number of key features which distinguish good leadership, and those in this model embody the values and ethics already discussed. They are: leadership through collegiality, leadership based on evidence, leadership for professional learning, leadership for sustainability, leadership building culture and community, leadership for effective change, leadership through networking and leadership building capability.

Leadership through collegiality requires the development of a culture and enabling structures which provide legitimate power to those staff best placed to make decisions about quality teaching and learning, recognising that all have a contribution to make. An explicit and owned sense of purpose builds on shared values and ethics and informs a shared understanding of what constitutes good practice. Staff hold one another, and students, accountable to shared standards.

Leadership based on evidence builds staff capacity by requiring the collection and analysis of relevant data which informs their planning and actions. It involves teachers taking a research stance in order to learn from their work. Good teachers and good schools collect data to reflect on their effectiveness. Effective Catholic schools develop a sense of the kind of evidence that is important and how to use it.

Leadership for professional learning is a driver of change and development. In fact unless there is learning there is no change in teacher behaviour. Fullan (2001) holds that an effective professional learning community is the key in building the capacity of a school. Effective Catholic schools make collaborative professional learning a focus of activity, encouraging conversation and innovation.

Leadership for sustainability recognises that unless leadership is implemented in ways that are sustainable, no efforts at improvement or ongoing change can be expected to persist in a school. Where leadership practice is unsustainable it places undue demands on those involved and can breach key values and ethics on which the school is built, such as equity, or the common good, or presence. This in turn can lead to alienation and wasted effort (Hargreaves and Fink, 2001). Effective Catholic schools provide resources and support which will promote diverse, activist and widespread leadership.

Leadership building community and culture is at the heart of the Catholic school. Every school community has a culture, built on its history and underlying set of unwritten expectations that shapes everything about it. A school culture influences the ways people think, feel, and act. In effective Catholic schools, leaders give explicit attention to the development of shared purpose, through explicit and commonly used language. They celebrate key events and achievements which reflect core values, expressed in behaviour, word and symbol.

Leadership for effective change – both internally and externally driven – is one of the major challenges for leaders in Catholic schools. It requires that change efforts embody a spirit of optimism, and that they be built on shared moral purpose, progressed with a keen sensitivity to the role of relationships, contribute to the increased knowledge in the school community and be consistent with the school's values and ethics (Fullan, 2001).

Leadership through networking ensures that the school not only taps into the resources of its staff, but looks to parents, parish and other educational providers. The Catholic school works in partnership with parents in its educative mission. It is a significant element of the work of the parish. The school also seeks to build constructive alliances with other partners in the education enterprise, in order to enhance its capacity to engage with the increasingly complex and demanding educational agenda in society and the Church.

Leadership building capability gives a school a 'dynamic capacity to respond to changing circumstances' (Duignan, 2006). A capability is not just having the capacity to act, but actually doing so. It involves the integration of knowledge, skills personal qualities and understanding. Leaders in Catholic schools are challenged to expand the reservoir of leadership capability in their schools, appreciating the complexity of leadership, and recognizing the capabilities of others. This calls for the challenge and support in a climate of trust.

Authentic learning

Authentic learning is the very heart of the enterprise in Catholic schools. It is the most profound manifestation of the moral purpose which is captured in its vision of transformed learners. Research has identified a set of focus points that have been shown (e.g. National Quality Schooling Framework (NQSF), Cuttance et al., 2003) to impact positively on learning outcomes. These are represented here as standards for learning, organising for learning, pedagogy, student engagement and assessment *for* and *as* learning. Each of these is a potential point of influence for the leader and its implementation needs to be in accord with espoused values and ethics, using the types of leadership behaviours already identified. Leaders looking for critical points of engagement with the learning agenda should begin by considering these.

Reflecting the value of excellence in particular, explicit, known and owned *standards for learning* are vital to the success of any school. Such standards are not limited to the formal academic curriculum, but should reflect the full range of outcomes for which the school strives.

Organising for learning impacts directly on outcomes. Effective schools make use of time, space, technology and groupings in ways which cater for individual difference, ensure equity and avoid waste in creating safe and stimulating environments (actual and virtual) for the pursuit of authentic learning.

The classroom encounter between the learner and that to be learned, between the learner and the teacher is often described as *pedagogy*. It is this act which the whole school is structured to enable. The research on teaching and learning tells us that the pedagogy which makes the greatest contribution to student outcomes is personalised, differentiated, goal focused, centred in relationship, built on prior learning, uses specific feedback and promotes self-responsibility. Structures to enhance the capacity of pedagogy include regular monitoring of student progress, and feedback. Where appropriate, this monitoring and feedback should give rise to purpose developed intervention programs, in the spirit of justice and the common good.

Student engagement is one of the marks of authentic learning. It reflects a genuine connection between the student and the material being learned, and is enhanced by building on prior knowledge and seeking to progress towards explicit individualised goals. It requires that students be self motivated and able to apply learnings to new situations.

Assessment is about more than giving marks in a summative exercise. An appreciation of *assessment for and as learning* is the basis on which the ideals of personalised learning can be built, and through which both students and parents can be informed of student progress. It is a way to help teachers and students decide what needs to be learned next (and how). It should be a key part of designing teaching.

The challenge for the future

This chapter has provided an overview of an emerging framework for understanding the privileged work of leading learning in Catholic schools. The LTLL pilot project revealed an enthusiasm among participants for working closely with the fundamental concerns of Catholic education in a way that is holistic, well-founded in the research and reflects accurately their unique values stance. Its explicitness, and its capacity to promote a common vocabulary and a common sense of the 'big picture' contributed to the development of shared understandings and processes among staff. These helped school staffs to engage with one another in ways that contributed to the provision of learning for both themselves and their students which was genuinely transformative, in the fullest Catholic understanding of that word. As one participant put it:

> the model for me has really emphasised … the moral nature of teaching, and I think … Catholics can grab hold of the model very easily and use it [as a] framework for their work.

This echoes, almost twenty years later, the sentiments of *The Religious Dimension of Education in the Catholic School (1988, n19)* which said:

> Teaching has an extraordinary moral depth and is one of man's (sic) most excellent and creative activities, for the teacher does not write on inanimate material, but on the very spirits of human beings.

The work of writing on 'the very spirits of human beings' is surely among the most privileged and the most daunting in which humanity engages. Leading this work, even more so. This chapter makes available some of the early learnings from an attempt to be as explicit and systematic about our moral purpose as Catholic educators as we have been (when we are at our best) about teaching and learning. The seriousness and complexity of the task of Catholic education drives some to over-simplification through recourse to the memories of a different era, in a world where both moral codes and movies were black and white. It is hoped that this chapter will open up a different way forward, calling perhaps for a compass rather than a map — one which draws on a deep sense of moral purpose and a sophisticated sense of learning and leadership to engage in deep thought, much conversation and an openness to learning from experience.

References

Andrews, D. and Lewis, M. (2004). Building sustainable futures: *Improving schools*, *7*, (2), PP129-150.

Bezzina, M. (2007) *Moral purpose and shared leadership: The Leaders Transforming Learning and learners* pilot study. Paper presented at the ACER Research Conference: The Leadership Challenge: Improving Learning in Schools. Melbourne. 12-14 August

Bezzina, M., Burford, C. and Duignan, P. (2007). *Leaders Transforming Learning and Learners: Messages for Catholic leaders.* Paper presented at the Fourth International Conference on Catholic Educational Leadership. Sydney, July 29-August 1.

Bishops of NSW and the ACT (2007) *Catholic Schools at the Crossroads.* Sydney. Bishops of NSW and the ACT.

Burns, J.M., (1978). *Leadership.* New York: Harper and Row.

Congregation for Catholic Education (1997) *The Catholic School on the Threshold of the Third Millennium.* Strathfield. St Pauls Press.

Crowther, F, Hann, L, & Andrews, D, (2002a). Rethinking the role of the school principal: successful school improvement in the post industrial era, *The Practicing Administrator. 24* (2) 10-13

Crowther, F, Kaagan, S S, Ferguson, M, & Hann, L (2002b). *Developing teacher leaders: how teacher leadership enhances school success.* California: Sage.

Cuttance, P., Stokes, S., McGuinness, K., Capponi, N., Corneille, K., Jones, T. and Umoh, C. (2003). *The National Quality Schooling Framework: An interactive professional learning network for schools.* Monograph. Melbourne: University of Melbourne

Duignan, P. (2006) *Educational Leadership.* Cambridge: Cambridge University Press

Duignan, P. and Bezzina, M. (2004) *Leadership and Learning: Influencing what really matters.* Presentation at the Teacher Education Council Conference, Strathfield. ACU National

Duignan, P. and Bezzina, M. (2006) Distributed leadership: The theory and the practice. Paper presented at the Commonwealth Council for Educational Administration conference, Lefkosia, Cyprus.

Duignan, P and McPherson, R.J.S. (1992). *Educative Leadership: A New Practical Theory for Administrators and Managers.* London: Falmer Press

Fullan, M, (2001), *Understanding Change: Leading in a Culture of Change,*. San Francisco: Jossey-Bass.

Hargreaves, A. and Fink, D. (2006), *Sustainable Leadership* Jossey-Bass, San Francisco.

Marzano, R., Waters, T. and McNulty, B.A. (2005). *School Leadership that Works.* Alexandria, VA: ASCD

MacBeath, J. (2005) Leadership as distributed: A matter of practice. *School Leadership and Management, 25 (4), pp.* 349-366.

Miller, M. (2005) The *Holy See's Teaching On Catholic Schools.* Keynote Address The Catholic University of America.

NCSL (2006). *Five pillars of distributed leadership* (Monograph 3.1,

Distributed leadership) Retrieved April 30, 2007 from www.ncsl.org.uk/distributedleadership

Pell, G. (2006) *Religion and Culture: Catholic Schools in Australia.* Keynote address to the 2006 National Catholic Education Conference, Sydney

Sacred Congregation for Catholic Education (1988) *The Religious Dimension of Education in a Catholic School.* Rome: Sacred Congregation for Catholic Education

Sacred Congregation for Catholic Education (1977) *The Catholic School*, Rome: Sacred Congregation for Catholic Education.

Starratt, R. J. (2004). *Ethical leadership*. San Francisco: Jossey-Bass.

17

Building leadership capacity in Catholic school communities: Is 'distributed leadership' really the answer?

PATRICK DUIGNAN

Much is written and talked about the theory and practice of distributed leadership in the area of educational leadership. The work of Spillane (2006), Harris (2006), Mulford (2006) and Elmore (2000) are pre-eminent among theorists in the area. In numerous workshops I conduct on the topic, many school leaders also report that they engage in distributed leadership practices.

I support the orientation and intentions of those theoreticians and practitioners who argue for greater sharing of the responsibilities and practices of leadership in school communities but wish to query the way in which the term 'distributed leadership' is often promoted and supported unquestionably and uncritically as 'the way to do it.' In fact, I argue that the label 'distributed leadership' may unwittingly, in both theory and practice, be supporting leadership mindsets, paradigms and practices that perpetuate control-oriented approaches to leadership and mitigate against building the breadth (wider net of leaders) and depth (deeper pool of leaders) of leadership in schools.

The idea of sharing leadership in a school community setting seems sensible and positive – the right thing to do. It promotes an image of people working purposefully together to achieve a school's goals and this surely is a good thing. The language, however, of distributed leadership may provide many practitioners with the comfortable and comforting sense that if they distribute duties, tasks and responsibilities, leadership capacity and density in their organisation will be greatly strengthened. They may indeed be right but there is also the distinct possibility that this is not the case.

While I do not wish to appear overly negative toward a possibly well-intentioned development in educational leadership (if it constitutes a genuine attempt to move away from hierarchical and control-approaches to leadership), I caution that we need to be clearer in terms of the meaning of the language of distributed leadership, its interpretation, and the approaches to implementation by some educational leaders whose intention is to grow leadership capacity in their schools. I will also propose an alternative framework for leadership, which, I argue, is more likely to build a greater breadth and depth of leadership in Catholic schools.

Drawing on recent research (Duignan, 2006; Duignan and Bezzina, 2006; Leaders Transforming Learners and Learning (LTLL), 2005-06), relevant literature, my own experiences as an educational leader, and my conversations with a large number of educational leaders in Catholic schools across Australia, I argue that:

1. The idea of a collective responsibility for leadership in Catholic schools is desirable and attainable

2. The concept of distributed leadership, which is widely promoted as the preferred model for sharing leadership in schools and school communities, needs to be critiqued and challenged as it may well involve conflicting assumptions and/or a clash of paradigms

3. A number of *Catholic imperatives* suggest an alternative paradigm that provides a framework for growing and nurturing the breadth and depth of leadership in Catholic schools; and

4. The concept of love-inspired leadership overcomes many of the shortcomings of distributed leadership and incorporates the essence of these Catholic imperatives.

Leadership is a Collective Responsibility

I support those who advocate spreading the net and deepening the pool of leadership talent in schools and educational systems, and I do so from the perspective that no single person (for example, the Catholic Education Office Director or principal) is capable of providing the quality of leadership required to lead complex contemporary organisations, such as Catholic systems and schools. It also seems sensible and practical to actively engage key stakeholders in important decision making so as to generate in them an increased sense of commitment, responsibility and ownership for the success of these decisions.

I believe that we all generally accept (at least the idea has become part of received wisdom) that many heads are better than one and that diversity of opinions and advice helps protect us from what is often referred to as 'group think.' There would seem to be a number of sensible reasons why leadership should be a shared phenomenon in Catholic systems and schools.

Leadership is too much for one person

Flockton (2001) suggested that in the school setting the principal is expected to be legal expert, health and social services coordinator, fundraiser, diplomat, negotiator, adjudicator, public relations consultant, security officer, technological innovator and top notch resource manager, whose most important job is the promotion of teaching and learning. Other labels that are relevant are confidante, marriage counsellor, architect, engineer, sanitary contractor.

Given the complexity of contemporary school communities, the multi-dimensional nature of the principal's role, and the very heavy workloads reported by incumbents in the role, it would seem both sensible and necessary for them to engage with others in meeting the expectations of the job. The 'Lone Ranger' approach is no longer, if it ever was, desirable or practical. The job has become too complex for one person.

Diversity matters in leadership and decision making

Another positive reason for collective activity in leadership is that diversity of perspectives and expertise actually matters in decision making. According to Surowiecki (2004, p.20), diversity of people and their information helps in coming to a better decision or resolution because it actually adds perspectives that would otherwise be absent and because it takes away, or at least weakens, some of the destructive characteristics of group decision making (e.g., group think). Grouping only smart people (experts) together, he states, does not work that well because they tend to resemble each other in what they can do. It is better to entrust a diverse group with varying degrees of knowledge and insight with major decisions rather than leaving them in the hands of one or two people, no matter how smart those people are (pp.30-31).

Surowiecki (p.31) also argues that there is no evidence that one can become expert in something as broad as 'decision making.' A group of diverse individuals will make better and more robust forecasts and more intelligent decisions than a 'skilled decision maker'.

The implications of what he is suggesting is that when important decisions have to be made in schools on, for example, the purchase and use of technology or the development of new literacy and numeracy programs, it is not advisable to rely only on experts in these specific areas for advice. It is important, he suggests, to engage with a wider spread of expertise and opinion in order to come up with more robust decisions.

Involvement leads to greater commitment and ownership

It has been long recognised in research and literature on educational change that it is wise to engage those affected by a decision or a change in its formulation. Those who are engaged in making key decisions about a change (or development) are more likely to be committed to its implementation. People feel valued when they are included and involved and this helps in building a culture of trust. Such a culture is necessary for a professional learning community to be developed and sustained.

Leadership is an influence relationship

Many current researchers and writers on leadership contend that effective leadership is, essentially, an influencing process (Hargreaves & Fullan, 1991: Rost, 1993). Rost (1993, p. 79), in a major review and critique of definitions of leadership, argued that 'if there are few other unifying elements to our collective thought about leadership, the notion of leadership as influence is one that clearly stands out.' From his comprehensive critique of numerous definitions of leadership, Rost (1993, p. 102) proposed that leadership is '. . . an influence relationship among leaders and followers who intend real changes that reflect their mutual purposes.'

Others to propose that leadership as an influencing process are Hoog et al. (2003) who claimed that leaders operate from a value set, which they use to influence the thoughts and actions of others, and Duignan (2006) who argued that leadership is, essentially, an influencing process because effective leaders have the capability to influence self, others and each other in order to attain worthwhile and agreed goals; engage in meaningful relationships to generate and live a shared vision; use scarce resources wisely and responsibly; and elevate the human spirit to higher levels of motivation and morality through actions and interactions that are ethical moral and compassionate.

If influencing is central to leadership, then the best way to influence others is to develop mutually rewarding relationships with them. Relationships are at the heart of influential leadership practice. Relationships, influencing and leadership are closely connected concepts. A simple connection among the concepts would suggest that without relationships there is unlikely to be much influence and without influence there is unlikely to be leadership in the way we have defined it here. This view of leadership suggests the need for a collective approach to leadership and is also important when we critique the concept and practice of distributed leadership.

Critique of 'distributed leadership'

While I support frameworks for sharing leadership in schools, I am not persuaded that the approach labelled 'distributed' leadership, as it is currently promoted and often practiced, necessarily fulfills its often lofty promises. Indeed, as currently practiced by some educational leaders, it may, in fact, promote and support mindsets and practices that are antithetical to what is actually intended. I now raise a number of issues related to distributed leadership that challenge its relevancy and usefulness in Catholic schools, especially for building their leadership capacity.

Problematic assumptions

It is unwise to assume because we share a common language or use a specific term that we all share a common meaning. The term 'distributed leadership,' even 'shared leadership,' can mean different things to different people within a system or organisation. One's view or perspective of leadership and, especially, distributed leadership, can be influenced by one's viewing point. Those who are located within system central offices may have a different perspective from those in schools, and even within schools teachers may have a different perspective or understanding of a concept like distributed leadership from members of the executive. Many in formal leadership positions in schools (e.g., principals) actually believe that when they distribute tasks (timetabling, discipline control) or delegate decision making, they are actually building the leadership capacity in their schools. As we shall see later, this is not, necessarily, a safe assumption. This raises the issue of what it is we are actually distributing when we say we are distributing or have distributed leadership.

What are we distributing?
When we talk about distributing or distributed leadership, are we referring to the distribution of knowledge, tasks, responsibilities, power, authority? Are we referring to delegating? Traditionally in schools, those in leadership pathways (e.g. subject coordinators, department heads, assistant and deputy-principals) have been delegated specific tasks and responsibilities; for deputies it often was (and still is) student discipline and/or timetabling. Is this distributed leadership?

Some research by d'Arbon et al. (2003) and Dawson (2003) seems to indicate that the answer is, 'not really'. D'Arbon et al. found that many of those in the pool from which principals are drawn (many were assistant and deputy principals) stated that they did not have the confidence to apply for the principalship. What does this say about their leadership capabilities? What does it suggest about our assumption that the position of assistant or deputy principal is part of the career-path preparation for the principalship?

Dawson (2003) surveyed every department head in state secondary schools in New South Wales as to the degree of their engagement in curriculum and pedagogical leadership and found that they did not see themselves performing this role. It would seem, therefore, that some of the traditional pathways toward principalship within schools, with their associated distributed tasks and responsibilities, may have failed to prepare many incumbents for leadership roles (or at least they have not given them the confidence to apply for them) or to generate the breadth and depth of leadership required to run complex contemporary schools. In the case of the department heads researched by Dawson, it would appear that if their principals believed that by distributing certain specific tasks related to curriculum and pedagogy they were distributing leadership, they may have been mistaken.

Can an influence relationship be distributed?

If leadership is, essentially an influence relationship, then it is fair to ask if talk of distributing it is meaningful. Are we actually asking the right question and using the right language? It can be argued that the words 'distributing' and 'distributed,' when used to qualify the word leadership, may actually reflect a centralist and/or control paradigm of leadership. Few could dispute that hierarchical, bureaucratic and control approaches to leadership are alive and well in many Catholic systems and schools. Yet the language of distributed leadership is everywhere in those same systems and schools.

It may be argued that the concept of leadership presented in this chapter (an influence relationship) may in fact come from a different framework, one that promotes and supports substantial involvement of all key stakeholders in the decisions that impact on their lives, one that allows and supports key stakeholders to grow as persons, professionals and leaders thereby helping them generate their own influence relationships. In this paradigm, it may be more productive to think of leadership as a phenomenon that is grown and nurtured through building networks of influence relationships and not as something that can be distributed, or even shared.

An alternative framework

I want to propose an alternative leadership framework for building of leadership capacity in Catholic schools. It constitutes a philosophically, theologically and scripturally driven framework for leadership using a number of *Catholic imperatives.*

There are a number of key Catholic concepts that are so engrained in scripture and Vatican documents that, in themselves, they form a framework for a different approach to leadership in Catholic schools. I select five that are central to the growth and nurturing of leadership in Catholic systems and schools.

The Catholic School as community

The Catholic school as a ministry of the Catholic Church is not just an organisation, it is a community of the 'People of God'. This is made absolutely clear in the *Declaration on Christian Education* (1965, par. 8):

> What makes the Catholic school distinctive is its attempt to generate a community climate in the school that is permeated by the Gospel spirit of freedom and love.

This is a view that has been repeated in a number of Vatican documents on the Catholic school in the ensuing years. Leadership in such a community requires a relational and collective framework and the use of the talents of all members. We are reminded in Romans 12: 4-5 that:

> Just as each of us has one body with many members, and not all the members have the same function, so too we, though many, are one body in Christ and individually members of one another.

The Catholic school is a community in another sense as well. David Ranson (2006) suggested that the Catholic school '. . . has become the primary manifestation of the local ecclesial community, the parish, and the principal means of that community to religiously enculturate its young members.' (p.417)

The concept of *communitas* is also a useful way of understanding a Catholic school as a community. It can be interpreted as an unstructured human community based on principles of unity (beyond the needs of individuals or groups) possessing a common purpose and experience as well as an intense unity and community spirit. The community members associate to achieve purposes and objectives that exceed individual capacities.

The common good

The Catechism of the Catholic Church points out that the good of each individual in a community or society is, of necessity, closely tied to the common good. The common good, according to the *Catechism* (S1906), is to be understood as 'the sum total of social conditions which allow people, either as groups or individuals, to reach their fulfilment more fully and more easily. The common good concerns the life of all. It calls for prudence from each, and even more from those who exercise the office of authority.'

The common good comprises three essential elements (italics in original):
1. It presupposes *respect for the person*
2. It requires the *social well-being* and *development* of the group itself

3. It requires peace, that is, the stability and security of a just order.

The idea of the common good is an important dimension of a framework for leadership in Catholic schools because it emphasises the requirement for individuals and groups to reach their fulfillment more fully and more easily through relationships based on respect and social well-being.

Positive subsidiarity

The Catholic Church has strongly enunciated the principle of *subsidiarity* (encyclicals *Rerum Novarum* of Leo XIII, 1891 and *Quadragesimo Anno* of Pius XII, 1931), which proposes that 'a community of a higher order should not interfere in the internal life of a community of a lower order, depriving the latter of its functions, but rather should support it in case of need and help co-ordinate its activity with the activities of the rest of society, always with a view to the common good' (CA 48 # 4; cf. Pius XI, *Quadragesimo anno* I, #184-186).

In practice it implies that a central authority should have a subsidiary function making those decisions that cannot be made more effectively at a more immediate or local level. Currently, it is a principle at the heart of European Union (EU) law (Treaty of Maastricht, 1992) stating that the EU may only make policy or decisions in situations where member states agree that action by individual countries is insufficient.

The concept of 'positive subsidiarity' demands that higher order institutions and communities create the conditions necessary for the full development of the human person and provide mediating processes and structures to empower individual and small group action, thereby linking them to their community and to society.

In education, it requires greater involvement of schools in making key decisions related to teaching and learning and, within schools, the greater involvement of teachers and community stakeholders in decisions focusing on the transformation of learners and learning.

Leadership as service

Scripture provides us with this important insight and perspective:

> … rather let the greatest among you become as the youngest, and the leader as one who serves. For which is the greater, one who sits at the table, or one who serves? Is it not the one who sits at the table? But I am among you as one who serves (Luke 22: 24-27).

There is an important symbolic meaning attached to the concept of leadership as service. When Jesus washed the feet of the disciples at the Last Supper he was making a deep and meaningful gesture about how we should treat each other in community. He wasn't merely implying that the disciples should copy what he had done, but was providing them with a broader framework for action and interaction based on respect for the dignity and worth of each individual and also on the need for the collective to behave as a community of love. As a servant leader, Jesus was driven by love and clearly demonstrated that leadership is above all else relational.

Robert Greenleaf (1977), the man usually acknowledged as introducing the concept of servant leadership to the business world, established the acid test for leadership as service when he asked:

> Do those served grow as persons? Do they, become healthier, wiser, freer, more autonomous, more likely themselves to become servants? (p. 14).

This is also a key test for any form of leadership in Catholic schools, which should be emancipatory, elevating, mutually empowering, and driven by love. It requires careful stewardship and husbandry of very valuable resources (people) in the tradition of Christian love as evidenced in the Jesuit philosophy and practice of leadership.

Love-inspired Leadership

Lowney (2003), explained that the Jesuit model of 'love-driven leadership' required their leaders to have their eyes open to the talent and potential in their organisation:

> Love was the lens through which individual Jesuits beheld the world around them. It changed not only the way Jesuits looked at others but what they saw. Their vision became more acute, their eyes open to talent and potential (p. 170).

He summarised love-driven leadership as:
- The *vision* to see each person's talent, potential, and dignity
- The *courage, passion, and commitment* to unlock that potential
- The resulting *loyalty and mutual support* that energise and unite teams (Lowney, p. 170, italics in original)

The Jesuits turned the notion of leadership as referring to those who are in charge on its head by exhorting them to '. . . stop behaving as if they're leading followers and start acting as if they're leading leaders by doing what helps others lead' (Lowney, p. 285). The Jesuit founders built their leadership and their 'company' by finding and nurturing 'as many as possible of the very best (*Quamplurimi et quam aptissimi*)'. This Jesuit passion about and commitment to *aptissimi* (excellence) ensured that they tapped into the talent and potential of the collective and elevated all to leadership in their company.

These ideas on leadership are exactly what is needed to grow and nurture the breadth and depth of leadership in Catholic systems and schools and is an important framework for responding to one key negative issue identified in leadership succession research (d'Arbon et al. 2003), namely, that many who are in assistant and deputy-principalship roles do not have the confidence to apply for the job (read have not been properly developed as leaders). A distributed approach to leadership, as it is currently promulgated and practiced by many leadership practitioners, will not deliver the type of love-inspired leadership required to grow leadership capacity in Catholic schools.

These Catholic imperatives require a sharing of leadership practices based on a leadership paradigm that is different from the one that I have argued often underpins contemporary approaches to distributed leadership in hierarchical contexts. These imperatives should inspire us all to embrace an approach to leadership that identifies (seeks out) and taps into the talents and expertise of all key stakeholders and helps them grow as leaders in their sphere of influence – classrooms, schools, school communities, systems.

Based on these imperatives, as well as on my critique of distributed leadership, I now propose some recommendations for a way forward for building leadership capacity in Catholic systems and schools.

Building leadership capacity in Catholic schools

A useful starting point is to critique the existing language, assumptions and meaning of leadership in contemporary Catholic systems and schools, including the concept of distributed leadership. The following points should assist in this critique:
- Do not assume too much about agreed meanings around leadership and surface and critique existing assumptions in open dialogue

- Create the conditions that encourage both principals and teachers to openly discuss meanings, purposes, anxieties about leadership (for example, distributed leadership) — this will help build an enabling and trusting culture
- Identify a moral purpose for sharing leadership practices around maximising opportunities and outcomes for all students
- Backwards map from a focus on transforming learners and learning (what would transformed learners look like?) to the type of pedagogy and teaching required for this transformation and then to the approach to leadership that best engages and empowers all key stakeholders in this exciting enterprise
- Use teachers as leadership ambassadors for other teachers with the intent of generating a critical mass and a 'tipping point' for whole-school staff engagement and involvement in leadership.

The Catholic imperatives I identified earlier can help you develop a specific frame for sharing leadership practices within your Catholic system or school. Leaders should ask themselves the following questions:

- Are you acting as if you're leading followers? If so, start acting as if you're leading leaders
- Are you open to the great talent and potential that is present in your organisation?
- Do you have a passion and commitment for *aptissimi* (excellence) in order to ensure that you are tapping into the talent and potential of all key stakeholders in your system and/or organisation?
- Are you broadening the net and deepen the pool of leadership capability in your system or school?
- Do those who work with you grow as persons? Do they, become healthier, wiser, freer, more autonomous, more likely themselves to become influential leaders?
- How well do you create the social conditions which allow people, either as groups or individuals, to reach their fulfillment more fully and more easily?
- Do you provide user-friendly and effective mediating processes and structures to empower individuals and small groups, especially with regard to making (or having major input into making) decisions that have a profound effect on their lives?

Conclusion

The key conclusion of the argument in this chapter is that leadership is an influencing relationship and, as such, does not lend itself to distribution, especially if this term is interpreted within a hierarchical and/or control paradigm. If you are intending to increase leadership capacity and density in your system or school, it is preferable to develop, grow and nurture leadership from the ground up. You need to create an *allowed-to-be-a-leader culture,* especially with new and younger staff. Seek out and nurture *aptissimi* and generate a *dare-to-lead* ethos. Have the vision, courage and commitment to see each person's talent, potential through love-inspired leadership.

It is not really a matter of distributing or distributed leadership, it is more a matter of developing capabilities in self and others and building capacities within groups and organisations. For some, such an approach comes easily, others may require a 'paradigm transplant'.

Let me conclude with a most insightful quote from Mother Teresa:

> You can do what I cannot do. I can do what you cannot do.
>
> Together, we can do great things.
>
> That's the result of partnership in Jesus.

References

Catholic Church Encycicals *Rerum Novarum* of Leo X111, 1891 and *Quadragesimo Anno* of Pius X11, 1931.

d'Arbon, T., Duignan, P. & Duncan, D (2003) Planning for Future Leadership in Schools: An Australian Study. *Journal of Educational Administration.*

Dawson, G. (2003) *Curriculum leadership and management,* Unpublished Doctoral Thesis, Sydney: University of Sydney.

Declaration on Christian Education (1965) *Gravissimum Educationis* Proclaimed by Pope Paul VI on October 28, 1965 paragraph 8.

Duignan, P. (2006) *Educational leadership: key challenges and ethical tensions.* New York: Cambridge Press.

Duignan, P. and Bezzina, M. (2006) Distributed leadership: the theory and the practice, CCEAM Annual Conference Hilton Cyprus Hotel, Lefkosia, Cyprus 12-17 October.

Elmore, R. (2000) *Building a New Structure for School Leadership*, The Albert Shanker Institute. Winter.

Flockton, L. (2001) Tomorrow's Schools: A World of Difference. Paper presented at the International Confederation of Principals,

Greenleaf, R.K. (1977) *Servant Leadership: A Journey into the Nature of Legitimate Power and Greatness,* New York: Paulist Press.

Hargreaves, A. and Fullan, M. (1991) *What's worth fighting for: Working together for your school.* Hawthorne: ACEA Paperbacks.

Harris, A (2006) Distributed Leadership: A Case of Theory Following Practice CCEAM Keynote Address Cyprus October 10th-13th

Hoog, J., Johansson, O., Lindberg, L., Olofsson, A. (2003) Structure, Culture, Leadership: Prerequisites for Successful Schools? *International Conference: School Effectiveness and Improvement.* Sydney, Australia. January 5-8, 2003.

Lowney, C. (2003) *Heroic Leadership.* Loyola Press, Chicago.

LTLL Project (2005-06) *Leaders Transforming Learners and Learning.* Sydney, ACU National.

Mulford, B. (2006) Leadership for school and student learning - what do we know? *BC* [University of British Columbia] *Educational Leadership Research, 4,* pp. 1-4.

Ranson, D. (2006) Forming a New Generation of Leaders for Catholic Schools. *Australasian Catholic Record, 83,* (4), 415-421.

Rost, J.C. (1993) *Leadership for the twenty-first century.* London: Praeger. South Korea, July.

Society of St Paul/Liberia Editrice Vaticana, Homebush/Vatican City. *The Catechism of the Catholic Church* (1906).

Spillane, J.P. (2006) *Distributed Leadership.* San Francisco, CA: Jossey-Bass.

Surowiecki, P. (2004) *The Wisdom of Crowds.* Anchor, a division of Random House, New York.

18

A Story of Hope: Holy Family Primary School

Brenda Kennedy and Tricia Carr

The story that follows about Holy Family Primary School echoes that of so many other Catholic schools throughout the country, each endeavouring in its own way to honour its mission to children and to the Church. In sharing something of the journey of one school, it is possible to understand others a little better. Holy Family is like each of these schools. It is also unique.

Preamble

Holy Family Parish in Emerton, Mount Druitt, in western Sydney, is situated in one of the most disadvantaged areas in Australia. Indigenous children represent 17% of its enrolment. For many years, the parish has opened its heart to the people in the community in a unique way, offering welcome, refuge, relief, advocacy, family support and non-formal education.

For a number of reasons, Holy Family Parish had not ever established a Catholic primary school. Early in 1997, the Director of Schools in the Diocese of Parramatta spent a full day in the parish as a guest of the parish priest at that time, Father Paul Hanna and the parish team. As a result of ongoing liaison between the parish and the Catholic Education Office over the next few years, the decision was taken by the Parramatta Diocesan Schools Board to establish a new school in the parish.

The founding Principal, Brenda Kennedy, a member of the Irish-founded Holy Faith sisters, brought 17 years' experience as a principal to the challenge of creating the new school. Assistant Principal, Tricia Carr, who joined her, likewise had a depth of experience and reputation as a teacher.

Getting started

During 2003, Brenda made preparations for the school to open for the 2004 school year. She was based in the parish centre during this time. After years of busy experience leading schools, she found herself in a vacuum, responsible for a school that as yet had no children, no parents, no teachers, no buildings: *she* was the school. Brenda describes this as one of the most frightening moments she can remember. There were many practical details to attend to as well as the larger ones of attracting students and staff.

An early step was to develop enrolment posters to let the broader community know about the school. The challenge in this task was to create an identity for a school which as yet had no motto or mission statement or history or story. The result was colourful and vibrant. With the assistance of one of the volunteers in the parish centre, Brenda drove around the shopping centres in the area and persuaded the shop owners to display the posters. Local newspapers carried advertisements for the new school.

Late in 2003, when there was still nothing physical on the site to show that a school was opening, Brenda spoke at weekend Masses and invited people to enrol their children. The first enrolments came very slowly. Brenda spent a lot of time with the families. She met with them in the parish centre, or visited families in their homes if they could not easily get to the Centre. Brenda still recalls vividly those conversations. For example, one young woman told Brenda about her partner who was in jail at the time while she was alone with their small children. She told Brenda, 'I think I am a Catholic. I do not know what to do and I want you to help me.'

Later in the year, when the Assistant Principal, Tricia, was appointed, the engagement with children started to get underway, with an orientation program in the Centre for the new children, using toys and equipment borrowed from friends in other schools.

The first weeks

There were delays in the building program and so when the school year opened in 2004, the fledgling school was without permanent buildings. The administration operated from a demountable inside the school fence. Kindergarten children were temporarily accommodated in an old cottage on the parish site, outside the school fence. This immediately raised issues regarding safety and supervision, especially for kindergarten children. The kindergarten room was small and musty. A fan helped the hot summer days in western Sydney and curtains given by another school made it look more like a classroom. Then someone gave the school an air conditioner to overcome the stuffiness. It was very crowded but the children loved it.

Those first children were really challenging for the staff to manage. Initially, the children seemed to have no sense of what happens when you go to school. And there were a few surprises. Holy Family Parish is a parish that has opened its doors to those in need. Unbeknown to teachers, the cottage initially used as a kindergarten room had previously been used as an Alcoholic Anonymous (AA) meeting place. It was not uncommon in those early days to have people in transit, knock on the door, or simply wander through, asking for electricity coupons or food vouchers. Or 'Where is the AA meeting?' They were unusual encounters, given they occurred in the middle of a kindergarten classroom!

Wild dogs had made their home underneath the administration building in the summer before the school opened and they had left a legacy of fleas. A number of remedies to get rid of the fleas failed. Brenda admits that she and her colleagues were stressed. After consulting further, Brenda made the decision to move completely off site so that the temporary buildings could be properly fumigated. With support from the education office, another primary principal offered the community a classroom. So Brenda, Tricia and the teachers commuted with their 38 kindergarten children further west to the suburb of St Clair for ten days.

At this stage, Brenda and Tricia experienced an extraordinary trust in the school from the parents. Brenda had written to parents to tell them what was happening. Not one parent questioned her about the situation. It was, after all, very unusual. Parents waved off their little kindy children (who had been at school for only about eight days), and accepted it. They did not ask, 'Why? Where are you going? What is happening?' Brenda realised then the respect that parents had in them as educators. In her words, 'It was the kind of trust that simply accepted what we said, because if we said we were going to do it, then they knew it must be all right. They just waved us off in the bus'. This was an extraordinarily positive statement about the kind of relationship that had already developed between the school and parent communities.

The children

The time spent in St Clair was one of welcome given by the children and teachers of Holy Spirit Primary School. Nonetheless, the sojourn at St Clair complicated the start of the school. It was apparent from the beginning that — as all good teachers do — the teachers in Holy Family needed to understand the particular needs and circumstances of the children given into their care with such unquestioning trust. The Principal and her staff admit that in the early days they were challenged in developing this understanding and the best way forward. Another first was for the teachers to come together as a staff for the first time, to get to know each other and to develop as a group and as team and ultimately as a community. This dynamism was also put on hold during the two weeks the school was off-site.

Back on their own site in Emerton, one of the first steps for the staff was to teach the children a little bit about being at school. Until they did that and brokered some understandings about the disciplines of formal schooling, school days were very stressful. There were only 38 children, but the staff found it necessary in the beginning to always have two adults with them on playground duty. The children brought with them to school a lot of physicality in their interactions. Staff had to keep them apart bodily. And being Principal did not save Brenda from children throwing rocks at her on one occasion.

Staff would work with children during the week, and then discover on Monday that all the discipline of the previous week was gone. So they changed their whole program to respond to this. One strategy the staff developed in the early days was to curtail children from running around on Mondays: they got to sit and eat, and be outside and talk to each other. Similarly, for those children sent to the principal's office — quite a common occurrence at first — Brenda would sit with the 'miscreants' and simply get them to play and to relax, to try and calm down. She would get them to draw for her and chat. This intervention eased the task of the teachers in the playground.

Since those early beginnings, teachers have noted tremendous changes. In the first place, they were very consistent in their expectations of what behaviours were acceptable from the children. 'Sure,' says Brenda, some years later, 'it almost wears you out, but we needed to be consistent.' However, there was more to it than just consistency of expectation regarding behaviour. Brenda and Tricia worked to develop in the school a mindset which always asked *Why* when a child misbehaved. Tricia's further comment is significant.

> I think what was critical was the relationship we developed with those children. You know, we came to know them so well. There was one child who was so violent especially on Thursdays and Fridays. As we observed him, we realized that something was happening at home and in his life on the weekends. He would come over to the office sometimes and just stand there and throw rocks at the window to get our attention.

Overall, those first children of Holy Family School were very resilient children, more resilient than most kindergarten children whom staff had previously taught. Because no one had told them about 'sick bay', children did not know to ask for ice packs or for time in sick bay. They had had lots of changes in their lives, lots of people in their lives who had come and gone. Nor did they get attached to their kindergarten teachers as readily as most children do.

The staff worked with Brenda and Tricia to build a relationship with the children. Sometimes, even now, they sense the children are a lot harder on themselves than the staff would be. Teachers will sometimes say to a child: 'Look, you made a mistake. You have done the wrong thing. What do you think your punishment should be?' They note that the children might put themselves out of play for a week, while the teacher would be thinking of just one day out.

The family and parents did not comment much to the staff about the changes in the children's behaviour. They accept the strict approach to discipline as part of their children being at school. The Principal and her colleagues communicate regularly with families, so there is good information flow. If children misbehave, then someone from the school talks with the parents who, in turn, are very co-operative with the school. Brenda describes the parents as 'being terrific.' She gives the example of her ringing a parent to tell them another child has hurt their child. The parent replied, 'Do not worry, my child's just as bad.' It was just a sensible kind of thinking. In this instance, the mum knew her son. That time he was the victim, but he was capable of doing the same thing to someone else.

The families

Discussion about religious matters has, if anything, been easier in this context where the Catholicism of parents is not taken for granted. On their first parent/teacher night held in the Parish Centre, Brenda asked the parents, 'What are some of the things that you enjoy about your children being at school?' She was delighted with the responses parents offered. 'We love them coming home and saying their prayers', said one parent. 'Sometimes the dinner is late because the children's prayers are so long', said another. At that stage, the school enrolments were probably about 50% Catholic.

Parents sometimes surprise the Principal when they enrol. Brenda recalls one young mum who had had a bad experience with another religious group. She asked to enrol her child because her cousin was here and she had come up a few times and liked the feel of the place. Brenda continues the story.

> She was very hesitant about religion. I remember saying, 'If you do come, you will have to take part in the community, and your daughter will have to take part in religious education.' The mother hesitated and checked with her husband. Much to my surprise, they enrolled the child. A bit later, when the mum told me that the family was moving to another suburb, she was adamant that the little girl was not going anywhere except Holy Family.

Teachers believe that the parents' enjoyment with their children's experiences at Holy Family school is partly because for many of them their last contact with school was not a happy experience. Some of the parents would have left school in Year 9.

Communication skills and literacy

Early in Term 1 in the new school, the teachers realised that the communication challenges experienced by the children were enormous. Children evidenced very limited experiences of conversation and teachers recognised that the children would need to do a huge amount of work in talking and listening before they would ever learn to read or write. Some children could not be understood, even when English was their first language. They were intelligent children and there was frustration and embarrassment on both sides when this happened. The staff set about to address this as a priority, while Brenda and Tricia as school leaders worked with staff to develop a shared understanding and approach.

As a result, Brenda invested heavily in professional development on talking and listening. In the first year, a specialist speech pathologist tested the children's speech so the school was able to get some funding to help them over and above what would normally have been available. In addition, the school was staffed above the normal formula with a special education teacher.

In the second year, Holy Family engaged a speech therapist for one day a week. This role has continued, and is regarded by the staff as one of the best investments they have made. Because she visits the school regularly, the speech therapist can assess children quickly, and the school is now able to assess children even *before* they come to school.

In 2007, 33 children of the total school population of 179 were assessed as being eligible for special education funding, with many of the needs being language-related. Brenda and Tricia describe the communication issue as a reality check for them in the early days. In Tricia's words,

> We came with assumptions that we were going to come in and give these students hope. There were so many things we wanted to do. I introduced them to beautiful books, thinking that they would love them. They did not love them. They had no value for them. They literally walked over them. We got crayons for them all and they would wind them up and then snap them all off.

The teachers and teaching

Again in the first year, teachers quickly learnt that approaches they might have used in another school were not going to work. Teaching in the school continues to be very structured and deliberate. English groups use very explicit teaching. Because few of the children are exposed to any depth of 'literary' experience at home, in kindergarten, teachers drill the alphabet every day in the English groups. They practise sight words so there is always a certain amount of reinforcement taking place. There is a focus on speaking and listening as a group. Each day there are two guided reading sessions, a shared book — a big book — and a computer group. In this program all the strands of literacy or English are being covered.

Interestingly, the teachers are enjoying this explicit approach to teaching. While the experience in this new school may have challenged their understanding of what good pedagogy is, so that they no longer assume that any *one* approach is the best approach to take. Teachers make no apology that they are teaching directly. Rather, they have moved to a view that considers 'good' pedagogy to be what best fits with a given group of children.

In its third year, the school received a grant which allowed them to engage a consultant to work with staff in helping the children in the classroom. Brenda and her colleagues have provided enriching opportunities for the children outside their immediate environment with excursions to experience live productions such as *Pinnochio*. Teachers measure the outcomes carefully. There is a tracking card for each child which continues on as the child moves into a new class. March and October are assessment times. Each class has decided which particular assessment tool they will use.

The school leaders are encouraged by the level of ongoing conversation amongst staff about teaching and learning. School starts at 8.00 am for staff. When teachers meet, they discuss teaching and learning rather than administration, leaving administrative matters to be handled in a very short briefing on Monday mornings. It is an interesting comment on the energy and morale within the school, that, notwithstanding a robust, sometimes even tough, classroom context, the attendance rate for teachers throughout 2006 was 98%.

Leadership

Leadership has played a critical role in the development of Holy Family Parish School. Teachers in the school are encouraged to develop their capabilities. They have grown; occasionally teachers might themselves admit they have changed from 'coasting along' to becoming far more effective, taking ownership of what they are teaching and how they are doing it. For Brenda:

> …leadership is about honouring the responsibility we carry. It is about respecting the trust that parents give us. It is not about me as principal saying to parents 'Do something because I say so'. We really do care what parents think and how they interact with us.' She continues, 'The staff here are hard working people. There is no place to hide so you would know if you have someone who is not pulling their weight. Here, they are actively working for the very best for the children and each other.

Brenda elaborates further on the understanding which she and Tricia have brought to their roles as school leaders:

To be an excellent leader is to know exactly where people are, what they are doing, what they should be doing and what their gifts and talents are. A good leader is innovative: someone can come to a principal and say, 'I want to try this' and she says, 'Why not?' A good leader is mentally young and agile and encourages innovation.

Good leaders are not closed off. Not everything that is new works. But a leader does not shut down and say, 'No, we do not do that. I have never done that before, so we are not starting it now!' Leaders are open to suggestions about the best possible education for the children. The authentic school leader is passionate about teaching and learning. They always want what is best for the children. And they can imagine possibilities for the children which even their families cannot articulate.

Holy Family community values leadership from people who have a clear vision. Vision is not confined to those in formal roles. Educational leaders have a mission for children, they have lots of ideas to make it happen and they value relationships. 'As school leaders at Holy Family School Emerton, we have sought to build relationships — with the community, with families and parents.'

Catholic identity and evangelisation

When Holy Family Parish School was established, the decision was made at diocesan level to have a more inclusive enrolment policy than applied normally in other diocesan schools. It is interesting to observe how this more open enrolment policy has impacted the school's Catholic identity and ethos.

The community clearly perceives Holy Family as a Catholic school. Enrolment interviews easily become opportunities for parents to name their desire to educate their children with values, and even to name their own desire to re-discover their own Catholicity. Brenda takes delight in being able to welcome families to the school, and explains clearly what attending a Catholic school means. She makes clear her expectations of parents that they support their children and connect actively with the community in some way. Only once has she had to refuse admission to a family because they were not prepared to meet this requirement. The

Assistant Principal observes, 'We are unapologetic about being Catholic. The school is very Catholic. As the school's leaders we are very strong about the Catholic identity.'

Prayer plays an important part for parents and children. The parents come for morning prayer, and ask the school members to pray for them. When one mum heard that the children and staff had prayed for her son when he was in hospital, she rang the Principal one morning at 7.30. 'I just want to tell you,' she said. 'He is well and he's home. Thank you for saying that prayer.'

In 2006, the parish and school cooperated in conducting a mini Rite of Christian Initiation of Adults (RCIA). Parents were invited to learn about the Catholic faith, not so much so that they would join the Church, but because their children were going to a Catholic school and receiving religious education. The program ended up with about 20 parents and parishioners involved in two groups. The baptism of six children flowed from the mini RCIA. It was a high point for the parish and school community. The baptisms took place during the day which allowed children from the school to attend. Five of those baptised were students in Holy Family. Two of those children have become school captains. Ever enterprising, the staff made a DVD of the baptismal ceremony which has been used as a teaching resource in other schools.

Interestingly, three of the children from the school who were baptised had been refused admission into another Catholic school because they were not baptised. Yet, they are all Catholic now. These children did not get baptised in order to get into the school. The baptisms came later.

Parents will sometimes tell the Principal during the enrolment process that their child has not yet been baptised. She assures them that their child is welcome, and encourages parents to consider arranging for the child's baptism. For some of those who ask her about the baptism of their children, Brenda believes it is a matter of practical help that is required — for these people to make time to go to the parish office. 'The enrolment policy,' she maintains, 'and the way we exercise it allows us to say something really powerful to people about the unconditional acceptance of the God of love.'

One of the important elements of the Catholic identity of Holy Family Parish School is its living link with the parish of which it is part. The relationship of the school with the parish is integral to the school's operation. The parish priest is very much part of the school. The children know him and love him. And the school is enriched by the quality of liturgy which he leads and the trust which he places in the school leaders and staff. One of the high points discussed in the school has been Christmas Eve mass. Many people attend, including those who are not Catholic, who through their association through the school, feel they belong.

The markers of success

The indicators of the quality of Holy Family School are present in its achievements since 2004, including the following awards:

- 2007 National Literacy and Numeracy Week Minister's Award for achievements resulting from the teachers' work to address the particular communication and literacy challenges faced by the students
- 2007 Award for Best National Achievement for Achievement for Excellence in Family-School Partnerships especially for the school's indigenous reading program linking Aboriginal culture and literacy
- 2007 Highly Commended Award for Outstanding National Achievement for Excellence in School Improvement under the Quality Teaching and Learning Program for the substantial improvement in the students' language
- 2007 Certificate of Merit, Dare to Lead Award for Excellence in Leadership in Indigenous Education for the gains made by the school's indigenous students in the areas of literacy, numeracy and school attendance.

In 2007, Holy Family Primary School was chosen from among the thousands of schools in the Sydney region to be one of a few schools to host a group of 25 educators from the USA-based Association for Supervision and Curriculum Development.

Other indicators of the school's achievements are parents' comments and the continuing growth in enrolments. Word of mouth is attracting new enrolments because parents perceive Holy Family as a very good school where all the staff do a good job and love their children. In Brenda's words, 'To them it is very much a community place. I think they see our values and that we believe in what we say.'

Leaders for the future

What are some of the challenges of leadership for a school such as Holy Family? The chapter concludes with Brenda's comments on leading such a Catholic school into the future:

> To lead a school like this, one has to be a person who really believes in it. And who believes in the whole acceptance of people, whether or not you agree with them. This kind of leadership is for a person in the second half of their faith life. They might be young in years, but they have to be very mature in their own religious development, so that they can see beyond the rules and regulations. According to Richard Rohr, the second half of religious development is characterised by freedom and an absolute certainty in your own faith. When you have that you can then be free not to judge people and to accept them whatever.
>
> We need rules of course, but the rules are there for guidance. They can never be the full story. Nor can they capture every possible situation. Life is complex and dynamic and it is certainly not black and white. The leader in a school like this needs to be clear about their responsibilities, but most importantly, the leader in a school like this needs to be comfortable enough in their faith to accept people and welcome them all into the community.

BIOGRAPHICAL NOTES

Hedley Beare is an experienced senior educator with an international reputation as a teacher, academic, school innovator, system administrator and writer. An authority on educational management and policy on educaton futures, he is Professor Emeritus of Education at the University of Melbourne and has been named by the national magazine, *The Bulletin*, as the nation's top educator in its Smart 100 Australians. He has been an active member of the Uniting Church of Australia and has served on its National Commission for Doctrine. He is the author of two books on prayer and spirituality, *Praying in Secret* (with wife Lyn) and more recently *God-in-the-Present-Moment* (John Garratt).

Anne Benjamin is an Adjunct Professor within the Flagship for Creative and Authentic Leadership in Australian Catholic University. She has been involved in Catholic education for around 40 years, as teacher in primary and secondary schools, as a teacher educator, in curriculum development and administration. For 16 years she held senior responsibilities in Parramatta Catholic Education Office and was Executive Director of Schools in Parramatta Diocese for nine years. She has served as a ministerial appointee to a number of key educational bodies, including the NSW Board of Studies, the Interim Committee for the Establishment of the NSW Institute of Teachers, the University of Western Sydney Board of Trustees, in addition to Commissions within Catholic Education.

Michael Bezzina has worked in Catholic education for over 36 years — as a classroom teacher, a school leader, a teacher educator, a system leader, a consultant and researcher. He is currently Head of School, Educational Leadership, and Director of the Flagship for Creative and Authentic Leadership at Australian Catholic University. He has had a long engagement in the professional development of teachers and leaders, and is currently one of the principal researchers in the *Leaders Transforming Learning and Learners* project. Michael has been made a Fellow of the Australian Council of Educational Leaders and has previously been an Adjunct Professor in Education at the University of Western Sydney, and in Educational Leadership at Australian Catholic University.

Kelvin Canavan is a Marist Brother and has spent the past 40 years with the Catholic Education Office (CEO) Sydney. He joined the fledgling CEO, Sydney in 1968, prior to government funding for students in Catholic schools. He was subsequently appointed Director of Primary Education and later Deputy Director. He was appointed Executive Director of Schools in 1987. In 2004 and

2007 the CEO, Sydney was a recipient of an Australian Business Excellence Award. In these awards recognition was specifically made to Kelvin's leadership. In 1994 his work was recognised by the Australian College of Educators as the inaugural winner of the Sir Harold Wyndham Medal for his 'outstanding contribution to the education of young people in New South Wales'. In 1997 Kelvin was made a Member (AM) of the Order of Australia 'for services to education as Executive Director of Catholic Schools in the Archdiocese of Sydney'. In 2008 he was awarded the degree Doctor of the University (*honoris causa*) by the Australian Catholic University.

Tricia Carr has been teaching since 1976 and as Assistant Principal is part of the foundation leadership team at Holy Family. Tricia has a great interest in infants' education and was a member of the Early Childhood Committee in the Diocese of Parramatta for a number of years. She was also a member of the Student Welfare Committee.

Timothy Cook has been an American Catholic educational leader in a variety of capacities. As Chief Administrator of a high school he succeeded in substantially changing its culture and performance. More recently he completed a three-year term as President of the Association of Catholic Leadership Programs (ACLP) in the United States. Tim is currently Associate Chair of the Education Department at Creighton University in Omaha, Nebraska. He is the author of *Architects of Catholic Culture: Designing & Building Catholic Culture in Catholic Schools.*

Brian Croke has been Executive Director of the Catholic Education Commission, New South Wales and a member of the National Catholic Education Commission since 1994, having previously been Director of Schools in the Diocese of Broken Bay. He is also currently a member of various national and state advisory councils including the new National Curriculum Board and the NSW Board of Studies, as well as being a Board director of the Australian Council for Educational Research, and the Australian Curriculum Corporation. He has published on various aspects of Catholic education, most recently a chapter on the challenges facing Australian Catholic schools in the new International Handbook of Catholic Education (edited by Gerald Grace [London] and Joe O'Keefe [Boston College], Dordrecht 2007). In his spare time Brian is Adjunct Professor of History at Macquarie University and the University of Sydney and was elected a Fellow of the Australian Humanities Academy in 1995.

Jim D'Orsa is a Catholic educator with an extensive history of teaching and senior leadership in schools and school systems. He was a pioneer in preparing lay leaders to take on the development of the vision and mission of Catholic colleges. Currently he provides leadership in pastoral planning in the Diocese of Sale and is extensively involved in the reviews of Catholic school systems.

Therese D'Orsa is a Catholic missiologist and educational leader. She is currently Head of Missiology at the Broken Bay Institute in Sydney and is a professorial fellow at Australian Catholic University. She has taught and exercised senior leadership in schools, tertiary institutions and school systems, including the roles of Director of Religious Education and Diocesan Director of Catholic Education.

Patrick Duignan is Emeritus Professor at ACU National and the President of the Australian Council for Educational Leaders (ACEL). During his career Patrick was a teacher, deputy principal, principal, lecturer, professor and dean in tertiary institutions in Australia and overseas. He is widely published in national and international refereed publications. He is co-editor of *Leading Australia's Schools* (2008), Canberra, DEST & ACEL and author of *Educational Leadership - Key Challenges and Ethical Tensions* (2006), Melbourne, Cambridge University Press.

Joan Hendriks is an adult educator and has worked since the 1980s in the field of Aboriginal Education. She has presented workshops in primary and secondary schools, local church and community organisations, government departments and internationally at the United Nations Indigenous Peoples forum. In 2007 Joan was awarded an Honorary Fellowship of the Australian Catholic University National and was also honoured with the 2008 Indigenous Research award for her research study *A Dialogue between Christian Theology and Indigenous Spirituality*, with specific reference to Aboriginal Traditional Ancestry. She also was awarded one of five 2007 DEST Indigenous Higher Education Advisory Council (IHEAC) Elder of the Year Awards.

Silma Ihram, education consultant and former school principal, has played a key role in the establishment of Muslim schools in Australia. Establishing the first Muslim school in New South Wales – also one of the first in Australia – in 1983, she set up a second school with her husband in 1995. She was a founding member and then Secretary General of the Australian Council for Islamic Education in Schools. She is currently working as a researcher and consultant while completing a Masters (Hons) degree. She was awarded the Centenary Medal in 2002 for service to the Australian Federation of Muslim Students Associations.

Brenda Kennedy is the foundation principal of Holy Family Primary School in Emerton, Mt Druitt, New South Wales. She is a member of the Holy Faith Congregation and has been involved in Catholic Education for 38 years, the last

28 working in schools in Western Sydney, and 22 of these years in leadership positions including three years as Area Administrator in the diocesan office in Parramatta.

Patrick Lynch, the CEO of the New Zealand Catholic Education Office, has served in national leadership positions in New Zealand education circles for over 20 years. He has been a member of the New Zealand National Commission for UNESCO for 12 years and has exercised public roles on behalf of the New Zealand Government and Non Government Organisations. Patrick is a De La Salle Brother and was awarded the 1990 New Zealand Sesquicentennial Medal and has also received the Queens Service Order for Public Services to New Zealand.

Michael Putney is a leading ecumenist, both nationally and internationally, being the Catholic Co-Chair of the International Methodist-Catholic Dialogue and a member of the Pontifical Council for Promoting Christian Unity. He is also very involved in inter-religious dialogue as Chairman of the Commission for Ecumenical and Inter-religious Relations of the Australian Catholic Bishops' Conference. He is a patron of the World Community of Christian Meditation. He is the Bishop of Townsville, Qld.

Dan Riley rejoined the University of New England after 10 years' working in Catholic schools in New South Wales and Western Australia. In 1997 he published a book with co-editor Ross Keane entitled: *Quality Catholic Schools: Challenges for Leadership*. In 2002 another co-edited book was published with Deirdre J Duncan entitled: *Leadership in Catholic Education: hope for the future*.

Kalo Sikimeti is a former principal and Director of Education of schools, Tonga. She entered the Sisters of Mercy in Christchurch, New Zealand in 1976. She continued to teach in secondary schools in Fiji, Samoa and Tonga, and at the University of the South Pacific in Tonga. She has also worked in Australian Catholic schools. Kalo was the first Tongan woman to be a director of a Tongan school system. She led the appeal to the Government of Tonga to give a fair distribution of government funds to the education of children in private schools.

Oona Stannard has been a prominent figure in English education for many years, firstly as one of the youngest members of HMI (Her Majesty's Inspector of Schools) and currently as Chief Executive and Director of the Catholic Education Service for England and Wales, the Catholic Bishops' agency for education. She has taught in both Catholic and community schools and lectured in higher education. Her responsibilities include advising the bishops on the formulation of their education policy and negotiating on their behalf with Government. Oona is familiar with Australian Catholic education following a number of professional visits which have included membership of the international panel of four education experts commissioned in 2004 to review and report on the work of the Catholic Education Office in the Archdiocese of Sydney. She also gave a key note address to the Australian Catholic University's International Catholic Education Leadership Conference in 2007.

Jerry Starratt is Professor of Education at Boston College. Starratt taught at Fordham University after serving as principal and teacher at Catholic schools in the United States of America. He is the author of numerous books and articles. Jerry has been a regular visitor to Australia since the mid-1980s and has strong links with the Flagship of Creative and Authentic Leadership and the School of Educational Leadership at Australian Catholic University National. He has also worked with many CEOs and schools across Australia. His recent book entitled *Ethical Leadership* is used as the focus text for the Leaders Transforming Learning and Learners project.

Christopher Toohey was ordained priest for the archdiocese of Sydney at St Mary's Cathedral, Sydney, in 1982, by Cardinal James Freeman, Archbishop of Sydney. He completed his post-graduate studies at Gregorian University, Rome specialising in Fundamental Theology. He was appointed Bishop of the diocese of Wilcannia-Forbes, and ordained in Holy Family Church, Parkes, on 30 August 2001 by Cardinal George Pell, Archbishop of Sydney. Presently, Chris is Chair of Catholic Earthcare, Australia and the Bishops Commission for Justice and Service.

Dan White is currently Director of Catholic Education for the Archdiocese of Hobart. He holds Masters Degrees in Leadership and Religious Education and has completed doctoral research in the area of brain-based learning and its implications for classroom pedagogy. He is the co-author of five educational resource books focusing particularly on higher order learning and thinking strategies. Dan represents Tasmania on the National Catholic Education Commission and is member of the National Catholic Religious Education Committee. He has also been appointed to the Tasmanian Qualifications Committee and serves on a number of governing bodies across Tasmania.